Monetary Statecraft in Brazil

T0359069

This book presents an analysis of the state's role in monetary policy from the latter days of Portuguese rule to the present day. Based on a variety of untapped archival sources, this study elaborates theories and concepts about monetary statecraft to reveal the open-ended, autonomous character of monetary politics, the complex, recursive phases of public policy and political development in the traditional sense of social inclusion. In the post-crisis world, still awaiting new perspectives on politics and monetary policy, this book traces how Brazilian policy makers and observers have sought, experimented with and reflected on a vast number and wide variety of forms and solutions for monetary policy since 1808.

This book will be of interest to economists, financial historians and those interested in the history and economy of Brazil.

Kurt Mettenheim is Professor at the Social and Legal Sciences Department, Getulio Vargas Foundation São Paulo Business School, Brazil.

Financial history

Series Editors: Farley Grubb and Anne L. Murphy

Monetary Statecraft in Brazil

1808–2014

Kurt Mettenheim

LONDON AND NEW YORK

First published 2016
by Routledge

2 Park Square, Milton Park, Abingdon, Oxfordshire OX14 4RN
52 Vanderbilt Avenue, New York, NY 10017

Routledge is an imprint of the Taylor & Francis Group, an informa business

First issued in paperback 2020

British Library Cataloguing in Publication Data
A catalogue record for this book is available from the British Library

Library of Congress Cataloging-in-Publication Data
Catalog record for this book has been requested

ISBN: 978-1-84893-619-5 (hbk)
ISBN: 978-0-367-59767-2 (pbk)

Typeset in Times New Roman
by Apex CoVantage, LLC

Contents

Figures

Tables

Acknowledgments

This book began thanks to encouragement from colleagues in a research group on the construction of monetary authority (funded by the São Paulo state research fund Fundação de Ámparo a Pesquisa do Estado de São Paulo, FAPESP); Lourdes Sola, Maria Rita Loureiro, Marques Moises and the late Eduardo Kugelmas. Ideas were first tested at a seminar on central banking at the Fundação Getulio Vargas Escola de Administração de Empresas (FGV-EAESP) with participation of Fernando Abrucio, Persio Arida, Mônica Baer, the late Geraldo Gardenali, Maria Rita Loureiro, Gustavo Loyola, Moises Marques, Alkimar Moura, Mailson de Nóbrega, Maria Clara Prado, Brasílio Sallum and Laurence Whitehead. The University of Oxford Centre for Brazilian Studies provided support for a second workshop and kindly published proceedings as *Statecrafting Monetary Authority in Brazil*. While a university lecturer in Brazilian studies and fellow of St Cross College, further comments and suggestions from Leslie Bethell, Valpy Fitzgerald, Rodney Bruce Hall, Rosemary Thorp, Laurence Whitehead, Leslie Corbett, the late Antonio Barros de Castro and visiting fellows and graduate students sharpened the manuscript. Access to historical materials in Oxford libraries, and assistance from André Carvalho at Oxford, and Cesar Mori, Danilo Lee and Tomas Anker at the FGV-EAESP, also proved essential, as was keen advice from Maria Antonieta del Tedesco Lins. Further support in São Paulo during 2008 from the FGV-EAESP research fund (GVpesquisa) permitted completion of chapter three.

The manuscript was then delayed by research on Brazilian federal banks, alternative banking and monetary channels for social inclusion. This proved beneficial, especially because many new sources became available online or to my attention. Support from GVpesquisa during 2010 and assistance from Marina Mansur permitted incorporation of primary materials from newly digitalized collections (primarily at the Brazilian Finance Ministry Library and Centre for Latin American Research Libraries) that improved the periodization of monetary orders and helped clarify how politics alternatively sustained currencies and produced change. Sabbatical from teaching in 2012 permitted revision of historical chapters, while suggestions from anonymous reviewers for Pickering and Chatto helped clarify the theory of monetary statecraft and, finally, complete analysis of the post-1994 period. Thanks are also due Benjamin Cohen, Leslie Armijo, Saori Katada and Carol Wise for suggestions at the seminar titled 'Financial Statecraft and

Ascendant Powers: Latin America and Asia after the 2008–10 Global Financial Crisis' in Los Angeles. Thanks are also due Maria Antonieta del Tedesco Lins for invitation to present the manuscript to faculty and graduate students at the Universidade de São Paulo International Relations Institute, and Maria Fernanda Freire de Lima for co-authorship of the article serving as basis for selected parts of chapter five (and the *Revista de Administração Pública* for permission to republish sections). Thanks are also due Bill Maurer and the staff and colleague grant recipients from the University of California, Irvine Institute for Money Technology and Financial Inclusion for help with field research in Guaianases, São Paulo. Thanks are also due to Lauro Gonzalez and Eduardo Diniz and the faculty, students and staff of the FGV-EAESP Center for Microfinance Studies. Thanks to all who have helped and my apologies for errors surely incurred in trespassing from political science into economics through monetary history.

Table 0.1 List of Brazilian currencies (1808–2014)

Currency	Symbol	Period	Equivalence
Real	R	Before 8 October 1833	R1$2000 = 1/8 oz gold 22k
Mil-Réis	Rs	8 October 1833 to 1 November 1942	Rs2$500 = 1/8 oz gold 22k
Cruzeiro	Cr$	1 November 1942 to 13 February 1967	Cr$1.00 = Rs1$000
Cruzeiro Novo	NCr$	13 February to 15 May 1970	NCr$1.00 = Cr$1,000
Cruzeiro	Cr$	15 May 1970 to 28 February 1986	Cr$1.00 = NCr$ 1.00
Cruzado	Cz$	28 February 1986 to 16 January 1989	Cz$ 1.00 = Cr$1,000
Cruzado Novo	NCz$	16 January 1989 to 16 March 1990	NCz$ 1.00 = Cz$1,000.00
Cruzeiro	Cr$	16 March 1990 to 1 August 1993	Cr$1.00 = NCz$1.00
Cruzeiro Real	CR$	1 August 1993 to 27 May 1994	CR$1.00 = Cr$1,000.00
Real	R$	Since 27 May 1994	R$1.00 = CR$ 2,750

Source: Central Bank of Brazil

1 Introduction

From the economics of politics
to the politics of monetary policy

[W]hile institutions respond to supply and demand or to economic necessity, as the Coase theorem asserts, they do so within a social and political structure that profoundly shapes the outcomes. Supply and demand propose . . . the social matrix disposes . . .
—Charles Kindleberger, *A Financial History of Western Europe*, p. 410

Monetary statecraft is a theory that accounts for the open-ended, autonomous character of politics, the complex, recursive phases of public policy, and political development in the traditional sense of social inclusion. Unfortunately, there are few precedents for this type of analysis. Since the testimony of US Treasury Secretary Douglas to Congress in 1941,[1] or the overview of finance in Western Europe by Ardant in 1975,[2] we were unable to find a compelling framework for analysis of monetary policy and *political development* that averts fallacies about central bank independence in economics or overemphasis on policy capture in sociology. Moreover, Ardant warned that European experiences do not apply to developing countries because 'numerous bottlenecks intervene between demand and any response of agriculture or industry', and therefore, 'solutions must be sought in different forms'.[3] This book traces how Brazilian policy makers and observers have sought, experimented with, and reflected on precisely such different forms and solutions for monetary policy since 1808.

Explaining how monetary phenomena constrain and enable government and political development proved easier said than done. This book began as an account of how gradual, muddling through policy making in 1994 ended inertial inflation and paved the way for modernizing monetary authority in Brazil.[4] These techniques of monetary statecraft (rather than heterodox shocks or big-bang reforms then in vogue) helped reverse the legacies of both mismanagement under military rule and capture by oligarchs that had delayed democracy and deepened monetary chaos. However, the seemingly endless series of currency crises faced by Brazil and other emerging economies (Mexico, 1994–1995; Asia, 1997; Russia, 1998; Brazil, 1999; Argentina and Turkey, 2001; Brazil 2002–2003) made it difficult to disentangle politics from markets, markets from policies and the pains of adjustment from advances produced by reforms. A historical approach provided relief in the form of distance and, more importantly, an analytic advantage by increasing the number of cases to elaborate concepts and theories about monetary statecraft.

Reconstructing the politics of monetary policy since the Portuguese crown arrived in Rio de Janeiro in 1808 extends and reinforces the central thesis of this book: that advances of central banking and monetary policy in Brazil since the mid-1990s (notwithstanding remaining obstacles to growth, democracy and social inclusion) were achieved by muddling through and *adapting ideas from abroad* to the particularities of underdevelopment in Brazil. We found this to be true of politics and monetary policy in previous periods of Brazilian history and submit that it reveals much about political economy in developing countries. Theories of domestic statecraft in comparative political economy uniquely explain how monetary policy makers in Brazil muddled through, reacted to circumstances and sought to balance political imperatives and market confidence by adapting theories and policy frameworks from abroad.

The chapters of this book use largely untapped primary materials and secondary accounts to trace the politics of monetary policy: during monarchy, independence and empire (1808–1889); a republic controlled by oligarchs and single-state parties (1889–1930); national populism and import substitution industrialization (1930–1945); post-war democracy wracked by disputes between developmentalists and monetarists (1945–1964); military rule that first imposed austerity but soon turned to state-led developmentalism (1964–1985); protracted transition and monetary chaos (1985–1994) and, finally, price stability and democratization (1994–2014). For each of these periods, historical-institutional analysis and policy process tracing[5] reveal how politics shaped monetary policy while controlling for alternative explanations from economics and sociology. Concepts and theories about the phases of public policy help explain further how problem identification and agenda setting shape the formulation, implementation and evaluation of monetary policies: phases that often become recursive when new problems begin the policy process once again.

Tracing the politics of money across political regimes and phases of public policy confirms the conclusions of Kindleberger, Allen and Gale, and Shonfield: that *political choices* shape national systems of money and finance in particular, path-dependent trajectories.[6] Statistical analyses of aggregate cross-national data have proven singularly unable to explain similarities and differences in the politics of monetary policy across countries – a typical result of excessive data aggregation that often conceals rather than reveals causes. Recent advances in case study selection and research design make it possible to skirt both these fallacies of aggregation and randomization that weaken statistical inferences about politics and monetary policy. Qualitative methods provide better tests of competing theories to leverage our causal findings about politics and monetary policy. To better control for competing explanations of politics and monetary policy, we draw causal inferences instead from in-depth case study, historical-institutional analysis, and process tracing.

The theory of monetary statecraft focuses on how the formulation and implementation of rules, policies and procedures by government agents mandate basic monetary functions and relations in society and markets.[7] From this perspective, monetary policy makes money by providing funds for government beyond taxes and tariffs by setting value and allocating resources in state and society, and by shaping markets and monetary phenomena. Monetary statecraft requires balancing domestic political support, economic realities, and market confidence.[8] Monetary statecraft is a specific type of economic statecraft that involves phenomena of money, prices, banking, finance, government accounts, foreign exchange *and politics*. Monetary statecraft, like most concepts and theories in the social sciences, cuts to essentially contested,[9] core ideas about money, markets, government intervention, public policy and politics.

Theories of money and monetary statecraft

Because money serves as a medium of exchange, store of value, unit of account and means of payment,[10] the stakes of monetary policy are high and theories are especially contested. Neo-classical approaches in economics are anti-politics; they conclude that *no politics* is the optimal monetary policy. In a broader sense, most sociologists and political scientists tend to agree by asserting, and often finding, that central banks and other entities responsible for monetary policy tend to be captured by banks and financial interests – the very entities that regulators should be regulating.[11] *Deregulation* in the United States and other advanced economies after 1970 did, in fact, facilitate capture of monetary policy through 'blood sport' lobbying, revolving door appointments, policy agenda setting and other mechanisms.[12] However, errors of deregulation in the United States should not be elevated to theory. Monetary policy is not always controlled by banks and corporate interests; this would ignore most periods of US history, other national experiences that have averted capture, and perhaps most importantly, lead us to underestimate prospects for reform. The mistakes of deregulation in the United States were expensive.[13] However, many experiences in Brazilian history, and the modernization of central banking amidst democratization in the country since the 1990s, cannot be explained as a result of political aggrandizement (as economic theories insist) or capture by bankers (as theories from sociology assert).

Understanding the politics of monetary policy is further complicated by the fact that theories of money are also deeply contested. Quantitative theories in the neo-classical tradition of economics suggest that central bank policies are exogenous determinants of the money supply.[14] Theories in the Keynesian tradition emphasize commercial banks as endogenous multipliers of money.[15] In the past, the 'currency school' argued that money must be backed by the real value of precious metals such as gold or silver. In opposition, the 'banking school' argued that the value of money was *not* determined by reference to the value of precious metals. Instead, money was a commodity, much like any other, and therefore subject to forces of supply and demand. The value of paper notes issued by commercial banks therefore extrapolated from fixed metallic references, because of market forces *and* the reality that bank credit multiplies money (albeit limited by fractional values of metallic reserves).

Disputes about the nature of money pervade the history of political economy.[16] For much of the 20th century, debates turned on differences between Keynesians and monetarists. The spectre of hyperinflation and debates about currency reforms in the 1920s gradually ceded, after 1945, under Bretton Woods arrangements that helped sustain several decades of more stable money, prices, and foreign exchange rates in advanced economies. However, once the US dollar was taken off a fixed exchange rate for gold in 1971, foreign exchange volatility and increasing uncertainty returned to produce reassessment of politics and monetary policies. The globalization of money markets, monetary unification in Europe, devastating currency crises across emerging and developing countries and the global financial crisis of 2007–2008 have placed money and monetary policy once again at the centre of research agendas in political economy, public policy and regulation.

Unlike most studies that focus on top global currencies, this book examines the politics of monetary policy in Brazil, a country traditionally lower in typologies of international currencies. The Brazilian case reveals both how monetary policies reinforced underdevelopment in the past and helped bring the country out of underdevelopment. A broader view of deeply contested theories about politics, money and monetary policy is required to explain this trajectory. Scholars and policy makers disagree, fundamentally, about whether money is, and should be, a private matter of free market exchange or, instead, that management of money is essential for state sovereignty and capacity. For most economists, money remains secondary to broader forces in the real economy unless it 'gets out of order'. And for most economists, politics and government policies are the prime suspects when inflation surges or money is devalued (or overvalued). Modern monetary theory argues that monetary phenomena are far more important in shaping real economic activity, but agree that politics and governments, almost inevitably, distort money and prices to produce bad equilibrium.

Chartalist theories of money provide an alternative explanation of how money is shaped by state policies such as the power to tax and the valuation and circulation of *fiat* money by force of law.[17] The origin and evolution of national currencies are inexorably related to the fiscal authority of governments. Modern national currencies arose with nation states and remain central to state sovereignty and policy making.[18] This differs fundamentally from neo-classical explanations of the origin of money in *private transactions.* For Chartalist theory, modern money arose from state mandates that payments (especially taxes) be paid in official currency. Chartalist theories of money help explain the origin and evolution of money in Brazil and clarify causal relations between politics and monetary policy.

State theories of money have suffered from association with Knapp, especially because he underestimated how German government policies produced hyperinflation in his lifetime.[19] Chartalist theories are nonetheless overwhelmingly supported by historical research into the origin of modern money. Moreover, Chartalist theory was recognized by classic authors such as Adam Smith (1776: 312): 'A prince, who should enact that a certain proportion of his taxes should be paid in a paper money of a certain kind, might *thereby give a certain value to this paper money*'.

For Bell, Smith's 'sagacious' observation identifies a crucial anomaly for met-allist theories of money: that government policy causes paper (with no inherent value and no necessary base or reference in precious metal reserves) to nonetheless become widely accepted as money at considerable values. Governments thereby allocate resources, use money for public policy, and determine the value of money in domestic and foreign transactions (this does not imply that governments can do anything they desire with money).

Ironically, state theories of money underestimate how politics and govern-ment policies shape money. State mandates for payment in official currency usually go far beyond taxes, such that *all* payments within a given territory must be paid in official currency is common. We therefore extrapolates from Chartalist theories to emphasize how other political phenomena such as war, domestic legitimacy, imperatives of political development and the realities of policy making also determine the value of money. Take, for example, the prac-tice of debasing metal coins. The following chapter of this book begins the his-tory of monetary policy in Brazil with the Portuguese crown in Rio de Janeiro (having fled Napoleon's advance in Iberia), stamping Spanish silver pesos at twice their value. Bell suggests that governments will necessarily object to the debasement of (their own) coins. This should not obscure the fact that one of the first 'Brazilian' currencies (before independence) was produced in the 1810s by stamping Spanish silver coin.

The many ways in which governments shape the value of money surely hold beyond Brazil. From Keynes' classic pamphlet on the economic consequences of the peace,[20] through many studies of politics and money since, it is clear that state interests, political forces and policy makers often do, in fact, opt to reduce the value of national currencies through domestic inflation or by fixing foreign exchange values below (or above) market prices.[21] Broadening the scope of state theories of money (by looking beyond taxation) also helps avert the recent fixation of economists and political scientists on *fiscal* questions. Theories of political development did indeed see taxation (after military mobilization) as the most important cause in the development of European states.[22] However, if the capacity of governments to define the value of money is central to theories of money, then it follows that this capacity must also be an important cause in the development of states – in Europe and beyond. Finding that monetary poli-cies are central to resource allocation and political development also provides fundamentally different explanations of economic constraints to change as dis-cussed below.

In sum, traditional accounts of the origin of money (Chartalist theories and modern monetary theory) provide alternative, often complimentary, explanations for phenomena of politics and money in Brazil. Modern monetary theorists provide parsimonious explanations based on forces of supply and demand; this often does indeed explain monetary phenomena. However, monetarist (and past metallist) accounts suffer from erroneous conceptions of (1) how states define legal curren-cies and (2) how politics and government policies shape the value of money and determine monetary phenomena.

Keynes and theories of money

Theories of money in the work of Keynes and post-Keynesian approaches help explain further phenomena of politics, public policy and money. Two contributions are critical: the importance of monetary policy for counter-cyclical smoothing of business cycles and the reality that banks and financial transactions may multiply money excessively to produce asset bubbles and, when they burst, cause financial and currency crises. Concepts and theories from Keynes, Kalecki and post-Keynesian economists such as Minsky are essential to explain the politics of monetary policy in Brazil. Indeed, since the global financial crisis of 2007–2008, research in monetary economics has returned to ideas about monetary circuits, excessive bank leverage and other problems in financial markets that multiply money (and monetary contractions) to exacerbate boom and bust cycles. One key idea in post-Keynesian approaches returns to an observation of the banking school and is critical for the theory of monetary statecraft: banks and other financial institutions *multiply money*.

Banks multiply money because credit, loans, and finance 'create' assets on the balance sheets of banks above and beyond the value of deposits or other liabilities. Even if deposits 'match' loans, loans can still be said to multiply money *by two*. Traditionally, the management of banks was seen as balancing liabilities and assets. From this perspective, the gradual accumulation of deposits and equity ownership on the liability side of bank balance sheets enabled the extension of credit, loans or finance on the asset side of bank balance sheets. However, contemporary banking theory suggests that banks no longer operate in this manner. Instead, banks are seen as profit-maximizing firms that serve as intermediaries between clients and investments in more lucrative and more efficient products and services traded on financial markets.[23] The theory of efficient markets has led banks, and theories of banks, to see banking as able to leverage much further, far beyond traditional limits set by liabilities and capital reserves.

This implies that banks are now able to multiply money far beyond the factor of two that arises from traditional bank management (that matches loans with deposits, equity and reserves). Indeed, current regulations free banks to *multiply money over ten times*. According to the capital reserve requirements of the Bank for International Settlements (BIS) Capital Reserve Accords II and III, banks and financial institutions are required to retain minimum capital reserves against risk of 8 percent (risk weighted) against total assets. These measures remain widely debated.[24] And recent reforms call for use of simpler measures of *liquidity* instead of complex calculations of capital reserve requirements. However, for core ideas about the multiplication of money, the point remains the same. Capital infusions, whether through sales of shares (in the case of joint stock banks) or cash from Treasury or official funds (in the case of state banks) or members (in the case of cooperative banks), permit banks to lend *over ten times* the value of fresh capital above minimum values required by the BIS Basel Accord guidelines and domestic regulations. From this perspective, the value of capital held in reserve by banks is seen to cover over *tenfold* the value of bank loans or other financial operations.

However, banks multiply money in yet another sense. Financial transactions such as repos or synthetic derivatives (that often retain no reference to the liability side of bank balance sheets) multiply money even further, indeed exponentially as a function of leverage. From the perspective of contemporary banking theory, banks *manufacture* these financial products and instruments. This can multiply money beyond the limit imposed by the 8 percent rule of the Basel II Capital Reserve Accord or other limits based on minimum levels of liquidity or leverage. Manufacture of assets may become excessive if banks buy, sell or trade repos or financial derivatives to third parties and, on this basis, declare asset values on (or off) balance sheets. Indeed, the value of financial products off balance sheets *surpassed* the value of assets held by banks on balance sheets in the years preceding the global financial crisis of 2007–2008. This suggests the importance of theories of how banks multiply money in the post-Keynesian tradition.

Post-Keynesian theories of how banks multiply money also help explain the conservative character of monetary policy, banking and central banking in Brazil.[25] Bad experiences in the past with easy credit and excessive leverage explain why conservative policies (both at commercial banks and monetary authorities) in Brazil restrict bank leverage; this is designed to reduce risk and *control the multiplication of money by banks*. In 21st century Brazil, conservative monetary policy, tight central bank supervision of banks and risk-averse commercial bank management cross the left–right ideological divide and are shared by participants and observers from diverse theoretical perspectives. This a legacy learned from the mismanagement of money and banking under military rule and delayed the transition that is seen as responsible for causing the monetary chaos that left Brazil vulnerable to currency crises abroad through the mid-2000s.

This book uses concepts and theories from all of the above theoretical traditions to test alternative explanations of politics and monetary policies. The empirical chapters that follow clarify how interest rate policies, supervision and control of banks, refinancing provisions, paper (and now electronic) currency emissions and most other means of managing money require balancing political support, market perceptions, and the vagaries of policy making. This does not invalidate laws of economics; it clarifies how politics and the realities of public policy make or break monetary policy.

From international realism to democratization

Research on international politics and money help further clarify the scope and limits to monetary policy in Brazil. Monetary statecraft began in Brazil as an instrument of political reaction used by Portuguese monarchs to defeat opposition and conduct war against neighbouring republics. Two centuries later, monetary statecraft proved essential for democratization and political development. Despite their focus on top global currencies and assumptions about realism in international politics, concepts and theories about politics and money in international relations do nonetheless apply to Brazil. Indeed, the political returns and risks of international money appear large in the record of Brazil precisely upon accessing international money and finance. The causal forces identified by studies of international politics and money are not exclusive to top currencies. Indeed, the evidence from Brazil suggests that the private and public functions of international money matter most upon first accessing international money markets.

Andrews defines monetary statecraft as the use of monetary policies to maximize national interests abroad.[26] Brazilian foreign policy makers have largely been unable to manipulate the currencies of other countries. However, broader views of politics and international money suggest that Brazilian policies have nonetheless produced returns (and risks) in each of the core functions ascribed to international money. Cohen describes the functions of international money in private and official spheres in terms of serving as medium of exchange, unit of account and store of value (see Table 1.1).

Large benefits (and risks) accrue to policy makers when their domestic currencies win acceptance abroad, even if this acceptance is limited and remains a very small portion of international monetary transactions. Political and economic returns from acceptance of money abroad are not linear or remote, in the sense of increasing gradually as countries scale the ladder of international currencies. Instead, large marginal returns, and risks, obtain upon entering the lowest rungs of the ladder.

Consider each function of international money in Table 1.1. Brazil still lacks a fully convertible currency. However, monetary authorities in Brazil nonetheless have reaped advantages as emphasized by Cohen: through seigniorage, macroeconomic flexibility, reputation and leverage. First, developing countries may obtain seigniorage in the form of subsidized or interest-free loans (and downward pressure on domestic interest rates) that arise when foreign countries acquire debt, bonds and currency reserves in US dollars (or sterling or francs in the past). Periods of world liquidity have repeatedly produced large inflows of money into Brazil, enabling domestic policy makers to take advantage of low interest rates and the valuation of the domestic currency to capitalize initiatives and direct funds toward development. Larger risks also ensued. The experience of Brazil is of interest precisely because of it's long history with experiments such as currency boards and other policies designed to ameliorate the consequences of large, often volatile foreign capital flows.

Second, Brazilian currencies never served as widely accepted international money for commercial transactions abroad. However, periods of improved terms of access to international money markets have indeed provided domestic policy makers with greater flexibility in terms of macroeconomic and fiscal policy.

Table 1.1 Private and public functions of international money

	Medium of Exchange	Unit of Account	Store of Value
Private	Forex trading, trade payment	Trade invoicing	Investment
Official	Intervention	Anchor	Reserves

Source: Cohen, Benjamin. 'The Macrofoundation of Monetary Power', (Florence: European University Institute, Robert Schuman Centre for Advanced Studies, Working Paper, 2005, no. 8).

Third, the international reputation of Brazil has suffered from the lack of a currency with international reserve and payment status. However, access to international capital markets has nonetheless improved the reputation of Brazil in the sense of lowering risk premiums and interest rates and improving the terms of foreign finance on international money markets. The, large marginal returns from gaining access to money markets abroad have proven critical for issue of corporate and sovereign bond issues abroad since the 19th century.

Fourth, access to money and finance abroad provides powerful advantages for policy making and state capacity. Indeed, large marginal returns accrue to Brazilian state and public entities from gaining access to capital markets abroad. Once again, the low acceptance of Brazilian currencies abroad causes the functions of international money to become more, not less, important.

Large marginal risks also obtain. Upon entry into international money markets, policy makers in developing countries such as Brazil face the same risks as governments with top global currencies, but at much greater levels. Underdevelopment involves more volatile capital flows and quicker changes in the economic and financial contexts for monetary policy. Accumulation of foreign liabilities may quickly produce excess debt, endanger the reputation of currencies, and force adoption of very high interest rates to regain the confidence of markets. Cycles of foreign investment and world liquidity have often left Brazil with excessive issue of sovereign bonds and debt abroad such that sudden stops of capital inflows caused currency crises.

In Brazil, large marginal returns also obtain from small increments of power to delay or deflect adjustment. Contrary to the idea that short time horizons of elected politicians make it impossible to reduce government spending and/or the money supply when necessary to adjust the economy and produce longer term growth studies of international politics and money suggest that benefits often arise from the power to delay or deflect adjustment (depending on international liquidity and 'underlying attributes and endowments' respectively).[27] Brazilian policy makers have often acquired powers to delay or to deflect adjustment, with the proviso again that large marginal returns (and risks) arise from small increments of power to delay or deflect.

Finally, inertia also holds for developing countries such as Brazil on a lower rung of international currency ladders. Inertia explains the long time necessary to improve reputations abroad and gain acceptance of domestic currencies for transactions, finance, banking and money markets. It is said to delay the decline of top currencies for decades (as in the case of the pound sterling); it also appears to delay the rise of developing country currencies for decades.[28] Economic historians of Latin America describe inertia with concepts such as original sin[29] and observation of 'erroneous' perceptions among foreign investors of the country as a bad debtor.[30]

The fact that concepts and theories from studies of international politics and money apply to Brazil confirms the analytic advantages of studying developing countries. Just as Katzenstein[31] argued that policy making in small states may indeed be more agile and more able to adjust to global market changes, this study of Brazilian policy makers since the 19th century suggests that volatility on the periphery of the world system provides a more effective natural experiments for understanding the politics of monetary policy. This is also reported by studies of money and political economy in other developing countries. Broz and Frieden argue that the more volatile macroeconomic conditions in Latin America increase the stakes of monetary policy decisions.[32] Canuto and Ghosh suggest the same by specifying the greater challenges of macro financial linkages in emerging market economies.[33] Bresser *et al.* also demonstrate that monetary phenomena such as Dutch disease, currency tsunamis and foreign exchange populism pose greater challenges for macroeconomic policy making in developing countries.[34]

Studies of international economics, from Kindleberger[35] through Krugman,[36] also raise critical questions about power, money and foreign exchange. However, once again, considerations of politics suffer from a bias toward fiscal questions, such that choice of foreign exchange policies is seen largely from the perspective of theories of optimal currency areas.[37] From this perspective, adoption of the euro and other fixed foreign exchange arrangements are seen as virtuous because they serve as anchors able to control inflationary expectations and impose fiscal and monetary control. Once again, for economic theories, the optimal monetary policy is no political discretion.

Empirical studies have explored how politics shape foreign exchange arrangements.[38] Whether governments fix or float or seek to appreciate or depreciate their currencies turns on domestic politics. Interest groups, social classes and political parties, and the institutional format of domestic political institutions and regimes all have been found to influence foreign exchange policies. However, aggregate statistical comparisons have also failed to clarify these causal processes. The imperative to adopt qualitative and low *n* comparative analysis also applies to understanding how politics shape foreign exchange arrangements; where too many causes and too many policy options impede statistical treatment. Over nine foreign exchange regimes are said to exist on a continuum that runs from a full float through fixed foreign exchange rates to a full currency union.[39] International business is said to favour fixed foreign exchange rates because this reduces foreign exchange risk and transaction costs. While fixed (or pegged) foreign exchange rates restrict monetary policy making, policy makers are nonetheless seen to *be forced to choose* between a fixed foreign exchange rate and monetary autonomy because of Mundell's impossible triangle principle. Because capital mobility (the third point of the triangle) is taken as a given in times of a globalized economy (especially in developing countries), most monetary economics suggest that the advantages of fixing foreign exchange rates far outweigh any advantages that arise from monetary policy autonomy.

From the perspective of the impossible triangle principle, a fixed foreign exchange rate (or monetary unification) are needed to impose discipline on politicians and policy makers so that money does not 'get out of order'. Serious doubts about these ideas have arisen in the wake of monetary unification in the euro and the global financial crisis of 2007–2008. Ceding monetary policy making prerogatives to the European Community and European Central Bank means that European states have forsaken traditions of democratic accountability and monetary policy that were so essential in the past to finance counter-cyclical deficits, ameliorate business cycles, and conduct monetary policy amidst democratic accountability.[40]

Moreover, since Milton Friedman, many economists emphasize that free or flexible foreign exchange rates are essential to permit economic adjustment through market pricing of currencies.[41] Liberal foreign exchange regimes help avert distortions (such as over- or under-valuation typical of fixed foreign exchange regimes) and eliminate the need for more complex and not necessarily effective central bank interventions into foreign currency exchange markets that require large amounts of hard foreign currency reserves. In Brazil, floating the real in 1999 and maintenance of a flexible foreign exchange rate regime alongside inflation targeting and fiscal control during the 2000s and early 2010s means that these three policies have become central referents for economic policy in the country. They certainly have been essential for modernization of central banking and monetary policy.

Monetary statecraft and political development

Monetary statecraft differs from all of the above concepts and theories by emphasizing the autonomy of politics and the complex, recursive nature of policy making. This returns to work that demarcated political science from the sister disciplines of sociology and economics decades ago. The title of this chapter paraphrases Giovanni Sartori's 'From the Sociology of Politics to a Political Sociology'.[42] His targets of Parsonian sociology and Marxist reductionism may no longer be influential. However, the core problem he identified remains. Phenomena of politics and public policy remain fair prey for mistaken explanations from neighbouring disciplines, especially sociology and economics. The statecrafting tradition in political economy and evidence from Brazil support the hard won findings of political scientists: monetary policy cannot be explained by constellations of social interests, as in sociological approaches, or as bad equilibrium caused by self-interested politicians and inattentive voters, as in economic theories.

The broader theoretical goal of this book is to counter the reduction of politics to either a sticky source of macroeconomic disequilibrium, or foreseeable result of microeconomic rational choice, or indeed the inevitable result of capture by banks and corporate interests. Monetary statecraft explains how policy makers muddle through, react to circumstances, try out ideas and policies and attempt to satisfice with limited resources, bounded rationality and incomplete information amidst often seemingly irreconcilable pressures from markets, social interests and political forces. Moreover, to the irritation of economists, sociologists and citizens at large, the politics of monetary policy making *never end*. Once implemented, effects of monetary policy often become causes that initiate new policy-making cycles.[43] Neither optimal solutions, nor capture, are definitive. Because circumstances change (often rapidly), policy making is endless and often recursive. The politics of monetary policy making require eternal vigilance, monumental patience, and epistemic communities able to understand the complexities of money, banking, public finance and economics. This book reconstructs how the politics of Brazilian monetary policy, since 1808, reflect these realities of statecrafting.

It is common sense that context matters. However, the trials and errors of adopting policy frameworks from abroad reveal another critical trait of monetary statecraft in Brazil. Brazilian policy makers have repeatedly *adapted* a wide variety of policy frameworks from abroad in ways consistent with influential accounts of modernism in the country. The anthropophagic movement in the 1920s remains a compelling reference for explaining how foreign genres are 'digested' in Brazil. Debate soon crossed from the humanities into the social sciences and authors continue to disagree fundamentally. Critical theories emphasize the perverse consequences of misplaced ideas.[44] The historical record of monetary policy making in Brazil provides examples of both the rigid imposition of misplaced ideas and of creatively adapting monetary policy frameworks in new ways.

Our focus on muddling through, adapting ideas from abroad, and the complexity of policy making leverages the analytic advantages of dealing with underdevelopment. However, far being exclusive to developing countries, these findings appear increasingly universal, given increasing pressures to reconcile democracy, market confidence and international economic pressures in all countries. The literature on political development brings clarity to this question. Since the 1960s, political development theory has focused on the inclusion and/or exclusion of social classes during economic development and social modernization. From this perspective, the politics of monetary policy turn on the consequences of policies for social classes and groups in terms of inclusion and citizenship. This remits to empirical democratic theory and political development, traditions that include Dahl, Sartori, Lipset, Rokkan, Linz, Huntington, Tilly and many others concerned with how social classes are, or are not, incorporated into political institutions during modernization.

Because Brazil has long been at the centre of political development studies, we also enjoy a well tested periodization of political regimes to frame this study. The chapters of this book turn on widely accepted accounts of political development, and reversals, in Brazil. Famously, Brazilian political history illustrates the challenges of incorporating demands of social classes as economic development produces social mobilization. Economic development causes social mobilization. However, this does not guarantee political development or democracy. Instead, a 'political gap'[45] emerges, whereby existing political institutions are challenged to incorporate new social classes. This concept clarifies the autonomy of politics and defines stages of political development in Brazil. Brazilian oligarchs overthrew monarchy in 1889, only to resist further inclusion until a paradigmatic 'middle class coup'[46] (the 1930 revolution) opened the door to the middle classes, only to close the door to further inclusion of popular classes by another military coup in 1964. From this perspective, military rule from 1964 to 1985 (and delayed transition from 1985 to 1994) *arrested* political development. Political development theory draws attention to the unfinished business of social inclusion in Brazil. Theories of statecrafting help explain how politics sustained economic reforms during democratization *and* how monetary policies provided new channels for change able to circumvent fiscal and structural constraints to change. The latter requires clarification.

Monetary channels of change

Although designed by monetary economists for other purposes, concepts and theories about channels of credit and interest rates help describe new patterns of change in Brazil. New monetary channels for change have proven critical for reducing the number of bankless Brazilians (those without bank accounts) from an estimated *80 to 45 percent* of the (190 million) population from 2000 to 2010. Once again, worse begets better. Large marginal returns obtain at the onset of financial inclusion. Theories that derive zero sum relations between social inclusion and optimal monetary policy are amiss in developing countries. To the contrary, high levels of financial exclusion may produce positive sum relations between monetary policy and social inclusion. This reverses conceptions of politics, money and central banking. Instead of seeking to ensure central bank independence from politics and social forces (Alesina and Summers, 1993) or free credit markets and private banks through privatizations and deregulation (Williamson, 1990), the construction of monetary authority in Brazil (Sola and Whitehead, 2006; Whitehead, 2002) involved a fundamentally different path. Liberalization produced instead a 'back to the future' modernization of large public banks and the use of these institutions as policy instruments for counter cyclical lending, financial inclusion and social policy provision (Mettenheim, 2010). Moreover, basic income policies (albeit conditional, see Soares *et al.,* 2010) and other social services have proved more important than private banking or non-governmental microfinance organizations for reaching the bankless. Chapter five traces policies that tapped new monetary channels of change to modernize central (and public) banking, reverse inequalities, improve monetary authority and maintain price stability amidst democratization.

New monetary channels make it possible to circumvent past constraints to change. Since the end of the electoral road to socialism exemplified by military coup in Chile against President Allende in 1973, social scientists and policy communities have fixated on *fiscal* constraints to social policies. For Gold, Lo and Wright (1975), new structural theories of the state replaced earlier instrumental and functional traditions by better describing how markets impose fiscal constraints on government social policies to veto change. Social scientists, mainstream and critical, have since stressed how social policies tend to pressure government fiscal accounts and require either tax increases or adjustment policies that reduce the profits of firms and, in turn, tax revenue. This structural cycle of fiscal constraints, in the worst cases, caused political-economic crisis and the breakdown of democracy in developing countries (O'Donnell, 1973). Similar forces in advanced economies led to stagflation in the 1970s and electoral turns to neo-conservative governments and neo-liberal policies in the 1980s designed to downsize Welfare States (Pierson, 1996).

These accounts of constraints to change are now incomplete. Old views of fiscal dominance fail to consider the implications of advances in monetary economics during the 1990s and the modernization of monetary policy making during the 2000s. Central bank modernization, new regulatory frameworks and better supervision of banks and markets (contrary to deregulation in the United States and a few tax havens and financial centres) provide a new setting for *monetary channels of change* and *financial roads to more social economies*. This can also be described as political development in the sense of social inclusion. Structural theories of the state and conceptions of fiscal constraints fail to account for new concepts and theories in monetary economics such as the credit channel and interest rate channel – concepts and theories that have been used to introduce more effective monetary policies since the 1990s.

Old views of fiscal dominance remain so prevalent that austerity often remains in place far beyond necessary. Many developing countries have accumulated large amounts of foreign reserves from sustained trade surpluses during decades of economic growth. Moreover, in Brazil, transparent policy frameworks such as inflation targeting and a flexible foreign exchange regime have been in place for over 15 years (Fraga *et al.*, 2004). The situation of many emerging and developing countries in the 2000s and 2010s differs from the 1970s. Central bank modernization, the accumulation of substantial foreign currency reserves and the consolidation of reforms have approximated markets and government policy. This provides new opportunities for public policies. Chapter five describes how new technologies, such as electronic card payment channels, have been used to deliver basic income grants and improved access to banking and public services *in vast numbers*. Contrary to expectations that liberalization and privatizations would market forces, and contrary to biases against government banks and public policy in microfinance studies, (1) provision of social services by a traditional government savings bank and (2) conceptions of citizenship and social justice have proved far more important for financial inclusion in Brazil than non-governmental organizations, private banks, or private microfinance firms or funds.

Debates about politics, central banking and monetary policy ignore the implications of new monetary channels for change. Because economic theories of central bank independence fallaciously affirm their consequence, they beg the critical question of how to improve monetary policy in developing countries.[47] The construction of monetary authority in Brazil during the 1990s and 2000s differed from theories of central bank independence in four ways. First, central banking in Brazil improved not through non- or antipolitical imposition of orthodox theories of money and prices but, instead, through development of alternative theories of inertial inflation in South America during the early 1980s.[48] Second, central bank independence in Brazil was not secured through legislation but, instead, constructed gradually and incrementally as emphasized in theories of statecrafting. Third, unlike the economic downturns seen as necessary to reduce inflation (because of higher interest rates, reductions in the money supply and cuts in government spending), alternative, heterodox anti-inflation policies based on the theory of inertial inflation accelerated growth and increased real incomes during the period of adjustment, especially among the poor. This produced political capital for further reforms. Fourth, central bank capacity emerged in Brazil in the *reverse causal order* expected by economists: the Central Bank of Brazil won prerogatives, better managed the money supply, improved monitoring and supervision of banks and began to set benchmark interest rates only *after* price stability was first secured by the gradualist implementation of heterodox policies in 1993–1994.

Theories of statecrafting in comparative political economy

Monetary statecraft remits to a long tradition in comparative political economy that focuses on how politics and government policies shape markets. Polanyi argued that laissez faire policies were first imposed through government policies then generated social movements of self-defense in the form of organized labour, tariffs and subsidies to protect agriculture and industry and *central banking* to protect banks from downturns and currency devaluation under the gold standard. Other interventions such as tariffs, imperialist adventures, and top-down social policies also prevailed over liberalism and free markets, especially after the 1873 crisis. In the 20th century, two world wars and economic depression meant that political imperatives continued to dominate monetary policy making. After 1945, Shonfield demonstrates how Continental Europeans reshaped monetary policies in response to the political and economic imperatives of recovery rather than ideology or nationalist design.[49] This emphasis on necessity and improvisation places the statecrafting tradition closer to Lindblom's theory of *muddling-through* than Marxist-Leninist or nationalist theories that see monetary policy as means to ideological ends.[50]

Recent research in comparative political economy has returned to core ideas of statecrafting. For Kirschner, because the effects of alternative monetary arrangements on welfare are often equal or unpredictable, politics rather economics explain both policy choices and market equilibria.[51] Research on statecrafting thus focuses on how coalitions support economic policies and how policies are adapted to domestic politics, markets and institutions.[52] However, a fundamental shift has occurred since the global financial crisis of 2007–2008. Statecrafting is not always about the politics necessary to implement liberalization, privatizations or deregulation to free market forces. For decades, scholars and policy makers have explored a global trend away from directed credit and monetary controls. Market-friendly reforms appeared to make central banking increasingly technical, free from political influence, and able to concentrate on policy frameworks such as inflation targeting to operate with a light touch through small marginal adjustments to interest rates. This changed in 2007. Emergency measures, bailouts, nationalizations of banks, vast sums of low-cost lending of last resort, massive measures of quantitative easing, and calls to regulate money markets, banks and financial markets have produced a profound reassessment of politics and monetary policy. This increases the importance of understanding the scope and limits to monetary statecraft.

From central bank independence to the construction of monetary authority

Since Alesina reported correlations in aggregate cross-national data between central bank independence, lower inflation and higher economic growth,[53] many economists and political scientists have argued that a strong causal relation exists.[54] From this perspective, the politics of monetary policy[55] are antipolitics; central bank independence (from governments and party politics) is seen as necessary to reduce inflationary expectations and wage demands by labour. Politics interferes with monetary policy because electoral cycles fuel inflation and excessive government spending slows economic growth. Globalization is seen to further constrain governments and increase the stakes for delegation of monetary authority to sustain the confidence of markets.[56] Central bank independence is thereby a type of contract whereby governments accept the delegation of monetary policy in return for better economic performance.[57]

The inability of economic theories of central bank independence to explain how central bank capacity is, in fact, created has led research outside advanced economies to focus on the *construction of monetary authority and central banking*. Johnson argues that independent central banks emerged quickly across the post-communist world during the 1990s because of a transnational epistemic community with neo-liberal ideas and sufficient resources to build these institutions.[58] In Brazil, a tempered, strategic, and reluctant support for central bank autonomy also emerged among political elites across the political spectrum during the 1990s and 2000s, but did so alongside support for state banks and other positions at odds with neo-liberalism. This heterodoxy, explored in chapter five, is typical of statecrafting and runs contrary to economic theories about politics and central bank independence.

In developing countries, boom-and-bust business cycles, volatile capital flows, unstable markets for capital and credit, and crises so frequent they become the norm sum to pose greater challenges. Brazilian monetary policy-making traditions have been forged amidst this greater volatility. From a methodological point of view, the greater frequency of financial crises increases the number of causal observations to help test competing theories about politics and monetary policy. Fortunately, greater instability of money and policy also increased the amount of press coverage, government documents and analyses from independent observers. This facilitates reconstruction of how policy makers, since 1808, have sought to reconcile political imperatives and market confidence to allocate resources through policies of money, credit, banking and foreign exchange.

Unlike the hard currencies, consolidated party systems and greater clarity of economic and social interest groups at more secure points on the Phillips curve, the politics of monetary policy in Brazil often required broad coalitions amidst crisis and shifting circumstances. By force of necessity, support for monetary policies is a more *ad hoc* process involving shifting alliances and seemingly end-less political negotiations. The tendency to overbuild coalitions in Latin America (just in case) amidst changing circumstances differs fundamentally from the com-paratively minor adjustments and allocation of smaller marginal gains and losses to labour, capital, state and society that traditionally defined the politics of monetary policy in advanced economies. The relation between monetary policy and politics in Brazil is more reactive than proactive, more *ad hoc* than ideological and designed to confront a seemingly endless series of crises, or near crises, that demand the attention of policy makers. That monetary statecraft since price stability and return to democracy in 1994 is a trajectory away from monetary chaos towards stability indicates not that Brazil somehow removed politics from monetary policy. Instead, this trajectory reveals how large marginal returns, and risks, shape the construction of monetary authority and central bank capacity in developing countries.

The emergence, since the 19th century, of an epistemic community of political economists, bankers, statisticians, journalists and policy makers specialized in mon-etary policy is another critical dimension of monetary statecraft in Brazil. This is part of a broader story of the separation of powers and specialization of government during development. Dornbusch, Aman and Baer argue that this holds for the recent periods of Brazilian history: the economists behind heterodox policy experiments from 1985 to 1993 developed technical knowledge and shared understandings that were critical.[59] Without the gradual emergence of policy debates on money, credit and finance in Brazil and the creation of specialized agencies capable of monitor-ing, regulating and supervising money, banks and financial markets in Brazil, the Real Plan and new policy frameworks and political support for price stability since the 1990s would have been unsustainable. Epistemic communities also emerged in previous periods of Brazilian history. This book explores the debates, experiments and experiences of cohorts and generations of monetary policy makers since 1808.

Historical institutional analysis of monetary orders and change

The following chapters use historical-institutional analysis and policy tracing to test the competing theories of politics and monetary policy introduced in this chapter. Evidence from primary and secondary sources, and concepts and theories about recursive cycles in studies of public policy, clarify how politics shape monetary policy: how ideas and public debate identify and define monetary problems; how politics and public disputes set agendas of monetary policy; how policy decisions are actually made in government agencies; how resources for monetary policy are allocated and spent; how (usually executive) agencies implement the rules, regula-tions and procedures for monetary policy (including minting and management of currency, interest rate policies, foreign exchange rates and transactions, bank super-vision and control, and credit policies) and, finally; how evaluation of policies and recommendations by government commissions, the financial press and public debate often begins the policy process anew in a recursive pattern. Focusing on politics in these phases of public policy opens the 'black box' of government to reveal more complex processes than assumed by theories in economics and sociology. Instead of inferring causation directly from social or economic interests, historical institutional analysis, case study, and tracing public policy are able to better reveal the causes and consequences of monetary policies.

Brazil is an effective laboratory to test competing theories both because of its long history of underdevelopment and, since 1994, successes in terms of price stability and the modernization of central banking amidst democracy. Economic failures and underdevelopment provide opportunities to understand the politics of monetary statecraft. Past experiences repeatedly belie simple formulas such as a gold standard, a hard currency, independent central banking or industry capture of public policy. Research on economic policy making in Brazil and other developing countries report similar insights. For Hirschman, studies of Latin America often revealed causal processes shared by more advanced economies precisely because stark realities, greater instabilities and crises make things more apparent.[60] In a different sense, Bates argued that coffee support programs in Brazil anticipated, by decades, policies later adopted by advanced economies and oil-producing states.[61]

Underdevelopment produced greater, earlier and qualitatively different monetary policies in Brazil. Policies were designed to counter the consequences of unfavourable trade relations, manipulation of export prices by foreign banks, severe credit crunches and finance shocks and volatile prices and demand for exports. Since the first national bank (Banco do Brasil) was founded in 1808, policies have sought to reduce radical price fluctuations and counter shocks that threatened farmers, exporters, importers, bankers, brokers and capital market operators, not to mention citizens at large and the careers of policy makers and politicians.

Brazil thereby stands opposite to the description of core beliefs in the United States by Louis Harz that 'all good things go together'.[62] Instead of early revolution, independence and industrialization, market-driven growth, deepening of markets for credit, finance and money, and the dollar that became global reserve currency, Brazilians experienced the contrary: colonialism, imperialism and political reaction, late industrialization, market failures and policy failures, persistent inflation and foreign exchange devaluation. Core beliefs in Brazil may thus be described as 'all bad things go together'. Monetary statecraft in Brazil is not just about debt crisis in the 1980s and currency crises during the 1990s and early 2000s, but about tough choices amidst crises and bad times since the early 19th century. Bad times and higher stakes for monetary policy in Brazil required resolution of more conflicting interests and the formulation and implementation of policies in different ways than in the history of advanced economies.

This provides another analytic advantage for study of monetary statecraft. Crises and economic hard times may uniquely prove *enabling constraints* in the sense of windows of opportunity to mobilize political support for monetary policies and reforms, whatever their stripe.[63] Theories of statecrafting clarify how greater challenges in Brazil often inspired greater creativity, while also discouraging wholesale adoption of simple formulas from abroad such as the gold standard or other orthodoxies about money.

Further analytic advantages ensue from studying how Brazil came out of underdevelopment. The empirical record of politics and monetary policy in Brazil reveals a critical digestion of ideas from abroad. The greater severity of shocks and market failures forced policy makers to extrapolate from economic laws and consider ideas from different schools of thought and policy frameworks from both sides of the North Atlantic. Again, this confirms insights from the humanities about cultural cannibalism in Brazil, a provocative concept that draws attention to how ideas about monetary theory and policy from abroad were adapted by policy makers to the circumstances of underdevelopment. From 19th century debates in parliament, annual reports from finance ministers, special commissions of inquiry into financial crises, and independent financial press and observers, through heterodox theories about the inertial character of inflation in the 1980s and 1990s, primary and secondary sources reveal an accumulated understanding (and episodes of ignorance) about the theory and practice of money and policy making in Brazil.

The following chapters of this book trace how politics, different political regimes and policies shaped periods of monetary order and change in Brazil. Table 1.2 summarizes this periodization. From 1808 to 1889, the exceptional experience of monarchy, empire and slavery in Brazil stands in stark contrast to

Table 1.2 Political regimes, monetary orders and statecraft in Brazil

Regime	Monetary Order	Policies and Politics
Empire		
1808–1829	Silver-Paper	Banco do Brasil
1831–1846	Stabilization	Reform and Recall
1846–1860	Plural Banking	Private Bank Emissions
1860–1889	Forced Currency	Central Government Monetary Authority
Old Republic		
1889–1898	Regional Banks	Federal Pact
1898–1906	Orthodoxy	Kemmerer Coalition
1906–1924	Paper	National Liberalism
1924–1930	Orthodoxy	Kemmerer Coalition
Populism		
1930–1937	Centralization	Revolution and Adjustment to Crisis
1937–1945	State Managed	ISI and National Populism
Democracy		
1945–1964	Developmentalist	Banco do Brasil > SUMOC
Military Rule		
1964–1967	Orthodoxy	Central Bank
1968–1982	Developmentalist	State-Led Finance
1982–1993	Inertial Inflation	Heterodox Adjustment Experiments
Democracy		
1994–2002	Price Stability	Construction of Monetary Authority
2003–2014	Developmentalist	Growth and Social Inclusion

neighbouring republics winning wars of independence from Spain. Financial revolution (a type of monetary statecraft),[64] explains the success of *political reaction* in Brazil. Creation of a national bank in 1808 and other techniques of monetary statecraft explain how political reaction secured monarchy in the New World against regional and liberal opposition groups to consolidate monarchy and empire in Rio de Janeiro. A Brazilian version of 'bank war' ensued between royal government and opposition.[65] Refusal of Parliament to renew the Banco do Brasil charter in 1829 and return of Pedro I to Portugal amidst revolution in 1831 settled the bank war in favour of the opposition but led, unexpectedly, to the disappearance of gold and silver in favour of copper coin. This required efforts to reverse monetary chaos during the late 1830s and early 1840s. Reassertion of central government control over currencies led to policies of conservative modernization in the late 1840s and 1850s that adopted liberal theories to free commercial (and government) banks to issue paper currency. However, by 1860, the consequences of crises caused money and monetary policy to once again be centralized until, in the last years of empire, reforms freed credit to help farmers adjust to abolition.

After military coup ended monarchy in 1889, republicans created regional banks to seal a federal pact. However, by 1898 a funding loan from London banks exemplified the turn to orthodoxies of quantitative theories of money. Orthodox policies imposed by 'Kemmerer coalitions'[66] thereafter alternated with periods of national liberalism that sought to spur growth. These two poles shaped the politics of monetary policy until revolution ended the Old Republic in 1930. Monetary policy during the national populist regime of Getulio Vargas (1930–1945) shifted to centralization, mobilization of domestic resources and directed credit to accelerate import substitution industrialization.

From 1945 to 1964, conflict over monetary policies set developmentalists centred in the Banco do Brasil against orthodox monetary authorities operating a proto-central bank (Superintendancy of Money and Credit, SUMOC). These tensions reinforced political disputes that escalated to produce economic crisis and the breakdown of democracy in 1964.

In 1964, military rulers imposed austerity and, emblematically, signed an agreement with the International Monetary Fund to create the Central Bank of Brazil, finally overcoming the veto of developmentalists. However, once again, change was not linear. By 1968, orthodoxy and adjustment gave way to state led finance under hardline rule designed to channel global liquidity to domestic capital goods production and complete import substitution industrialization. This cycle of unprecedented annual gross domestic product (GDP) growth of 10 percent ended after global liquidity dried up and moratorium on foreign debt payments by Mexico in 1982 stopped foreign finance. Thereafter, until 1994, dual foreign debt and fiscal crisis produced monetary chaos and inertial inflation that were accelerated by capture of state government banks (and policy making) by regional oligarchs during the (far too long) transition from military rule to democracy (1974–1994).

Price stability under the Real Plan in 1994 vindicated heterodox theories of inertial inflation and sustained political support for reforms of liberalization, privatization and fiscal control designed to dismantle the developmental state that had been hijacked under military rule and captured by traditional elites. During the late 1990s, the *ad hoc* formulation of monetary policy by a small group of economists gave way to modernization of the Central Bank and other entities responsible for money, banking and finance policy. After 2002, Presidents Lula and Dilma of the Partido dos Trabalhadores (Worker's Party, PT) unexpectedly kept core policies introduced during the 1990s (inflation targeting, fiscal control, flexible foreign exchange) to reap a sustained period of growth after 2004. This made it possible to accelerate social inclusion through new monetary channels for change by introduction of basic income policies and the modernization of government bank operations.

Monetary statecraft explains the causes and consequences of monetary order and change across these periods of Brazilian history. Substantial evidence from primary and secondary materials demonstrate that economic theories of politics and sociological theories of capture fail to explain how policy makers react to circumstances and political imperatives; choose from options advocated by epistemic communities; adapt ideas from abroad; and muddle through to satisfice amidst bounded rationality and imperfect information to shape money, credit, banking, markets and development in Brazil.

Notes

1 Douglas, William O. *Democracy and Finance: The Addresses and Public Statements of William O. Douglas as Member and Chairman of the Securities and Exchange Commission* (New Haven, CT: Yale University Press, 1941).
2 Ardant, Gabriel. 'Financial Policy and Economic Infrastructure of Modern States and Nations', in Charles Tilly (ed.), *The Formation of National States in Western Europe* (Princeton, NJ: Princeton University Press, 1975), pp. 164–242.
3 Ibid., p. 241.
4 Lindblom, Charles. 'The Science of "Muddling Through"', *Public Administration Review*, 19/2 (1959): 79–88.
5 Collier, David. 'Understanding Process Tracing', *PS: Political Science and Politics,* 44/4 (October 2011): 823–830.
6 Kindlberger, Charles P. *A Financial History of Western Europe* (London: George Allen, 1984); Allen, Franklin and Gale, Douglas. *Comparing Financial Systems* (Cambridge, MA: MIT Press, 2000); Shonfield, Andrew. *Modern Capitalism* (Oxford: Oxford University Press, 1965).
7 Our focus on domestic politics and monetary policy differs from realist approaches to monetary statecraft in international relations. See, Baldwin, David A. *Economic Statecraft* (Princeton, NJ: Princeton University Press, 1985). Our view of domestic monetary statecraft is based on approaches in comparative politics, especially: Conaghan, Catherine and Malloy, James. *Unsettling Statecraft: Democracy and Neoliberalism in the Central Andes* (Pittsburgh, PA University of Pittsburgh Press, 1994).
8 'The governments of many new democracies are heavily dependent upon access to international capital markets in order to maintain the economic stability necessary to address the other demands of the electorate. In such conditions it becomes a high political priority to design and manage a system of monetary authority that can command "credibility" in financial markets'. Whitehead, Laurence. *Democratization: Theory and Experience* (Oxford: Oxford University Press, 2002), p. 136.
9 Gallie, Walter B. 'Essentially Contested Concepts', *Proceedings of the Aristotelian Society*, 56 (1956): 167–198.

10 Further functions include serving as numeraire, as measure of wealth, as credit–debt relation, as 'a delayed form of reciprocal altruism, a reference point in accumulation, an institution, or some combination of these'. Bell, Stephanie. 'The Role of the State and the Hierarchy of Money', *Cambridge Journal of Economics*, 25 (2001): 50.

11 Capture of regulatory agencies has been at the centre of studies in political science and policy making since Lowi, Theodore. 'American Business, Public Policy, Case Studies and Political Theory', *World Politics*, 16/4 (1964): 677–715.

12 The Financial Crisis Inquiry Commission. 'The Financial Crisis Inquiry Commission Report' (Washington, DC: US Government Printing Office, 2011).

13 Mettenheim, Kurt. 'Back to Basics in Banking Theory and Varieties of Finance Capitalism', *Accounting, Economics and Law*, 3/3 (2013): 357–405.

14 Friedman, Milton (ed.). *Studies in the Quantity Theory of Money* (Chicago: University of Chicago Press, 1956).

15 On endogenous theories of money, see, Wray, Randall. *Money and Credit in Capitalist Economies: The Endogenous Money Approach* (Aldershot: Eduard Elgar, 1990).

16 Shumpeter, Joseph. *History of Economic Analysis* (London: Routledge, 1954).

17 Bell, Stephanie. 'The Role of the State and the Hierarchy of Money', *Cambridge Journal of Economics*, 25 (2001): 149–163; Wray, Randall. *Money and Credit in Capitalist Economies: The Endogenous Money Approach* (Aldershot: Eduard Elgar, 1990); Foley, Duncan. 'Money in Economic Activity', in Eatwell *et al.* (eds.), *The New Palgrave Dictionary of Economics* (New York: WW Norton, 1987), pp. 519–525.

18 Goodhart, Charles. 'Two Theories of Money', *European Journal of Political Economy*, (1998), 14: 407–432.

19 Knapp, Georg. *Staatliche Theorie des Geldes* (Munich: Duncker & Humblot, 1905).

20 Keynes, John M. *Economic Consequences of the Peace* (New York: Harcourt, Brace and Howe, 1920).

21 Feinstein, Charles (ed.). *Banking, Currency and Finance in Europe Between the Wars* (Oxford: Oxford University Press, 1995).

22 Tilly, Charles (ed.). *The Formation of Nation States in Western Europe* (Princeton, NJ: Princeton University Press, 1975).

23 Berger, Allen, Molyneux, Phillip and Wilson, John (eds.). *The Oxford Handbook of Banking* (Oxford: Oxford University Press, 2010); Bhattacharya, Sudipto and Thakor, Anjan. 'Contemporary Banking Theory', *Journal of Financial Intermediation*, 3 (1993): 2–50.

24 Lall, Ranjit. 'From failure to failure: The politics of international banking regulation,' *Review of International Political Economy*, (2012), 19(4): 609–638.

25 On conservative policies generally, see Admati, Anat R., DeMarzo, Peter, M., Hellwig, Martin F. and Pfleiderer, Paul. 'Fallacies, Irrelevant Facts and Myths in the Discussion of Capital Regulation: Why Bank Equity Is *Not* Expensive' (Stanford University, working paper, 2011).

26 Andrews, David (ed.). *International Monetary Power* (Ithaca, NY: Cornell University Press, 2006).

27 Cohen, Benjamin J. 'The Macrofoundation of Monetary Power' (Florence: European University Institute, Robert Schuman Centre for Advanced Studies, Working Paper, 2005, no. 8); Cohen builds on Andrews, David M. 'Capital Mobility and State Autonomy: Toward a Structural Theory of International Monetary Relations', *International Studies Quarterly*, 38 (1994): 193–218; Henning, C. Randall. 'Systemic Conflict and Regional Monetary Integration: The Case of Europe', *International Organization*, 52 (1998): 537–573; Kirshner, Jonathan. *Currency and Coercion: The Political Economy of International Monetary Power* (Princeton, NJ: Princeton University Press, 2003); Webb, Michael C. 'Capital Mobility and the Possibilities for International Policy Coordination', *Policy Sciences*, 27 (1994): 395–423; Strange, Susan. 'The Politics of International Currencies' *World Politics,* 23/2 (1971): 215–231. Strange, Susan. *Sterling and British Policy* (London: Oxford University Press, 1971).

28 Armijo, Leslie and Katada, Saori. (eds.), *The Financial Statecraft of Emerging Powers* (New York: Palgrave Macmillan, 2014).
29 Eichengreen, Barry, Hausmann, Ricardo and Panizza, Ugo. 'Currency Mismatches, Debt Intolerance and Original Sin: Why They Are Not the Same and Why It Matters', *Capital Controls and Capital Flows in Emerging Economies: Policies, Practices and Consequences* (Chicago: University of Chicago Press, 2007), pp. 121–170.
30 Paiva Abreu, Marcelo. 'On the Memory of Bankers: Brazilian Foreign Debt, 1824–1946', *Political Economy, Studies in the Surplus Approach*, 4/1 (1988): 45–82.
31 Katzenstein, Peter. *Small States in World Markets: Industrial Policy in Europe* (Ithaca, NY: Cornell University Press, 1985).
32 Frieden, Jeffry. *Currency Politics: The Political Economy of Exchange Rate Policy* (Princeton, NJ: Princeton University Press, 2014).
33 Canuto, Octaviano and Ghosh, Swati (eds.). *Dealing with the Challenges of Macro Financial Linkages in Emerging Markets* (Washington, DC: World Bank, 2013).
34 Bresser-Pereira, Luiz C., Oreiro, José L. and Marconi, Nelson. *Development Macroeconomics: New Developmentalism as a Growth Strategy* (London: Routledge, 2014).
35 Kindleberger, Charles P. *Power and Money* (New York: Basic Books, 1970).
36 Krugman, Paul. *Currencies and Crises* (Cambridge, MA: MIT Press, 1992).
37 Mundell, Robert. 'A Theory of Optimum Currency Areas', *The American Economic Review*, 51/4 (1961): 657–665.
38 Frieden, *Currency Politics*.
39 Frankel, Jeffrey. 'No Single Currency Regime Is Right for All Countries or At All Times' (NBER Working Paper no. 7228, 1999).
40 Scharpf, Fritz. 'Monetary Union, Fiscal Crisis and the Preemption of Democracy' (Cologne: Max Plank Institute for the Study of Societies, MPIfG Discussion paper, 11/11, 2011).
41 Friedman, Milton (ed.). *Studies in the Quantity Theory of Money* (Chicago: University of Chicago Press, 1956).
42 Sartori, Giovanni. 'From the Sociology of Politics to a Political Sociology', *Government and Opposition*, 4/2 (1969): 195–214.
43 Pierson, Paul. 'When Effect Becomes Cause: Policy Feedback and Political Change', *World Politics*, 45/4 (1993): 595–628.
44 Schwartz, Roberto. *Misplaced Ideas* (London: Verso, 1996).
45 Deutsch, Karl. 'Social Mobilization and Political Development', *American Political Science Review*, 55/3 (1961): 493–514.
46 From this perspective, the military is paradigmatically middle class and, therefore, coups to end oligarchic rule and open the door to the middle class but coups, once again, to veto further moves to include popular classes in political institutions. See Nun, José. 'The Middle Class Military Coup', in Claudio Veliz (ed.), *The Politics of Conformity in Latin America* (Oxford: Oxford University Press, 1967), pp. 66–118.
47 See, Sola, Lourdes and Whitehead, Laurence (eds.). *Statecrafting Monetary Authority: Democracy and Financial Order in Brazil* (Oxford: University of Oxford Centre for Brazilian Studies, 2006).
48 Bresser-Pereira, Luiz C. and Nakano, Yoshiaki. *The Theory of Inertial Inflation.* (Boulder, CO: Lynne Rienner, 1987).
49 Shonfield, Andrew. *Modern Capitalism.* (Oxford: Oxford University Press, 1965).
50 Lindblom, Charles E. 'The Science of Muddling Through'. *Public Administration Review*. 19/2 (1958): 79–88.
51 Kirschner, Jonathan (ed.). *Monetary Orders: Ambiguous Economics, Ubiquitous Politics* (Ithaca, NY: Cornell University Press, 2003).
52 Conaghan, Catherine M. and James M. Malloy. *Unsettling Statecraft: Democracy and Neoliberalism in the Central Andes* (Pittsburgh, PA: University of Pittsburgh Press, 1994).
53 Alesina, Alberto, Roubini, Nouriel, and Cohen, Gerald. *Political Cycles and the Macroeconomy* (Cambridge, MA: MIT Press, 1997).

54 Cukierman, Alex, Web, Steven., and Bilin, Neyapti. *Measuring Central Bank Independence and Its Effect on Policy Outcomes* (World Bank Economic Review (1992) 6 (3): 353–398); Cukierman, Alex and Lippi, Francesco. 'Central Bank Independence, Centralization of Wage Bargaining, Inflation and Unemployment: Theory and Some Evidence', *European Economic Review*, 43 (1999, June): 1395–1434; Barro, Robert. *Determinants of Economic Growth: A Cross Country Comparison* (Cambridge: Cambridge University Press, 1977).

55 Alesina, Alberto F. and Stella, Andrea. 'The Politics of Monetary Policy' (May 2010), Harvard Institute of Economic Research Discussion Paper No. 2183.

56 Clark, William R. and Hallerberg, Mark. 'Mobile Capital, Domestic Institutions and Electorally Induced Monetary and Fiscal Policy', *American Political Science Review*, 94 (2000): 323–346; Garret, Goeffrey. *Partisan Politics in the Global Economy* (Cambridge: Cambridge University Press, 1998).

57 Walsh, Carl. 'Optimal Contracts for Central Bankers', *American Economic Review*, 85/1, (1995): 150–167; Rogoff, Kenneth. 'The Optimal Degree of Commitment to and Intermediate Monetary Target', *Quarterly Journal of Economics*, 100/4 (1985): 1169–1190; Jensen, Henrik. 'The Credibility of Optimal Monetary Delegation', *American Economic Review*, 87/5 (1997): 911–920.

58 Johnson, Juliet. 'Financial Globalization and National Sovereignty' (Paper delivered at the 2002 Annual Meeting of the American Political Science Association, Boston, September 2002).

59 Dornbusch, Rudiger. 'Brazil's Incomplete Stabilization and Reform', Brookings Papers on Economic Activity, No. 1, 1997; Amann, Edmund and Baer, Werner. 'The Illusion of Stability: The Brazilian Economy Under Cardoso', *World Development*, 28/10 (2000): 1805–1819.

60 Hirschman, Albert O. *Essays in Trespassing: Economics to Politics and Beyond*, (Cambridge: Cambridge University Press, 1981).

61 Bates, Robert. *Open-Economy Politics: The Political Economy of the World Coffee Trade* (Princeton, NJ: Princeton University Press, 1998).

62 Hartz, Luis. *The Liberal Tradition in America* (New York: Harcourt Brace, 1955).

63 Gourevitch, Peter. *Politics in Hard Times: Comparative Responses to International Economic Crises* (Ithaca, NY: Cornell University Press, 1986).

64 Dickson, Peter. *The Financial Revolution in England* (New York: St Martin's, 1967).

65 'Bank war' refers to disputes between supporters of Andrew Jackson and Nicholas Biddle, president of the Bank of the United States, culminating in refusal to renew the bank's charter in 1833; Hammond, Bray. *Banks and Politics in America, from the Revolution to the Civil War* (Princeton, NJ: Princeton University Press, 1957).

66 On Kemmerer coalitions, see, Drake, Paul. *The Money Doctor in the Andes: U.S. Advisors, Investors, and Economic Reform in Latin America from World War I to the Great Depression* (Durham, NC: Duke University Press, 1989).

2 Monetary statecraft under monarchy and empire (1808–1889)

Monetary statecraft explains the core anomaly of 19th century Brazil: that Portuguese monarchs defeated regional and liberal opposition at home and Hispanic republics next door to sustain slavery and empire in the New World until 1888–1889. Clipping silver coins, printing paper currency and founding a national bank in 1808 (14 years before independence from Portugal) confirms Dickson's thesis about financial revolution, with the proviso that, in Brazil, financial revolution funded political reaction.[1] Politics continued to shape monetary policy after independence, exemplified by Parliament's refusal to renew the national bank charter in 1829; by government issue of coin, paper currency, bonds and loans in Brazil and abroad; by periods of enforced official currency and plural banking; by monetary reforms in 1833, 1846, 1860 and 1888; and finally, by government (and national bank) lending of last resort and other policies to counter financial crises that erupted in 1837, 1853, 1859, 1864 and 1875. Considerations of monetary statecraft pervade primary materials such as State Council meeting transcripts, Finance Ministry reports, parliamentary commissions of inquiry on money, finance, banking and crises; legislative proposals and debates; analyses in the independent financial press; and accounts of foreign and domestic observers.[2]

This chapter traces the rise and fall of monetary regimes from 1808 to 1889 to isolate political causes and control for alternative explanations. Politics comes to the fore. War and competition between European states caused Britain to help transfer the Portuguese crown and court to the New World in 1808. Independence in 1822 brought elements of economic liberalism in terms of trade and banking. However, underdevelopment, slavery, corruption, and dependence on primary exports meant that monetary policies confronted government deficits, devaluation of the mil-réis abroad, volatile prices (and demand) for Brazilian exports and costly transactions on distant European markets. However, notwithstanding colonial legacies, the blight of slavery, and the high cost of military mobilization, monetary policies nonetheless sustained monarchy and imperial government in the New World.

Monetary statecraft by monarchs in 19th century Brazil may appear distant from central banking and democracy in the 21st century. However, tracing the political economy of monetary policy making in 19th century

Brazil reveals the autonomy of politics and policy making and a long record of attempts to address the volatility of markets, money flows and the allocation of value amidst under development. Policies in the 19th century were inspired by ideas from abroad about national banks, paper money, metal standards, free and plural banking, and government control of money, credit and banking. The record from 19th century Brazil reveals a particular tradition, or epistemic community, of monetary statecraft honed by finance ministers, national bank presidents, parliamentary debate, policy experiments and a financial press attuned to how policy makers sought to reconcile theories from abroad about money and policy with realities of politics, market constraints and underdevelopment.

This chapter traces monetary statecraft in Brazil from 1808 to 1889 as follows. After reviewing gold depletion and monetary chaos as legacies of colonial rule, we trace the emergence and collapse of three monetary regimes (gold, silver and copper-paper), focusing on how political conflicts shaped these monetary regimes, from independence in 1822 through revolution and departure of Pedro I in 1831. The first national Banco do Brasil (1808–1829) remained at the centre of political conflicts, seen as agent of empire and object of liberal and regional opposition to absolutism. After a period of conservative modernization under the regency (1831–1840), monetary policies inspired by liberal theories freed commercial banks to print and manage the supply and circulation of money. However, recreation of the Banco do Brasil as national bank in the early 1850s suggests how a mix of ideas from abroad reinforced monetary prerogatives of the central government. Liberal theories of money also faded as a series of financial crises delegitimized plural banking and led to centralization of government and monetary policy in 1860. Further financial crises in 1864 and 1875, and obligations from war with Paraguay (1864–1870) reinforced centralization thereafter. In the final years of empire, monetary reforms and generous credit policies sought to help agriculture adjust to abolition before military coup by republican forces ended monarchy on 15 November 1889. Evidence from each of these periods clarifies how politics, state policies and the emergence of an epistemic community of monetary policy makers shaped Brazilian development.

Colonial legacies: gold depletion and monetary chaos

Portuguese control of trade and industry, slavery, semi-feudal patterns of production and exchange and decimation of native groups[3] left an estimated 1 million free subjects, 2.5–3.0 million slaves and 300,000 Amerindians just before independence in 1800.[4] Portuguese occupation was limited to large, self-sufficient farms and urban trading centres in Bahia, Rio de Janeiro, Recife, São Luis, Fortaleza, Belem, Goyaz and Minas Gerais. Prohibition of industry in 1774 further repressed credit, money, investment and commerce. Non-monetary exchange such as *Mutuo* and *comodato* predominated over free labour and markets.[5] Underdevelopment encouraged piracy, contraband and loan sharking – phenomena that produced aversion to usury, seen to be associated with foreigners, and exacerbated conflicts between farmers and urban groups exemplified by the Mascates War (1710–1711) between Recife and Olinda.[6]

It is ironic that the end of colonial rule coincided with the depletion of gold in Brazil. Scholars have long emphasized the triangular relations between colonial exports from Brazil and English trade with Portugal.[7] Indeed, large supplies of gold from colonial Brazil helped the metal emerge as a global standard. Gold and diamond production did indeed produce booms in colonial Brazil.[8] However, the export of a thousand tons of gold and 3 million karats of diamonds generated neither lasting patterns of domestic trade and production nor a stable currency in Brazil.[9] Although the volume of gold production averaged 146 tons per year between 1740 and 1760, production fell to *1.5 tons* a year by 1800. This left Brazil without gold before independence.[10]

Monetary chaos prevailed in colonial Brazil. Gold, silver, copper and a plethora of unofficial coins, monetary units and exchanges flourished[11] (contrary to Gresham's law that posits flight to a single currency). Vieira argues that colonial rule and trade monopolies reinforced monetary chaos.[12] Proto-currencies such as gold powder and bullion, silver, sugar, salted meat, hides, cotton skeins, flour, tobacco, cloves or coconuts continued to serve as money. Large, self-sufficient *fazendas* (farms) reduced demand for money and reinforced barter and exchange of pseudo-currencies to settle transactions. Portuguese colonial authorities first stamped Dutch florins and Spanish dollars as official coinage. Provincial colonial mints were founded in 1694 in Salvador (moved to Rio de Janeiro in 1698, to Recife in 1700, then back to Rio de Janeiro in 1703, opening again between 1741 and 1830) and 1720 in Minas Gerais (closed 1730).

Monetary statecraft of monarchy and empire in the New World

In 1808, João VI arrived in Brazil, having fled the approaching armies of Napoleon under escort of the British Navy. On 28 January 1808 (six days after arrival in South America), a royal decree raised the status of the Brazilian territory to kingdom, ended prohibition of industry and opened Brazilian ports to free trade.[13] Funds to organize crown, court and government in Rio de Janeiro were short, given the loss of Iberian revenue and accumulation of debts from war with France.[14] Monetary statecraft nonetheless enabled Luso-Brazilian monarchs in Rio de Janeiro to fund government defeat opposition, and shape three monetary regimes from 1808 to 1831. This is consistent with Chartalist theories of how state mandates explain the origin and circulation of money.

Monetary statecraft explains the rise and fall of three monetary regimes in Brazil from 1808 to 1831 as follows. First, stamping Spanish silver coin produced transition from the colonial 'gold' monetary regime during the 1810s. This created a second 'silver' monetary regime that lasted from 1810 to 1826. Finally, a third period of coexistence between national bank notes and copper coin (a third 'copper-paper' monetary regime, 1826–1831) was shaped by

Table 2.1 Monetary regimes under monarchy (1822–1831, contos [000 mil-réis])

Year	Coins from Rio de Janeiro Mint		Copper	BB Notes	Forex: Mil-Réis/ Pence
	Gold	Silver			
1703–1767	130,508.8				
1768–1809	74,128.2	222.8	20.1		
1810	1,278.3	1,026.7			
1811–1821	6,385.8	12,205.9	1,013.5	6,330.9	52.2
1822	141.8	1,755.1	280.9	7,430.9	48.5
1823	88.5	380.8	237.2	7,330.9	50.5
1824	153.2	384.0	532.5	9,530.9	48.0
1825	84.7	56.8	534.1	11,130.9	51.1
1826	36.6	225.6	547.6	11,230.9	47.0
1827	35.1	23.3	1,390.9	20,230.9	35.5
1828	4.1		2,637.7	20,180.9	32.7
1829	5.8		3,099.3	17,780.9	25.3
1830	5.8	1.3	2,878.8	17,623.4	23.0
1831				953.9	24.6
Total	212,857.3	16,282.7	14,126.8	122,370.0	

Source: Sturz, J.J. *A Review, Financial, Statistical, & Commercial, of the Empire of Brazil and Its Resources: Together with a Suggestion of the Expediency and Mode of Admitting, Brazilian and Other Foreign Sugars into Great Britain for Refining and Exportation* (London: Effingham Wilson, 1837), p. 58.

political tensions that culminated in revolution and departure of Pedro I to Lisbon in 1831. Table 2.1 presents the value of official coin and Banco do Brasil notes from 1810 to 1831. The first column reports the value of gold coin minted in Rio de Janeiro from the discovery of gold in 1703 to 1767, totalling 130 contos (thousand mil-réis).

From 1768 to 1809, gold served as the primary medium for exchange. Sturz estimates the total value of gold coin struck in Rio de Janeiro to be over 74 contos (000 mil-réis). However, by 1810, gold coin minted at Rio de Janeiro declined to 1,278.3 contos, while stamped silver coin reached 1,026.7 contos. During the second silver monetary regime based on stamped Spanish silver coin (1811–1821), the amount of silver coin minted (12,205.9 contos) overshadowed gold coin (6,385.8 contos), copper coin (1,013.5 contos) and paper notes issued by the Banco do Brasil (6,330.9 contos). Finally, the third monetary regime combined copper coin and bank notes and lasted from 1822 to 1831. During this period, Sturz estimates a total of 14,126 contos of official copper coin from the Rio de Janeiro mint (and 10,300 contos of provincial and illicit coin). In comparison, Banco do Brasil paper notes in the period 1822–1831 totalled 21,711.1 contos.

Politics shaped these periods of monetary order and transition. Transition from gold to silver coincides with the opening of ports and arrival of crown and court from Portugal. The monarchy met expenses of setting up court by purchasing and stamping silver coin from cargo ships stopping at Rio de Janeiro while en route from Chile and Peru. Sturz estimates that Spanish dollars stamped 900 réis netted a profit of 5–6 percent for government. Stamping silver coin would thereby have netted a minimum of 2.4 contos for the monarchy (5 percent of 12,205.9). This is consistent with state theories of the origin of money.

However, monetary theory also points to the limits of government policies, for stamped silver also produced the disappearance of gold. Sturz notes, '[M]erchants had recourse to remittances in gold in preference to bills and soon drained Brazil of nearly all her large and small gold pieces'.[15] The fact that this largely escaped debate in Brazil suggests the absence of an epistemic community or cohort of policy elites and financial press.[16] In this respect, transition from gold to silver coin in Brazil during the early years of monarchy serves as a blank slate or point of departure for the emergence of debates about money and monetary policy.

In the 1820s, transition ensued from the 'silver' monetary regime to a third period of 'copper-paper', the latter more an unstable situation than a regime or order. Politics also explains this transition. The turn to copper coin between 1827 and 1830 was caused by relations between Rio de Janeiro and provincial governments. During the late 1820s, the central government increasingly drew on accounts in anticipation of revenue from the provinces. Then, as Sturz notes:

> [T]he presidents of the Province and Treasury of Pernambuco, not know-ing how to devise means for paying drafts of this kind, called a meeting of merchants, at which they presided, when the fatal resolution was adopted of calling in all the copper currency then in circulation in the province, in order to re-issue it with a stamp of double the value it had previously borne.[17]

Stamping copper coin at double its value, in the short term, doubled the resources of provincial governments. This indicates, once again, the importance of Chartalist and state theories of money. However, restamping copper coin in Pernambuco also quickly created an unanticipated flow of copper coin into the province. This is consistent with both a core idea in public policy (that of unintended consequences) and confirms the importance of market valuation of money as a commodity as emphasized in modern monetary theory.

Much of this influx of copper came in the form of counterfeit coin carried by North American cargo vessels 'who thus, to their great discredit, realized enor-mous sums'.[18] Moreover, the flow of copper coin to Pernambuco produced short-ages elsewhere. Sturz notes:

> Thus copper coin soon became superabundant in Pernambuco, from whence it could no more find its way into the place from which it had been imported. It therefore oppressed the circulation, became an article of merchandise and took a discount against silver in that province.[19]

This situation of copper coin induced new government policies. In the face of shortages of copper coin outside Pernambuco, appeals ensued from provincial governors to produce greater quantities of copper coin, in Rio de Janeiro, as *official* currency:

> The Portuguese-Brazilian financiers hailed this request as an unexpected blessing; and having immediately bought up all the sheet copper in Brasil and given orders for large quantities from England, they coined out the pound of copper, which cost them 400 reis, at 1280 reis; and in proportion as this coin was sent to the treasuries of the provinces, they drew on them for the value in silver coin; and these drafts had in Rio de Janeiro a premium of 15 to 20 percent against bank notes.[20]

For the imperial treasury in Rio de Janeiro, *profits at fourfold costs* obtained from coining copper proved far more advantageous than the 5 percent gain from restamping Spanish silver dollars. Copper coin thus became widespread, reaching an estimated 24.9 contos by 1832 (of which official copper coin reached 14.6 contos). The early currencies of gold, silver and copper thereby were shaped by the policies of central and provincial government – and realities of trading these currencies in the context of a vast uncontrolled terrain.

After coin came paper. Paper currency emissions by the Banco do Brasil also reinforced transition away from gold coin and stamped silver coin. Sturz notes:

> In 1819, the paper currency was felt to have become redundant; the monetary equilibrium was destroyed; and the bank not being able to take up its notes in coin, it became necessary to give these notes a forced *legal* currency. They thus became the regulators of the exchange and went to a discount shortly after against silver, which became merchandise and acquired a premium. The exchange then continued to fall as the discount on the bank paper increased. This state of things began in 1819 and exists to this day [1837]; and the fluctuations in the discount of paper, or rather in the premiums on gold and silver, have been continual, sudden and ruinous.[21]

Imperial government policies defining Banco do Brasil notes as legal tender has since been described as transition to fiduciary currency or, in Brazil, as *curso forcado* (forced acceptance).[22] Although this term is critical, it nonetheless recognizes realities of monetary statecraft to the extent that the Brazilian government, in fact, set the value of notes.

These developments evidence the importance of monetary statecraft. They cannot be disregarded, as in most accounts in economic history, as dysfunctional deviations from ideals of hard currency management. Instead, Chartalist and state theories of money (that emphasize government mandates for payment of taxes and other transactions in official currencies) provide a more compelling explanation of the origin and evolution of money in early Brazil. Monetary statecraft and politics caused the rise and fall of three monetary regimes. Money was shaped by government stamping silver coin, minting copper coin and printing national Banco do Brasil notes – policies designed to meet political imperatives of war, regional revolts, and the lack of circulation of money in the provinces. In a broader sense, monetary statecraft helps explain the core anomaly of 19th century Brazil: the fact that political reaction, prevailed in the New World.

Upon independence in 1822, the negotiation of foreign loans and capitalization of the national bank provide further examples of monetary statecraft. Recourse to London bankers enabled crown and court in Brazil to build government institutions, mobilize military forces against Buenos Aires over Montevideo, and confront regional and liberal revolts.[23] Treaties and resolution of debts between England, Portugal and newly independent Brazil were not completed during 1823–1824. Nonetheless, Sturz reports that 600,000 pounds sterling were nonetheless remitted from London to the Banco do Brasil in species and bullion (while remittances of bills of exchange reached 400,000 pounds sterling).[24] As newly independent monarch, Pedro I used these funds to purchase warships from England and the United States and stock arsenals in Rio de Janeiro and Bahia with over 500,000 pounds sterling of military equipment.

In August 1825, treaties between England, Portugal and Brazil settled finances. Instead of Brazil paying Portugal's claim of 2 million pounds sterling for palaces and warships left in Brazil, treaties transferred to Brazil the obligations of Portugal arising from a 1.5 million pound sterling loan taken out in London in 1823. Given that Portugal had paid or redeemed 100,000 pounds sterling, Brazil thereby assumed 1.4 million pounds of debt upon independence to be paid in 50,000 pounds sterling annual payments.

This cleared the way for finance from abroad. The value of loans from London banks to the Brazilian monarchy reached 5 million pounds during the first empire under Pedro I (1822–1831). A loan contracted in 1824–1825 added 3.68 million pounds to the 1.4 million pound balance of Portuguese loans; a second loan in 1829 added 769,000 pounds summing to 5.85 million. Subtracting 732,000 pounds paid by Brazil, the stock of debt remained at 5.13 million pounds (28.5 million contos at 43.2 exchange rate).

These are large numbers that presented an opportunity to stabilize the currency, economy, and new national institutions. The opportunity was lost because of expensive diplomatic missions, purchase of military equipment, and wasteful spending on war with Buenos Aires. Hiring of Irish mercenaries alone cost 50,000 pounds sterling (despite their return to Ireland without seeing service), while the cost of bringing the second empress to Brazil is also cited by Sturz.[25] The United States and England also won compensation of 4,500 contos for vessels detained during Brazilian blockade of the Plata River (apparently paid through domestic note issues).

Policies sought to decrease the cost of debt and remittances to London. Proceeds from a 400,000 pound loan were left in London to pay dividends and obligations without the high cost of currency remittances by sea. The Brazilian government also tapped changing market conditions. While Brazilian bonds traded in London at 47–48 percent face value, news of negotiations for a new loan both increased the market value of old bonds and made it possible for the Brazilian government to issue new paper at 54 percent face value. This increased the market value of Brazilian bonds in London to 767,000 pounds sterling.[26] The London Stock Exchange refused to accept the loan (because the Exchange barred 'any loan raised for the purpose of paying the dividends of another' and 'that Brazil had not fulfilled her engagements with respect to the Portuguese loan').[27] Nonetheless, competition between London banks made it possible for the Brazilian government to negotiate and improve terms. Rothschild first refused to extend a loan at 50 percent. However, once Thomas Wilson & Co. signed at 54 percent of face value, Rothschild chose to also participate in the loan at 54 percent of face value.[28]

The first monarchy (1822–1831) also tapped domestic finance. By 1831, domestic debt summed to 56.5 contos, with Banco do Brasil notes (16.0), copper coin to be withdrawn (19.0), budget arrears (3.5), unfunded debt (38.5) and funded debt in a 'great book' of public debt (18.0) together reaching well over the value of 28.5 contos in foreign debt. However, the centrepiece of monetary statecraft in early Brazil was the creation of a national bank.

The Banco do Brasil (1808–1829)

On 12 October 1808, the Portuguese monarchy commissioned a Banco do Brasil to provide funds for Treasury, supply credit to government ministries, issue legal tender for acceptance at public agencies and encourage the use of official currencies. From its creation in 1809 until refusal of parliament to renew its charter in 1829 (and liquidation by 1837), the Banco do Brasil remains at the centre of monetary statecraft. Despite the depletion of gold, a weak tax base and little access to foreign finance (in 1808), King João VI nonetheless raised government funds by selling shares for a national bank granted monopoly of paper currency emissions. In addition to paying debts from war on the Iberian Peninsula, the invasion of Guiana by the French in 1809 required further funds to mobilize military forces through Pará provincial authorities.[29] The River Plate War (1823–1825) and war with Argentina (1826–1828) forced Emperor Pedro I to mobilize military forces in the far south. Regional uprisings throughout the first Empire also pressured government finances. From the 1817 revolt in Pernambuco through the abdication of Pedro I in the face of the 1831 revolution, serious challenges wracked the new imperial government in Rio de Janeiro.[30]

The design of the Banco do Brasil followed experiences abroad (the Bank of England and the Swedish Riksbank) and attempted to reduce monetary chaos by consolidating policy in a national bank granted monopoly over currency emissions and exchange as well as commercial bank operations such as discounting currency exchange letters, commissions, loans and mortgages, accepting deposits and making government interest payments and sales. Money and currency operations were also ascribed to the bank: emissions of coin and paper money; trading of short- and mid-term promissory notes; and transactions involving gold, silver and other precious metals and coins. Banco do Brasil notes were limited to minimum of 30$000 to avert their use in small retail transactions.

The end of the gold cycle in Brazil and substitution of gold coin for restamped Spanish silver dollars meant that the new imperial government failed to accumulate metal reserves to anchor paper money issued by the national bank.[31] This lack of gold, a hard currency, and proper reserve requirements notwithstanding, Sturz notes the counterintuitive stability of Banco do Brasil deposits and liabilities:

> And it is a curious and singular fact in the history of banks that, although the issue of notes by the Rio de Janeiro bank exceeded ten times the capital origi- nally deposited in metal, no one holder of its notes ever thought of demanding cash for them.[32]

The Banco do Brasil provided policy options and funds for government. The national bank printed notes, loaned to government entities, and used stewardship of gold reserves in its vaults to retain market confidence and maximize the supply of finance and credit.

The Banco do Brasil raised capital through issue of shares. Investors first refused to buy shares during 1810–1811. A royal offer of Order of Christ commendations for subscribers also failed to increase sales in 1812. Thereafter, a commercial bank tax funded Treasury purchase of shares. By 1816, the end of war in Europe, the elevation of Brazil to status of kingdom, the opening of bank branches in Bahia and São Paulo, and payment of 189$607 per share dividends finally stimulated voluntary purchase of national bank shares. By 1818, the government was able to double the capital base of the national bank to 2.400.000$000.

Despite political and military challenges at home and abroad, a weak tax base, and lack of precious metals to anchor the value of paper money, the Portuguese crown used the Banco do Brasil to consolidate a monarchy and empire in the New World. This was political. Viera reports a 0.97 correlation between political chal- lenges to the government and currency emissions in following years.[33] The costs associated with repressing the 1817 revolution in Pernambuco were met through emissions in 1818 and 1919. The costs of war in the south during 1825–1825 were met through further emissions of Banco do Brasil notes in the following years. This correlation appears after three years of bank operation: by 1817 the government had depleted funds at Treasury and began printing money. Thereafter, Banco do Brasil reserves against currency issues decline dramatically: paper money increased from 75 percent of reserves in the first year of operation (1810) to 117 percent (1811) to 287 (1812) and 305 percent (1813). Reversing the calculation thereafter, reserves as a percent of paper notes declined from 48 percent in 1814 to 8.47 percent by 1828, the last year before parliament refused to renew the national bank charter.

Data reported by Calogeras confirm this course of paper money emissions. The already slim prospects for building a convertible currency were dashed as issues of paper money quickly outpaced metal reserves. Emissions of paper money increased while metal reserves declined from an estimated 10 contos[34] (two-thirds gold) in 1808 to an estimated 1.3 contos in 1821. The first paper money to circu- late in Brazil was fiduciary. The relation between deposits and loans also failed to observe the banking prudence called for in the royal decree founding the national bank in 1808. By 1821, private deposits are estimated at 245 contos; government deposits are estimated at 482 contos. Loans surged to 3.3 contos during 1821, a full 2.3 contos of which originated from simple verbal orders by the royal treasurer. Before departing for Portugal in 1821, João VI decreed that all government debts and obligations acquired through the bank were to be guaranteed by future government receipts, mixing further the already tangled relations between politics and monetary policy.[35]

An epistemic community of monetary policy

Monetary statecraft in 19th century Brazil also involved the emergence of an epistemic policy community and specialized agencies for money, banking and finance. The first official responsible for Portuguese finances in the New world was Fernando José de Portugal (Marquês de Aguiar II). As administrator of crown finance from 1808 to 1816, he prohibited gold dust as means of exchange, closed the Gold Bar Exchange Bank (Banco do Troco das Barras de Ouro), introduced taxes, and supervised capitalization of the Banco do Brasil. After serving in sub-secretarial posts, Martim Francisco Ribeiro de Andrada became responsible for finance and money from July 1822 to July 1823. Despite João VI having returned to Lisbon (taking with him the entire stock of reserves in the Royal treasury and Banco do Brasil), Minister Andrada nonetheless secured a domestic loan (oversubscribed) to purchase warships and cover obligations during these first months of independence from Portugal.[36]

Manoel Jacintho Nogueira da Gama (Marquês de Baependi) succeeded Andrada in 1823, and returned as Finance Minister in 1826 and 1831 to, among other policies, introduce a pension fund for government employees in 1834.[37] From November 1823 to November 1825, Mariano José Pereira da Fonseca (Marquês de Maricá) negotiated the first foreign loan of Brazil abroad, negotiating 3 million pounds sterling with London banks by mortgaging import receipts (1 million pounds at 75 percent face value and 5 percent interest and 2 million pounds at 85 percent face value and 5 percent interest).[38] Although in office only 11 months during 1827, Finance Minister João Severiano Maciel da Costa (Marquês de Queluz) cut taxes on gold, wrote the first budget laws, and consolidated government debt (12.000:000$000) in a Book of Public Debt (Livro da Dívida Pública), finally, and liquidated obligations (including the 1828 budget deficit) with treasury paper. Maciel da Costa also created the first Currency Board (Caixa de Amortização) and drafted the 1828 Finance Ministry Report.

Miguel Calmon du Pin e Almeida (Marquês de Abrantes) was nominated finance minister in November 1827, a post he would hold again on four occasions through January 1843.[39] Minister Calmon prohibited export of copper coin from Bahia, fixed the fiscal year from July–June, supervised the liquidation of the Banco do Brasil, created standardized tax receipts and sold bonds at home to avert taking on further foreign loans. In 1827, he secured a 400,000 pound loan in London at 4 percent interest and 52 percent of face value to cover obligations from previous loans signed in 1824 and 1825. In 1838, Calmon Du Pin created a state credit facility that provided 3,700 contos (1838), 6,500 (of 15,800 contos in 1939) and 12,459 (of 16,500 contos in 1840) for government budgets. To meet payments on foreign debt, Calmon du Pin contracted a loan in 1838 of 312,500 pounds in London at *76 percent face value and 5 percent interest* and, once again, in 1842 to settle disputes with Portugal (732,600 pounds).

Felisberto Caldeira Brant Pontes de Oliveira e Horta (Marquês de Barbacena) was finance minister on two occasions, from November 1825 to January 1826 and again during 1830. Minister Caldeira Brant freed gold and silver imports, nominated a commission to propose policies for the organization of the monetary system and, as special minister in London, negotiated other Brazilian affairs.[40] Caldeira Brant was the first Finance Minister to present a budget to Parliament (1830) detailing financial accounts, money stocks, and a proposal to balance the budget and reform monetary arrangements.[41] Despite support from parliament and fellow ministers, Pedro I removed Brant from the Finance Ministry in 1930, further escalating confrontation with regional and liberal opposition groups.

José Antonio Lisboa served only a month as finance minister in late 1830, but published several works on the Banco do Brasil, money, and statistics.[42] José Inácio Gomes also served briefly in 1831 while government finances deteriorated. Parliament rejected his proposal to suspend payments on foreign debt but approved a proposal to prohibit export of copper coin.

Finally, amidst revolution and withdrawal of Pedro I to Lisbon, Bernardo Pereira de Vasconcelos served as finance minister from July 1831 to May 1832. He created a new National Treasury Court and Provincial Treasuries charged with registry and control of receipts and budget lines.

Bank war in Brazil: parliament vs Pedro I

From 1821 to 1831, liberal and regional opposition groups perceived the Banco do Brasil as agent of absolute monarchy and central government in Rio de Janeiro responsible for corruption and the uncontrolled printing of paper currency. Refusal of parliament to renew the Banco do Brasil charter in 1829 reflected liberal opposition to abuses of the national bank, a close parallel to the bank war between US president Andrew Jackson and Nicolas Biddle, president of the first US Bank. In Brazil, these perceptions informed a turn to liberal doctrines of free banking and the delegation of currency emissions to private commercial banks.

Opponents were right: the capacity of the national bank to serve monarchy confirms the importance of monetary statecraft. Despite return of João VI to Portugal in 1821, the Banco do Brasil nonetheless provided funds and policy alternatives for Pedro I upon declaration of independence in 1822.[43] Capitalization of the national bank was the first item on the agenda of the State Council in 1822 and seen as critical to reinforce the newly independent monarchy.[44] The return of João VI to Portugal (1821) had produced a crisis of confidence that forced the Banco do Brasil to limit withdrawals to 80 percent paper (permitting 15 percent silver and 5 percent copper). However, having declared himself emperor of an independent Brazil,

Pedro I also proclaimed to the Constitutional Assembly (shortly before closing it in 1823) that concern about the solvency of the national bank was unfounded and that his government would restructure its finances. Only 200 contos in metal reserves remained to cover an estimated 8,872 contos of paper money in circulation. However, sale of bank shares in 1823–1824 were oversubscribed to increase the capital of the national bank to 3,600 contos.

Two explanations appear in primary and secondary sources for the trajectory of paper note printing at the national bank. One emphasizes the rents extracted and fraud wrought on the bank by privileged members of the court. A second explanation emphasizes the objective weight of government obligations (from war and repression of rebellions) that forced spending to be covered by emissions of paper currency by the national bank. Parliamentary commissions of inquiry are rife with accusations of the former. Data tend to support the latter.[45]

The cleavage between, on the one hand, shareholders and directors of the national bank and, on the other hand, depositors and subjects provides further evidence how money and banking caused political conflicts to escalate in the 1820s. Indeed, this cleavage continued even after the national bank was closed: during liquidation of the bank (1830–1837), shareholders were paid while depositors were not.

Closing the national bank was followed by inflation, foreign exchange devaluation, return of illicit copper coin, contraband, high interest rates and flight to precious metals. Demonetization is widely reported during the late 1820s and early 1830s. Reports of parliament, Finance Ministry commissions and secondary analyses concur. During 1829, paper notes lost 40 percent against copper coins, 110 percent against silver coin and 190 percent against gold coin. The mil-réis also fell from averages of 96 pence in 1812–1814, to 41 pence (1826), 31 pence (1827) and 28.5 pence (1828), to bottom at around 20 pence per mil-réis between 1829 and 1831 (see Figure 2.1).

Finance ministers and members of parliament proposed several plans to reorganize the national bank during the 1820s. Minister Visconde de Baependy proposed channelling 576 contos in taxes and 76 contos of government deposits. In 1827, Finance Minister Marques de Queluz proposed discounts in metal exchanges (100 percent against gold and 40 percent against silver in 1827, followed by another 190 percent against gold and 110 percent against silver in 1829) to bring the bank back to solvency. Gonçalves Ledo also proposed to reorganize the bank, while Calogeras asserts that liquidation of the bank was unnecessary and costly, leaving Brazil without a national banking for decades. Vieira seems more convincing: he argues that capital flight (to precious metals and from the country), a lack of confidence among investors, high government debt and regional revolts against imperial government during the 1820s made restructuring of the bank *politically* impossible.[46]

The politics of liquidation shifted questions of monetary statecraft to the allocation of losses. Despite objections from liberal opposition groups, the government paid four-fifths of shares by 1835 and the rest by 1839. Banco do Brasil debts to creditors close to the court were notoriously difficult to collect.

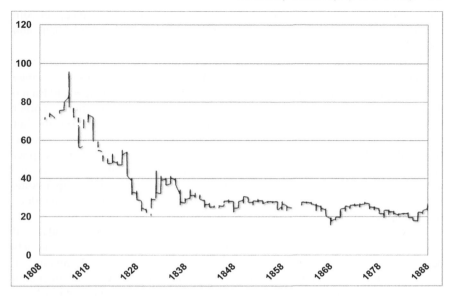

Figure 2.1 Foreign exchange rate (1808–1888, mil-réis/pence)
Source: Ipeadata

Differences between the government and bank (turning on 500 contos government capital in the bank, 420 contos of earnings due the government and pardon of past due fees owed to the bank by the government) also required negotiation. Payments to shareholders suggest that the bank was a good investment. The same cannot be said about deposits or recalls and/or conversions of coins and notes. Setting rates for recalled notes far below market value led to criticism of both the autocratic method of intervention and the redistributive impact of bank liquidation.[47] Further legislation in 1833 recalled notes in exchange for new notes issued by Treasury.[48]

Legacies of liquidation: 1831 revolution evolution and copper coin redux

The void left by liquidation of the national bank caused flight of gold and silver coin and the return of copper and illicit *xenxem* (copper) coin, especially in the provinces. Demand for coin in the interior, especially the north, increased contraband of copper from abroad. Parliamentary commissions repeatedly debated these phenomena and proposed various measures to combat the circulation of illicit copper coin. From Coutinho's 1826 legislative proposal, through parliamentary commissions of inquiry held in 1827 and 1828, and schemes from Pires Ferreira, Calmon and Rebouças presented to parliament in 1830; the central government in Rio de Janeiro sought to reverse the spread of illegal copper coin and promote use of official legal tender (paper notes from the national bank and official copper coin).

The interaction between government policies and money suggest, once again, the validity of both Chartalist and monetarist theories. Four programs to exchange notes and copper coin were pursued during the 1820s. One exchanged old Banco do Brasil notes for new notes issued by the liquidation commission. Another program exchanged commission notes for new treasury notes. Yet another exchanged copper coins for treasury notes at a gold base of 2$500 (increased from 1$600). Finally, Bahia province printed treasury notes to exchange copper coins. A 5 percent discount on legal copper coins exchanged for new treasury notes, 50 percent discount for marking (thereby legalizing) illicit copper coins in Rio de Janeiro (25 percent discount in the provinces) also attempted to reduce use of copper coin.

The spread of copper coin was also political. The aversion of regional and liberal opposition groups to the use of official imperial currencies were part of conflicts between provinces and central government that culminated in the 1831 revolution. For Falcão, the political consequences of this flight to and inflation of copper coin were nothing less than the 1831 revolution: '. . . copper inflation peaked in 1827, becoming the principal cause of the revolution of 7 April 1831'.[49]

Finance Minister Bernardo de Vasconcelos also begins his account in 1832 of political decay and revolution with the disappearance of gold and silver coin and the insolvency of the national bank:

> the disappearance of precious metals; the emptying of the bank; the increase in prices together with that lost in the balance of trade and business relationships; interest rates raised to an extraordinary level; an exchange rate almost on par with zero; opulence greater than private fortunes but demanded by a court to concealed its little merit; judicial iniquity, moral corruption, staff embezzlement; blind fondness of the crown for some and the unlimited depredation by those favored; unwarranted and foolhardy war; the extraordinary issue of currency with no value; the persistence of abusive practices and the abundance of Treaties that dealt a mortal blow to our trade, shipping and industry.[50]

The collapse of money during the 1820s, liquidation of the bank to save shareholders but sacrifice depositors and recall of paper notes from the national bank below market prices suggest how monetary policies drove disputes between opposition groups and the monarch in Rio de Janeiro culminating in revolution in 1831.

For liberal and regional opposition groups, private commercial banks would provide an alternative to absolute monarchy and these monetary policies of the central imperial government in Rio de Janeiro. However, adoption of liberal policies would await another decade of conservative modernization under the Regency imposed after the 1831 revolution.

Conservative modernization under regency (1831–1841)

Monetary policies under the regency (1831–1841) attempted to sustain the foreign exchange value of the mil-réis and counter proliferation of copper coin and monetary chaos at home. Unintended consequences ensued. Instead of consolidating a single currency, the attempt to control money encouraged the circulation of commercial bank notes, especially in the provinces. Ideas from abroad about consolidating a single convertible government currency thereby entered into conflict with liberal and regional opposition groups who sought to reverse demonetization in the provinces. After Pedro I returned to Portugal in 1831, those responsible for financial policy under the regency (1831–1841) confronted illicit copper coin, a lack of confidence among creditors and bondholders, and devaluation of the mil-réis. Brazilian government bonds traded at 45 percent face value in Rio de Janeiro and 47 percent in London. The mil-réis fell to 19 pence while reserves at Treasury in Rio de Janeiro approached zero. Emergency policies reduced government deficits by cutting the number of standing armed forces and refusing to let British merchants pay in copper coin.

Policies focused on recovering the value of the mil-réis abroad, reducing the circulation of copper coin in the provinces, and centralizing monetary policies in Rio de Janeiro. Reforms in 1833 increased the gold parity of mil-réis from 1$600 to 2$500, lowered the official exchange rate from 67.5 to 43.2 pence and set a schedule for recall of copper.[51] From 1833 to 1837, Treasury exchanged over 9.6 contos of paper for copper coin (1833 estimate = 16.6 contos legal and 8 contos illicit copper coin). Policies thereby attempted to move towards a single paper money reference and overcome the myriad coins and currencies that had appeared in the decade after closing the national bank.

However, recalls often produced shortages of legal tender. By 1835, the government had achieved its goals of increasing confidence in treasury operations. Nonetheless, Finance Minister Calmon announced a new program for the recall and destruction of paper currency in 1837 to control inflation. This is a turning point in the politics of monetary policy in early Brazil. Instead of seeking to ensure the supply of coin and reap gains from stamping Spanish coin or printing paper notes at the national bank, *control of the money supply* became the goal, a goal that continued to be pursued despite clear signs of currency shortages. Indeed, contraction of the money base after 1835 worked against the goals of reducing use of copper coins by producing a new phenomenon: the use of private commercial bank promissory notes (*vales*) as currency.[52]

This shift to control of the money supply involved a fundamental change in the epistemic community of monetary policy makers.[53] After conservative party leader Joaquim José Rodrigues Torres (Visconde de Itaboraí) and Nicolau Pereira de Campos Vergueiro served briefly as finance ministers in 1832, Cândido José de Araujo Viana (Marquês de Sapucaí) remained Minister from December 1832 to June 1834.[54] Araujo Viana set a new currency parity, sought in vain to reopen the Banco do Brasil[55] and closed the Bahia mint. In 1833, he introduced major monetary reforms proposed by a commission charged in January that attempted to build on fiscal gains. Reforms included a new gold parity for the mil-réis (2$500 per 1/8 ounce), recall of copper coin and exchange of Banco do Brasil notes for treasury notes.[56] Manuel do Nascimento de Castro e Silva served as Finance Minister from October 1834 to May 1837.[57] He sought to control what he perceived as an excessive circulation of money and to reform customs houses. Castro e Silva created a currency board (Caixa de Amortização) for recall of bonds, notes and certificates of deposits, as well as Banco do Brasil notes for Treasury notes. Castro e Silva also replaced three exchange rates (67.5, 60 and 54 pence) with the new 43.2 pence exchange rate. These policies led Brazilian bonds abroad to reach 88 percent face value; a substantial recovery from below half face value during the 1831 revolution.

Manoel Alves Branco (II Visconde de Caravelas) served as Finance Minister from May to September 1837 and returned to the post three times (1839–1840, 1844–1846, 1847–1848). As Treasury Accountant General in 1837, Alves Branco introduced double-entry budgeting, reformed the Finance Ministry secretariat, regulated lotteries and proposed two policies that were adopted only decades later – creation of a gold fund to guarantee currency convertibility (adopted under Joaquim Murtinho in 1899) and creation of Accounting Courts (adopted under Rui Barbosa in 1890). Manoel Alves Branco continued to advocate transition to a gold standard and convertible currency from 1844 until the 1846 monetary reform.

Finance Minister from April to September 1839, Cândido Batista de Oliveira later published *Sistema financial do Brasil* (1842) advocating the organization of a bank to be charged with emission of a convertible currency. Although Finance Minister for only two months (May–July 1840), José Antonio da Silva Maia left five publications on monetary policy and financial management.[58] After Calmon served for a fourth time as Finance Minister from March 1841 to January 1843, Joaquim Francisco Vianna served from January 1843 to February 1844 to introduce proportional stamp taxes and a temporary progressive tax on earnings from government bonds.[59]

In sum, after departure of Pedro I in 1831, the government cut spending, sought to increase revenue, revalued the gold parities of the mil-réis and gradually removed copper coin from circulation.[60] Monetary policies were part of a broader conservative modernization of government. Consolidation of national and provisional treasuries, liquidation of the Banco do Brasil, improved government budgets, and creation of a private pension fund for public servants (and creation of a savings bank to encourage savings by labourers) defined the politics of monetary policy as the reassertion of central government during the 1830s.

The two latter proposals were brought to Brazil by José Bonifácio and other Brazilians trained in European universities. Savings banks were founded in Rio de Janeiro (1831), Bahia (1835) and several other provinces during the regency. The evolution of deposits, withdrawals and accumulated capital at the Rio de Janeiro Savings Bank 1831–1837 suggest that this institution played a significant role in political economy. By June 1837, deposits at the Rio de Janeiro Savings Bank surpassed 2,500 contos (Bahia Savings Bank reported 220 contos). Moreover, Sturz estimates that the Rio de Janeiro Savings Bank held one-fifth of Brazilian domestic government debt. Designed along lines of European institutions, the Rio de Janeiro

Savings Bank paid 6 percent interest on savings and ensured its downmarket retail mission by limiting accounts to 100 contos. The second measure of modernization was creation of a pension fund for public sector employees in 1835. Of 4,800 government employees (1,357 civil and 2,902 military), this shift away from public pensions as treasury obligations to private funds are estimated to have reduced the cost of pension payments incurred by the imperial government from 1,057,942 mil-réis in fiscal year 1835–1836 to 604,693 mil-réis by 1838–1839.

In sum, the mixture of monetary policies under the regency from 1831 to 1840 reflected tensions between conservative modernization of government in Rio de Janeiro, while regional opposition groups began to circulate commercial bank notes.

Liberalism, plural banking, and financial crises (1840–1859)

From 1840–1859, monetary policies shifted away from efforts to consolidate a single official currency to a fundamentally different approach: the delegation of money management to commercial banks and use of bank notes (*vales*) as currency. Liberal theories from abroad informed this turn to the use of private commercial bank notes as money. This changed the politics of monetary policy. From reforms in 1842 and 1846 through financial crises in 1837, 1853, 1857, and 1859, debates and policies turned on the excessive emissions of unregulated promissory notes and their acceptance as de facto currency. Beginning in the 1830s, the vices and virtues of plural commercial bank notes came to dominate debates about money, credit and banking until the financial crisis of 1859 led to centralizing reforms that largely ended plural bank note emissions. Legislation in 1833 first freed commercial banks to issue 15-day coupons that thanks to demand, quickly became used as means of payment far past their due date. After a government ban failed to stop use of bank notes as currency, policies attempted to regulate use of coupons by setting minimum values for notes (500$000 in 1842, 200$000 in 1852) and limiting notes to a third of bank capital. The second official Banco do Brasil (discussed below) received preference (5-day notes instead of 15 and limit of half bank capital).

A new generation of policy makers supported private commercial bank note issues. Bernardo de Souza Franco, who served temporarily as Finance Minister (August–September 1848) and then formally (May 1857–December 1858), was a proponent of free banking, free use of British coin and advocate of customs reforms. Since Joaquim Nabuco, many cite Souza Franco as representative of one pole in debates about finance, banking and monetary policy during the 1850s: defender of free banking and plural commercial bank management of the money supply.[61] Plural banking was also advocated by Honório Hermeto Carneiro Leão (Marquês de Paraná) as Finance Minister from September 1853 to January 1855 and from January 1855 to August 1856.[62] Carneiro Leão stressed the need for more credit to encourage commerce after the end of the slave trade abroad in 1850, and, towards this end authorized a threefold increase in currency emissions by the Banco do Brasil and new branch offices for the national bank in provincial capitals. He nonetheless stabilized the mil-réis against foreign currencies.

Bank notes first circulated in provinces where supply of official money was short and constituted a type of rebellion against central government. Circulation of notes from a savings bank in Ceará state during 1836 led other provinces to follow suit. The 1837 financial crisis in Rio de Janeiro further encouraged private bank note issue, now seen as necessary to maintain bank liquidity and help firms through the crisis. Bank promissory notes thereafter circulated widely and contributed to financial market bubbles and speculative fever in Rio de Janeiro.

A boom in banking ensued. Major banks were founded such as the Banco Comercial do Rio de Janeiro (1838), the Banco Commercial da Bahia (1845), the Banco Commercial do Maranhão (1849), the Caixa Commercial da Bahia (1850) and Banco de Pernambuco (1851). In 1853, the Banco Comercial de Rio de Janeiro, Banco Commercial do Pará and Banco Rural e Hipotecário followed. All of these printed notes were widely used as currencies. After the 1857 crisis, plural commercial bank emissions continued, with 14 new banks founded in 1858 alone. It is of note that foreign banks founded affiliates *after* the 1860 monetary reform, such as the London and Brazilian Bank (1962) and Brazilian and Portuguese Bank (1863).

Monetary reform in 1846 attempted to regulate commercial bank notes as part of Finance Minister Vasconcelos's plan to move Brazil gradually toward a metal standard. Reforms combined opposing theories and principles: a convertible currency based on a gold standard and free banking designed to encourage commercial banks to issue and manage money. While this undermined transition to a convertible currency, 1846 reforms were effective because the fixed exchange rate of 4$700 mil-réis per pence was more in tune with markets. Moreover, legislation in 1849 that sought to move toward currency convertibility and a gold standard by limiting silver coins to values under 20$000 helped reduce the multiplication of currencies. Progress also continued during the 1850s and 1860s because world surpluses of gold stemmed flights from Brazilian paper currencies and reduced use of illicit currencies. This mixture of opposing policies is typical of monetary statecraft in Brazil.

Ministers also changed sides. Finance Minister Itaborai criticized private bank issues in 1846, however by 1850 recognition of the need for money due to economic growth altered his position and, in 1853, he defended the free circulation of private commercial bank notes. Itaborai also proposed commission of a new national bank that could gradually increase government influence over money, credit and banking. This is an example of how policies combined apparently incompatible principles in an attempt to reduce the profusion of unregulated private bank emissions and create propitious circumstances to move gradually, in the future, toward a single national convertible currency anchored to gold reserves. The comparatively benign consequences of the 1853 financial crisis also legitimized this framework of plural commercial bank issues. Instead of simply printing money to relieve crisis, interest rates appear to have played an important role for the first time, increasing from 4 to 5 percent short term and 10 to 12 percent long term.

Moreover, a second official Banco do Brasil was created during this period of plural commercial bank issues that would remain central to the politics of monetary policy until the end of the empire in 1889. Like the first national bank, the government commissioned sale of bank shares and set a variety of regulations to increase control over money, credit and banking while retaining private shareholder ownership of the bank. Maua's Banco Commercial do Rio de Janeiro and the (already existing private) Banco do Brasil promptly merged in 1854 to meet the minimum sale of 50,000 shares (of a total 150,000) for registry of the new Banco do Brasil.[63] Maua's private Banco do Brasil purchased 50,000 shares, the Banco Comercial do Rio de Janeiro purchased 30,000 shares, while 40,000 shares were reserved for provinces willing to fund branch offices. A further 30,000 shares were sold in Rio de Janeiro (10 percent over the 200 mil-réis face value), suggesting the level of interest in the new bank.

A strategy of gradually increasing control over diverse monies continued to inform policy during the 1850s. Inspired by the Austrian experience of reducing plural emissions, the 1853 bank law reduced the variety of notes issued by commercial banks and recalled coins and notes left from previous periods. The Banco do Brasil's new charter required it to recall 2 contos per year in exchange for treasury notes earning 6 percent interest until 20 contos were removed from circulation. Vieira suggests that the national bank fell just short of targets during the 1855–1864 decade. Further measures sought to reduce the money supply. Currency recalls were to be paid in full by Treasury, while *one-third* of Banco do Brasil capital increases were earmarked for recall of bank notes. Legislation also gave the government prerogative to nominate the president and vice president of the bank, while requiring the election of 15 directors by shareholders in secret ballot in assembly, alongside three independent inspectors charged with submitting monthly accounting reviews of bank operations.

Amidst a regime of plural commercial bank issues, the second official Banco do Brasil sought to bring the country closer to a gold standard. The government achieved progress in the sense that copper and silver coin diminished. However, the mil-réis never gained convertibility. Instead, it remained a fiduciary currency, anchored to a specially designed *fundo disponível* (available fund) that banks were required to set aside as additional reserves to ensure confidence in the currency. Banks were required to maintain *half* the value of their bank notes in precious metal, coin, and treasury notes in reserves against risk.

The new Banco do Brasil also moved quickly to acquire regional banks or open new branches to assert greater monetary authority over the provinces. The Banco de Pernambuco was acquired in 1855, the Banco Comercial da Bahia in 1856, the Banco do Para in 1856 and the Banco do Maranhão in 1857. The financial crisis of 1857 reversed this trend briefly while the government permitted regional banks to print notes twice their reserve funds to ensure liquidity. Soon thereafter acquisitions continued. In 1862, the Banco do Brasil acquired the Banco Agrícola do Rio de Janeiro. Prohibition of emissions by the Banco Rural and HipotecaRio de Janeiro meant that the national bank had acquired a monopoly of currency emissions in Rio de Janeiro. Liquidation of the Banco do Rio de Janeiro Grande do Sul left only the Banco do Para, Banco do Maranhão and the Banco Comercial da Bahia (sold in 1860) as banks emitting notes widely traded as currencies.

Table 2.2 Treasury and bank currency emissions (contos)

Fiscal Year	Treasury	Banco do Brasil	Bank Subtotal	Total
1853–1854	46.6	8.6	15.5	62.2
1854–1855	46.6	16.6	21.0	67.7
1855–1856	45.6	25.0	40.1	85.8
1856–1857	43.6	49.6	51.5	95.2
1857–1858	41.6	46.5	50.5	92.5
1858–1859	40.7	40.6	55.1	95.8

Source: Calogeras, J.P. *La Politique Monétaire du Brésil* (Rio de Janeiro: Imprimerie Nationale, 1910), pp. 107–108.

This consolidation of money management by the national bank differs from other experiences of free banking and plural commercial bank issue. From the beginning of operations in April 1854 to year-end, the Banco do Brasil emitted 15.5 contos of notes. In 1855, emissions surpassed reserve requirements, leading the government to request increasing caps on emissions to three times the reserve fund. Some monetary authorities counselled caution.[64] A parliamentary commission charged with analysis of the 1857 crisis repeated the warnings of Finance Minister Parana about the dangers of liberal doctrines of paper currency.[65]

The evidence from 1839–1860 confirms the central arguments of the monetary principle school; that multiple commercial emissions inflate currencies and disorganize commercial transactions, with one addendum: the second national Banco do Brasil remained the primary source of bank notes after 1854 (see Table 2.2).

Recall of notes by the national bank pale in comparison. From 1855 to 1860, total bank emissions averaged over 90 contos per year, while Banco do Brasil recalls averaged under 2 contos.[66] Treasury notes also declined from 46 contos in 1853–1854 to just above 40 contos in 1858–1859. However, commercial bank emissions of currency increased from 15 to 55 contos. The increase in a variety of notes, paper, promissory certificates and trading of private bank issues has been emphasized by virtually every analyst of this period.

Figure 2.2 suggests how money creation in Brazil after 1852 changes from a phenomena of government paper currency to the multiplication of money by banks. The major source of increased money before the 1864 crisis (and subsequent crises in 1890 and 1913) are bank deposits. Increases in paper currency ensue *after the financial crisis*. We take that the value of bank deposits are a proxy for the multiplication of money by banks. The rapid accumulation of money in banks appears to be as important as changes in the supply of paper money during financial crises. Debates among contemporaries and money statistics suggest that banks multiplied money to fuel financial bubbles and crises.

Despite a run on the mil-réis in foreign exchange markets in January 1858,[67] emissions of commercial bank notes proceeded apace. During 1859, foreign exchange devaluation continued, domestic inflation increased and another financial crisis

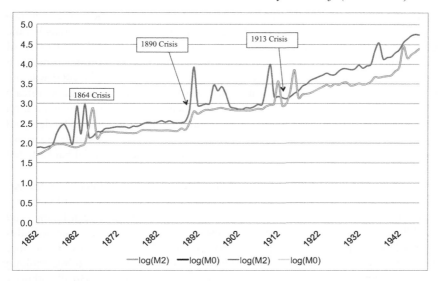

Figure 2.2 Paper currency (M0) and bank deposits (M2) (1852–1947)
Source: Ipeadata

ensued. The mil-réis in London fell from trading at 27.5–29.25 pence in 1853 to trade between 23.25 and 27.0 pence during 1859. Financial crisis in Rio de Janeiro in 1859 finally produced consensus to the need to end commercial bank emissions of paper currency. First, registry was refused on 2 April 1859 to 18 new applications to create commercial banks able to issue paper money. On 30 April, limits to Banco do Brasil paper currency emissions were reduced from thrice to twice deposits. On June 15, the Finance Ministry set a schedule for recall of notes to reduce the excess offer of private commercial bank notes. However, further policy change would await the 1860 election and change of government to the more aggressive and interventionist Finance Minister Silva Ferraz.

Recentralization: 1860 reforms, war with Paraguay (1864–1870) and crisis in 1875

In 1860, liberal theories of plural banking were repudiated to reassert central government control over money management. Financial crisis in 1864, finance of war with Paraguay (1864–1870) and counter-cyclical policies to avert crisis in 1875 reinforced thereafter both a shift to central government control over monetary policy and abandonment of the ideal of reaching a convertible currency in Brazil. In 1860, legislation recalled notes below 50$000, required guarantee of paper notes by bank reserves (*fundo disponível*), scheduled monthly limits to bank emissions and required deposit of bank reserves at Treasury. In 1864, the most severe financial crisis of the 19th century coincided with declaration of war on Paraguay to complete this turn away from liberal policies and toward centralization of monetary authority. In 1866, geopolitics and the depth of crisis led the government to transfer monopoly of currency emissions from the Banco do Brasil to Treasury. The empire thereby returned to beginnings, with military spending driving monetary policy much like the 1820s. One difference in 1860 was the creation of an imperial government pawn and savings bank (Caixa Econômica e Monte de Socorro), once again based on European experiences. This institution was designed to encourage popular savings and reduce illicit moneylenders and pawn shops. Remarkably, amidst the 1864 crisis (only four years after creation), deposits flowed *into* the official savings bank as private commercial banks failed and depositors sought safety.

A new generation of policy makers advocated and implemented recentralization of monetary policy after 1860. However, designs to move toward currency convertibility and a gold standard were tempered by the needs of war finance and liquidity during and after the financial crises of 1864 and 1875. Francisco de Salles Torres Homem (Visconde de Inhomirim) served as Finance Minister December 1858–August 1859 and August 1870–March 1871.[68] An opponent to free banking and plural currency emissions, Torres Homem reduced Banco do Brasil authority to print notes from three times to twice reserves. However, Salles Torres Homem also contracted a loan in London to liquidate debts from 1829 and finance two major railways, the Pedro II and União e Indústria railroads.

Angelo Moniz da Silva Ferraz (Barão de Uruguaiana), Finance minister from August 1859 to March 1861,[69] attempted to increase government tax revenue and created government secretaries for agriculture, commerce and public works. Silva Ferraz supervised the centralization of monetary authority, creation of the official savings and pawn bank and introduced responsibility clauses for debtors to Treasury and exams for public employment. José Maria da Silva Paranhos (Visconde do Rio de Janeiro Branco), Finance Ministry from March 1861 to May 1862 and March 1871 to June 1875,[70] cut spending and required budget lines to specify the origin of funds.[71]

In 1864, crisis reinforced the turn to centralized monetary policy. Crisis in the United States first produced a run on the Banco do Brasil and mil-réis. A loan in London proved insufficient to regain the confidence of depositors and markets. Given that the level of reserves appeared unlikely to be sufficient to stay the flight of deposits, the bank requested permission to *temporarily* emit four times reserves. The national bank thereby survived. However, many other banks and firms did not. The collapse of the private bank A.J.A. Souto in September left depositors with losses of over 41 contos. Failure of 118 banks by year-end produced estimated losses of 110 contos.[72]

The financial crisis of 1864 coincided with the onset of war with Paraguay, a development that shifted debates in parliament and government away from matters of money and finance to geopolitics and military mobilization.[73] Table 2.3 reports the financial sources for war with Paraguay and its aftermath (1864–1872). The value of foreign loans (61.7 contos) remained far below domestic paper loans (171.8 contos) and paper note emissions (113.2 contos).

Table 2.3 Finance sources for war with Paraguay (1864–1872)

Foreign Year	Domestic Loan	Domestic Gold Loan	Domestic Paper Loan	Notes	Other	Total
1864–1866	35,219		15,154	3,017		53,390
1866–1867			36,433	22,677	2	59,112
1867–1868			22,782	53,911	7	76,700
1868–1869		27,000	27,288	17,910		72,198
1869–1870			44,031	5,480	180	49,691
1870–1871	26,522		26,146	10,220	700	63,588
1871–1872			21		1,225	1,246
Total	61,741	27,000	171,855	113,215	2,114	375,925

Source: Carreira (1980), p. 469.

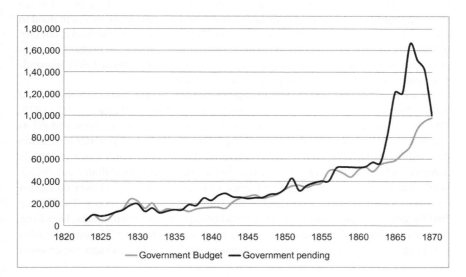

Figure 2.3 Government revenue and spending (1823–1870, million mil-réis)
Source: Ipeadata

Figure 2.3 illustrates the increase of expenditures from war covered by these largely domestic sources. Domestic monetary statecraft proved far more important for conduct of war than international finance. Moreover, given the tightening of foreign credit in the face of Brazilian war debts, domestic sources such as acquisition of government bonds (then called domestic paper loans) by the imperial savings and pawn bank suggests a different domestic political economy. The accumulated deposits of popular classes in the imperial savings bank were instrumental for paying debts from war with Paraguay.

The turn to war finance reflected the ideas and policies of a new generation of finance ministers. Carlos Carneiro de Campos (Visconde de Caravelas III) served as Finance Minister from August 1864 to May 1865, authoring the 1865 Finance Ministry report on the 1864 financial crisis.[74] He proposed laws to reform mortgage contracts, increased the reserve fund of the Banco do Brasil threefold, created rules for the establishment of royal credit societies, and once again forced acceptance of Banco do Brasil notes as legal tender and regulated convertible bond issues. As Finance Minister March–August 1866, João da Silva Carrão liquidated the Banco do Brasil department responsible for currency and note emissions, purchased metal reserves and promoted treasury notes. Zacaraias de Góes e Vasconcelos (Cabinet Minister and Finance Minister August 1866–July 1868)[75] raised existing and created new taxes and tariffs to cover war expenses, while opening Brazilian Treasury offices in London.

In sum, the centralization of monetary policy began in response to excesses of private commercial bank note issues during the 1850s seen as responsible for financial bubbles and crises. Centralization was reinforced by government need to cover war expenses with Paraguay. Crises in 1875 and 1885 would lead monetary authorities to provide emergency loans and credits to ensure liquidity. This suggests the mix of opposing principles typical of monetary statecraft that responds to circumstances rather than imposing theory or ideology.

Financial crisis abroad in 1873 produced depression in Europe and the United States. This cut Brazilian access to foreign finance and reduced exports.[76] By 1875, Brazilian monetary policies focused on rediscounting to alleviate firms and printing of money to ensure liquidity. Sale of government bills at 6 percent in London drained deposits from banks and accelerated the crisis of confidence in Rio de Janeiro bank branches. In May, the Mauá bank and German-Brazilian Bank failed, while alarming estimates of only 5 contos in reserve at banks to cover 68 contos in deposits fueled crisis. President of the Imperial council Viscount Rio Branco first failed to convince parliament to extend emergency credits to banks. However, deepening crisis led the Senate to authorize Treasury to emit 25 contos in bills and print 25 contos of paper mil-réis to ensure bank liquidity and stay the crisis of confidence in the banking system.

The end of empire: monetary reforms, recovery and adjustment to abolition

The military coup that ended the monarchy in 1889 was caused more by militarization of government after war with Paraguay and the emergence of new republican elites than economic trends or monetary policy.[77] To the contrary, the evidence suggests that monetary reforms during the 1880s produced economic recovery and a certain optimism, especially after abolition was completed in 1888. Moreover, the provisional republican government declared by military coup 15 November 1889 honored the foreign and domestic debts of monarchy and retained the framework for monetary and economic policy.[78] Indeed, emergency credits to farmers who were bankrupt by the end of slavery and other sources of easy money and liquidity at the end of empire drove a bubble in capital markets that would burst in 1891, the first year of republican rule.

Recovery of economic activity and trade surpluses from strong coffee harvests in the late 1880s produced an optimism that, in retrospect, appears at odds with the coming end of empire and turn to republican rule. The influential republican Finance Minister Leopoldo Bulhões emphasized the importance of reforms in monetary policy and finance that had produced growth in the last years of empire. The emancipation of slaves in 1888 followed two record years of coffee exports at high prices that stabilized the mil-réis near 28 pence and inspired Rothschild to extend a funding loan that converted debt from 1883, 1886 and 1888 at 5 percent into a 19 million pound loan at 4 percent with longer terms.[79] The fact that imperial debt was renegotiated weeks before a military coup ended the monarchy indicates how political regime change and monetary statecraft ran parallel courses.

Optimism about business and economic conditions pervaded parliamentary debate during 1889.[80] Minister Visconde de Ouro Preto introduced new credit policies to help farmers adjust to abolition only weeks before the 15 November 1889 coup that ended empire. Treasury emitted interest-free notes to banks as liability base for twice the value of notes in long-term loans to farmers at interest rates of 6 percent. This continued the efforts of his predecessor at the Ministry of Finance, Joao Alfredo, who sought to appease farmers and avert their shifting support from the emperor to republican clubs. An estimated 726 of 773 farms in the southeast states of Sao Paulo, Minas Gerais and Espirito Santo were 42,000 contos in debt.[81] Minister Ouro Preto also ordered monthly recall of 1,000 contos in paper currency to be exchanged by the Banco Nacional do Brasil (an institution recently nationalized)[82] and secured 100 contos in gold from domestic sources to finance the above loans to agriculture and measures to alleviate drought in the northeast. Decree 10.262 of 6 July 1889 also regulated metal reserves at banks according to a law passed by parliament on 24 November 1888.

This wave of money and credit policies in the late 1880s suggests the political dilemma faced by imperial government as described by Vieira:

> Either care for bankrupt farmers through loans and advances, thus steadily increasing the amount in circulation from the Treasury (and in that case incurring criticism from the republicans for causing inflation) or hold off the increase in circulation, not easing credit, not supporting farmers, and thus worsening discontent and giving cause to join the republican campaign and bring about the end of the Empire.[83]

The general improvement of economic conditions therefore concealed the consequences of massive credit to farmers. After 1887, government deficits declined, trade surpluses surpassed 54 contos, the mil-réis reached 27 pence, foreign credit flowed and government paper in London neared face value.

However, as Keynesian approaches to money and banking would suggest, the infusion of credit and liquidity at the end of empire produced a boom in capital markets. The Rio de Janeiro financial paper commented:

> There is no way to ignore the unusual increase in stock exchange transactions during the quarter August to October [1889]. Without reason or plausible explanation, bonds rose 30 percent in a day and 150 percent in a month. At a quickening pace, fortunes were made in a few weeks, sometimes in just a few days.
>
> (*Jornal do Comércio*, 18 December 1889)

The financial press suggested that two factors fuelled this valuation of capital markets amidst regime change: the farm credit program announced on 7 July 1889 and reforms that freed banks to emit fiduciary notes to increase liquidity and avert bankruptcies. The first republican Finance Minister Rui Barbosa would agree:

> The speculation fever on the stock exchange was thus not born from republican finances. It was a pre-existent disease, which during the last weeks of the Monarchy, became exacerbated to the proportions of acute delirium.
>
> (Barbosa, *Finanças e Política da República*, p. 24)

Improved access to financial markets abroad also permitted consolidation of debts on favourable terms. As mentioned above, the value of outstanding loans dating to 1865, 1871, 1875 and 1886 at 4 percent interest (down from 5) and longer (19-year) terms suggests that banks failed to perceive the coming financial crisis in 1890.

Pragmatic monetary policies and conservative modernization thus prevailed during the last years of empire. Gaspar da Silveira Martins served as finance minister from February 1878 to February 1879 and[84] imposed budget cuts to reverse deficits from funds used to alleviate drought in the Northeast. Upon refusing to increase currency emissions, Silveira resigned under pressure from opposition to austerity. Affonso Celso de Assis Figueiredo (Visconde de ouro Preto) served as finance minister through March 1880 and again from July to November 1889.[85] During his first ministry, Figueiredo designed a plan to amortize paper currency, further separated budgets by ministry, increased transparency by consolidating official publications in a printing office (Tipografia Nacional), introduced a transportation tax (known as the vintém tax repudiated by taxpayers) and proposed administrative reform. During his second term, Figueiredo also held the post of Ministerial Council President and managed the aftermath of emancipation in 1888 by helping farmers adjust to free labour.

José Antônio Saraiva served as Finance Minister from March 1880 to January 1882 and again from May to August 1885. He imposed fiscal austerity and attempted to reverse tax increases designed for drought relief. Saraiva authored the 1880, 1882 and 1885 Finance Ministry reports to Parliament.[86] Martinho Álvares da Silva Campos was Finance Minister January–July 1882, during which time he continued policies of Saraiva designed to value the mil-réis abroad and reduce government debt.

As president of the council of ministers, João Lustosa da Cunha Paranaguá (Marquês de Paranaguá) assumed the Finance Ministry July 1882–May 1883, adopting policies modeled on the liberal cabinet's program of 1868 (reduction of paper money and interest rates on the public debt). Lafayette Rodrigues Pereira similarly held both posts May 1883–June 1884 and continued policies designed to reduce government deficits and improve the terms of government debt. From June 1884 to May 1885, Manuel Pinto de Sousa Dantas occupied the Finance Ministry while Director of the Banco do Brasil (and other ministries) in the Sinumbu cabinet to pursue closer control of government income, spending cuts and attempts to increase tax revenue. Francisco Belisário Soares de Souza held the Finance Ministry from August 1885 to March 1888 and served as Banco do Brasil Director from 1873 to 1878.[87] An opponent of free banking and paper currency, he sought to concentrate monetary authority in the national bank to substitute treasury notes for new notes convertible into gold.

In sum, the politics of monetary policy during the last years of empire involved emergency measures to avert crisis in 1885, generous credit flows to farmers after abolition, positive perceptions of the country abroad, a speculative bubble in domestic capital markets and, in the midst of all this, designs to pave the way for transition to a convertible currency.

Conclusion

Monetary statecraft explains the core anomaly of 19th century Brazil. Dickson describes the modernization of public finance in England as a financial revolution. In Brazil, however, creation of a national bank and government bond issues financed political reaction; financial revolution by enabled Luso–Portuguese monarchs to defeat regional and liberal opposition forces. Monetary statecraft in later periods of Brazilian history would involve different political imperatives. However, the persistence of slavery, the defeat of opposition to central imperial government and what Carvalho has described as bestialisation of the Brazlian people are distinguishing features of 19th century Brazil. Monetary statecraft explains how money and finance policies were critical for this anomaly of monarchy and empire in the New World.

Tracing monetary policy making in 19th century Brazil reveals the greater challenges and creativity of policy making on the periphery; notwithstanding the reality of political reaction in the country. Primary and secondary sources reveal both a dynamic history of monetary policy amidst times of boom and bust and how ideas about money, banking and government policy were adapted from abroad to more volatile conditions on the periphery of the world system. This is the analytic advantage of studying underdevelopment. This chapter has reported significant evidence of how politics shape monetary phenomena amidst markets and phenomena of public policy such as unexpected consequences.

Creation of a national bank in 1808 *before* independence demonstrates the importance of monetary statecraft. The national bank remained at the core of money and politics. It's policies and performance explain how monarchy was able to prevail in the New World and became the object of conflicts between absolute monarchy and regional movements; such that this bank-anti-bank cleavage was a central cause of revolution and abdication of Pedro I in 1831. Thereafter, conservative modernization and liberal measures first decentralized government during the 1830s but soon reasserted central government and monetary authority in the 1840s. From this trajectory emerged a peculiar top-down two-party system of patronage that lasted from 1836 to 1889.[88] These political institutions would be unthinkable without the policies of money, credit and banking used to create and sustain them.

Despite the flow of capital from the slave trade to financial markets after the ban on naval slave traffic in 1850, slavery nonetheless sponged capital away from banking and credit to reproduce underdevelopment and reinforce coffee exports as primary motor of the economy for most of the 19th century. And unlike banking and industrialization in Europe and North America, industrial goods were imported and agrarian exports, especially coffee, predominated. This produced persistent trade deficits. Need to secure large foreign loans to finance trade deficits set the context for the politics of monetary policy during the latter 19th century.

Monetary statecraft in early Brazil was shaped by geopolitics, war and the need to obtain money for monarchs. Thereafter, the liberalization of commercial banking and the development of plural emissions was first encouraged, then countered by policies designed to recover authority over money through creation of a second official Banco do Brasil. Government policies designed to channel private commercial bank currency issues into a bank able to monopolize currency emissions led to the fusion of Maua's private Banco do Brasil with the Banco Comercial do Rio de Janeiro in 1853. Thereafter, the course of monetary policy and politics has to do with this second official Banco do Brasil. Domestic financial crises in 1837, 1853, 1859 and 1864 also brought government policy responses that shifted between polar opposite doctrines; sometimes defending free markets for issue of paper currency and opposing theories seeking to anchor currencies against a gold standard.

From attempting to monopolize currency issues in the third Banco do Brasil in 1853, to the 1857 law under Finance Minister Souza Franco that encouraged once again multiple commercial bank emissions, to the 1860 *entraves* law under Salles Torres Homem that once again sought to consolidate currency emissions in the Banco do Brasil, policies changed quicky and radically. Finally, in 1866, currency emissions were delegated to Treasury, a prerogative it retained until the end of the empire. War with Paraguay (1864–1870), the reversal of foreign trade deficits through coffee exports, financial crisis in 1875, and immigration of wage labour also changed the context for the politics of monetary policy. Finally, financial reforms, crisis in 1885, massive credits for farmers to recover from abolition, and a funding loan (in 1889 weeks before the end of empire) produced optimism and a financial market bubble before military coup ended monarchy on 15 November 1889. The evidence reported in this chapter suggests how politics shape money, banking and finance; how ideas from abroad were adapted to local conditions; and how monetary phenomena mix with realities of politics and public policy making.

Notes

1 Dickson, Peter. *The Financial Revolution in England* (New York: St. Martin's, 1967).
2 Of particular value are sources digitalized and placed on the Brazilian Ministry of Finance website titled 'Memória Estatística do Brasil'. For an overview of Brazilian 19th century history see: Bethell, Leslie (ed.). *Cambridge History of Latin America* (Cambridge, Cambridge University Press, 11 vols., 1984–2008), and Stein, Stanley. 'Historiography of Brazil, 1808–1889'. *Hispanic American Historical Review*, 15/2 (1969). On imperial political institutions, see: Graham, Richard. *Patronage and Politics in Nineteenth Century Brazil* (Stanford: Stanford University Press, 1990); Beiguelman, Paula. *Formação Política do Brasil* (São Paulo: Pioneiro, 1976); Carvalho, José M. *Teatro de Sombras – A Política Imperial* (Rio de Janeiro: IUPERJ-Vértice, 1998); Carvalho, Jose M. 'A Composição Social dos Partidos Políticos Imperiais' (Cadernos DCP, Vol. 2, 1974, pp. 1–34); Prado, Jr. Caio. *A Evolução da Política Brasileira* (São Paulo: Brasiliense, 1986, 13th edition); and Vianna, Oliveira. *Instituições Políticas Brasileiras* (Rio de Janeiro: José Olympio, 1951). For monetary, financial and economic data over time, see: Peláez, Carlos M. and Wilson, Suzigan, *História Monetária do Brasil* (Brasília: Editora da Universidade de Brasília, 1976) and Goldsmith, Raymond W. *Desenvolvimento Financeiro sob um Século de Inflação* (São Paulo: Harper & Row, 1986) and Castro Carreira, Liberato. *História Financeira e Orçamentária do Império do Brasil* (Brasília: Senado Federal/Casa Rui Barbosa, 1980). Essential secondary analyses of 19th century finance are: Calogeras, J. P. *La Politique Monetarie du Bresil* (Rio de Janeiro Imprimerie Nacional, 1910); Cavalcanti, Amaro. *O Meio Circulante Nacional* (Brasília: Editora da Universidade de Brasília, 1983); Ónody, Oliver. *A Inflação Brasileira (1820–58)* (Rio de Janeiro: 1962); Vieira, Dorival T. *Evolução do Sistema Monetário Brasileiro* (São Paulo: FCEA/Universidade de São Paulo, 1962). The standard work on 19th century Brazilian economic development remains: Furtado, Celso. *The Economic Growth of Brasil* (Berkeley: University of California Press, 1963).
3 Machlachlan, Colin M. 'The Indian Labor Structure of the Portuguese Amazon, 1700–1800', in Dawrirl Aldan (ed.), *The Colonial Roots of Modern Brazil* (Berkeley: University of California Press, 1973), pp. 199–230.
4 On legacies of colonial rule, see: Caio, Prado. *The Colonial Legacies of Modern Brazil* (Berkeley: University of California Press, 1973); Simonsen, Roberto. *História Econômica do Brasil (1500–1820)* (São Paulo: Editora Nacional, 1962); Barman, Roderick J. *The Forging of a Nation, 1798–1852* (Stanford: Stanford University Press, 1988); Graham, Richard (ed.), *Brazil and the World System* (Austin: University of Texas Press, 1991); Schwartz, Stuart B. *Sovereignty and Society in Colonial Brazil* (Berkeley: University of California Press, 1973). For a review of independence, see: Malerba, Jurandir. 'Esboço Crítico da recente historia sobre independência do Brasilo (desde 1980)'. University of Oxford Centre for Brazilian Studies Working Paper CBS-45–03.
5 Cavalcanti notes, 'the loan and the lending contracts thus dispensed with the use of money with which things of primary need or the means to satisfy them were obtained. And in 1808 we still ignored world trade, consisting of the wholesale buying and sending of colonial goods to the ports of the kingdom' (Cavalcanti, *O Meio Circulante Nacional*, p. 9).
6 On the Mascates War: Vainfas, Ronaldo. 'Guerra dos Mascates', in *Dicionário do Brasil Colonial (1500–1808)* (Rio de Janeiro: Objetiva, 2000), pp. 272–274.
7 Duguid, Paul. 'The making of Methuen: The commercial treaty in the English imagination', *História: Revista da Faculdade de Letras (Universidade do Porto)* [Portugal], 3/4 (2003): 9–36
8 Bernstein, Harry. *The Brazilian Diamond in Contracts, Contraband, and Capital* (Lanham, MD: University Press of America, 1986).
9 Gold exports before independence follow: for Eschwege, 130 million pounds sterling (1600–1820), Calogeras 190 million (1700–1801), Humboldt 194 million (1500–1803)

and Alexandre del Mar 181 million (1680–1820). Source: *Historia dos Bancos e do Desenvolvimento Financeiro do Brasil,* p. 31.

10 The irony of exporting gold under colonial control only to hear repeatedly from abroad, after independence, that holding to a gold standard was the only means to a hard currency was not lost on Brazilian policy makers.

11 The term *monetary chaos* is taken from Souza, *A Anarquia Monetária e suas Consequências.* Portuguese colonial coins included: gold of 1,222 mil-réis and 4,000 mil-réis; silver of 640 réis, 320 réis, 160 réis, 80 réis, 40 réis and 20 réis and copper of 40 réis, 20 réis and 10 réis. Total money supply is estimated not to exceed 10 million cruzeiros.

12 Vieira, *Evolucao do Sistema Monetaria Brasileiro.*

13 Given the lapse between these measures in 1808 and restoration of peace and commerce by the Congress of Vienna in 1815, English merchants gained a strong foothold in Brazil.

14 '[T]he country was not financially or economically prepared for the excess expenses involved in its being raised to the status of kingdom, transforming Rio de Janeiro overnight from a modest and poor city into a court of the Portuguese dynasty, headquarters of European diplomacy, a senior civil service, a large garrison and sumptuous courts of justice. The funds of the government revenue could not cope with this sudden growth in expenditure, which was kept up, however, through the Bank's unlimited right to issue money without having to look at the solidity of its deposits in the conversion of the issue, which transposed the strength of the coverage to be later transformed, as it was so transformed, into legal tender coverage' (Felisbelo Freire, *História do Banco do Brasil* (Rio de Janeiro: Tipografia do Economista Brasileiro, 1907).

15 Sturz, *A review, financial, statistical, and commercial, of the Empire of Brazil and its resources: together with a suggestion of the expediency and mode of admitting, Brazilian and other foreign sugars into Great Britain for refining and exportation.* (London: Effingham Wilson, 1837) p. 4.

16 Sturz notes: 'But the evils of this and later tamperings with the currency were only gradually felt; for Brazil had no political economists, nor Rio de Janeiro a well conducted periodical press, which could open the eyes of the people to the robbery about to be committed on them' (p. 4).

17 Sturz, p. 5.

18 Ibid., p. 6.

19 Ibid., p. 6.

20 Ibid., p. 7.

21 Ibid., pp. 5–6, italics added for emphasis.

22 *Curso Forçado* is the title of an influential book from the late 19th century: Dunlop, Julio R. *Curso Forçado* (Rio de Janeiro: Laemmert, 1888).

23 On British finance of independence in Latin America, see: Dawson, Frank G. *The First Latin American Debt Crisis: The City of London and the 1822–25 Loan Bubble* (New Haven, CT: Yale University Press, 1990). As Sturz notes: 'Brazil – following the example of the Spanish colonies, her neighbours, then struggling like herself for independence and who had not found difficulty in raising money on the credit of their *future* revenue – contracted a loan for 3,000,000L sterling: 1,000,000 at 75 percent in August 1824 and 2,000,000 at 85 percent in January 1825, making the amount of bonds issued 3,686,000L' (p. 10).

24 Ibid.

25 Sturz, p. 12

26 Ibid., p. 13

27 Ibid.

28 Shaw, Caroline. 'Rothschilds and Brazil'. *Latin American Research Review,* 40/1 (2005), pp. 165–185.

29 Novais, Fernando A. *Portugal e Brasil na Crise do Antigo Sistema Colonial (1777–1808)* (São Paulo: Hucitec, 1985); Maxwell, Kenneth. *Conflicts and Conspiracies, Brazil &*

Portugal, 1750–1808 (Cambridge: Cambridge University Press, 1973); Malerba, Jurandi. 'Esboco critico da recente histoRio de Janeirografia sobre indepêndencia do Brasil (desde 1980)' (Oxford: University of Oxford Centre for Brazilian Studies Working Paper, 2003).

30 Castro, Jeanne B. *A Milícia Cidadã: a Guarda Nacional de 1831–1850* (São Paulo: Editora Nacional, 1977).

31 Sturz notes: 'But the constitution of that establishment was such, that Government could draw from it according to its pleasure; and it made such a free use of this facility that in 1821 it was a debtor to the bank for above 15,000,000,000, worth 3,000,000L. sterling' (p. 4).

32 Ibid., p. 5.

33 Vieira, p. 68.

34 Contos = 000 mil-réis. On the origin of this term, see: Azevedo Azevedo, J. Lúcio, *Novas epanáforas: estudos de história e literatura* (Lisbon: A.M. Teixeira, 1932), p. 92.

35 In 1821, João VI himself admitted that the bank on several occasions had contributed with extraordinary and large advances to his treasury, and considering himself the creditor of various public coffers by the discounting of bills of exchange signed by his treasurers, and by the payment of expenses for works that were to be carried out from those coffers, declared that disbursements for similar transactions were national debt and all public revenue of the kingdom was liable for them.

36 Bulhões, Leopoldo de. 'Os Financistas do Brasil'. 1913 conference, Biblioteca Nacional.

37 Rocha, J. J. *Biografia do Marques de Baependi* (Rio de Janeiro, 1821).

38 Bulhões, p. 452.

39 Minister Calmon's publications reflect his long tenure as Finance Minister: *Relatório (exercício de 1827)* (Rio de Janeiro, 1828); *Documentos, com que instruiu o seu Relatório o Ministro da Fazenda, na sessão de 1828* (Rio de Janeiro, 1828); *Falas sustentando o orçamento do Ministério a seu cargo (da Fazenda) nas sessões da Câmara dos Deputados de 21 a 28 de agosto do corrente ano* (Rio de Janeiro, 1829); *Proposta e relatório do Ministério da Fazenda apresentados à Assembléia Geral Legislativa* (Rio de Janeiro: Tipografia Imperial e Nacional, 1863).

40 Minister Caldeira Brant's publications include: *Defesa dos negociadores do empréstimo brasileiro em Londres* (Rio de Janeiro, 1826); *Conta geral da Caixa de Londres, desde a sua instalação no ano de 1804 até o fim de 1830* (Rio de Janeiro: Tipografia de Tomaz B. Hunt & Comp., 1831–1832); *Relatório do Ministro e Secretário de Estado dos Negócios da Fazenda; na sessão de 15 de maio de 1830* (Rio de Janeiro: Tipografia Imperial e Nacional, 1830).

41 The 1830 Finance Ministry report to Parliament was published as: *Relatório do Ministro e Secretário de Estado dos Negócios da Fazenda; na sessão de 15 de maio de 1830* (Rio de Janeiro: Tipografia Imperial e Nacional, 1830).

42 José Antonio Lisboa is author of *Reflexões sobre o Banco do Brasil* (Rio de Janeiro, 1821); *Observações sobre o melhoramento do meio circulante no Império do Brasil* (Rio de Janeiro, 1835) and *Projeto de lei sobre o sistema monetário* (Rio de Janeiro, 1835) and *Estatística do Brasil* (Rio de Janeiro, 1822).

43 The monetary cost of the return of crown, court and entourage to Lisbon is disputed. Nationalists argue that João VI took the entire treasury and liquid assets of the national bank back to Portugal. Simonsen estimates that although 20 contos (6 million pounds sterling) left Brazil, 22 contos were brought with king and court from Portugal in 1808.

44 Atas do Conselho do Estado, 1822, p. 1.

45 Data collected by Calogeras, Castro Carreira, and other secondary sources suggest that excessive emissions were indeed the central cause of bank insolvency. But given that emissions follow political developments so closely, political necessity seems more important than fraud. Cavalcanti places the cost of court at a sixth of total government spending (p. 19). However, spending by ministry suggests that the royal office *does*

not outpace other ministries and agencies. Instead, the war office is responsible for increases.

46 Major regional revolts include Pernambuco (1817, 1832–1835, 1848–1849), Ceara (1831–1832), Para (1831–1833,1835–1837), Bahia (1837–1838), Minas Gerais and Sao Paulo (1842), Maranhao (1838–1841), Alagoas (1844) and Rio de Janeiro Grande do Sul (1835–1845).

47 The Marquis of Queluz, reporting to the Chambers on the Finance Ministry in 1827: 'He was appalled, and would have disappeared had the government not come to his rescue as it did, but in what way? By a despotic act, ordering the Bank not to pay the players, the holders of promissory notes, any more than the amount he set out in a table, even determining how such payment should be made, which was the same as admitting to the insolubility of the Bank to pay its notes in cash'.

48 Having decreed liquidation, the following measures were adopted: substitution by new standard bank notes of those issued by the bank and in circulation; state guarantee of the bank's notes, which were in circulation until they were substituted, and the new ones following the substitution circulating as currency, being legal tender until their full redemption; and the obligation by the state for the payment of the bank notes, all assets and income having been mortgaged.

49 Falcão, Waldemar. *O Empirismo Monetário no Brasil* (Rio de Janeiro: Companhia Editoria Nacional, 1931), p. 149.

50 Carvalho, José M. (ed.). *Bernardo Pereira de Vasconcelos* (São Paulo: Editora 34, 1999), p. 66.

51 Minister of Finance Viscount of Sapucaí set up a gradual and stable plan: 'On June 1 1833, the resolution of the General Assembly was approved, which authorized the government to set the period for the end of circulation of the old bank notes and the substitution of the new standard bank notes in use from the extinct Bank of Brazil by treasury bank notes; On October 3, the law ordered the substitution of the copper coinage in circulation, setting out the respective procedure. On October 8, the new monetary standard was set up; a currency and deposit bank was set up; the government was authorized to sign contracts with individuals or companies for the mining of the nation's lands; the stamp duty was changed; and an annual tax on slaves was creates'.

52 By 1839, Finance Minister Oliveira argued in a report to parliament: 'amortization progresses so quickly that, unless provision is made as soon as possible to fill the vacuum left annually by the progressive contraction of monetary circulation, drawbacks would shortly be felt due to the scarcity of currency in the market, or even worse, the presence of new agents of circulation of doubtful credit'.

53 Needell, Jeffrey D. *The Party of Order: The Conservatives, the State, and Slavery in the Brazilian Monarchy, 1831–1871* (Stanford, CA: Stanford University Press, 2006).

54 Publications of Cândido José de Araujo Viana include: *Relatório sobre o melhoramento do meio circulante; apresentado à Assembléia Geral em sessão extraordinária de 1833* (Rio de Janeiro, 1833).

55 Araujo Vianna proposed recreating the Banco do Brasil by selling 40,000 shares (Bulhões counts this as the fifth proposal to recreate the national bank since 1829).

56 Bulhões, p. 453.

57 Castro e Silva published *Guia do novo manual dos coletores e dos coletados* (Rio de Janeiro, no date); *Relatório* (Rio de Janeiro: Tipografia Nacional, 1835) and *Proposta e relatório* (Rio de Janeiro: Tipografia Nacional, 1836–1837).

58 *Memória da origem, progresso e decadência do quinto do ouro na Província de Minas Gerais* (Rio de Janeiro, 1827); *A Lei de 04 de outubro de 1831. Da organização do Tesouro Público Nacional e das Tesourarias das Províncias* (Rio de Janeiro, 1834); *Guia dos Procuradores da Coroa* (Rio de Janeiro, 1841); *Apontamentos da legislação para uso dos Procuradores da Coroa e da Fazenda Nacional* (Rio de Janeiro, 1846) and *Decreto n. 736, de 20 de novembro de 1850. Reforma o Tesouro Público Nacional*

e as Tesourarias Provinciais, com notas explicativas e justificativas de suas disposições (Niterói, Tipografia. Fluminense de C. Martins Lopes, 1852).

59 Francisco Viana authored the 1843 budget proposal and report: *Proposta e relatório apresentados à Assembléia Geral Legislativa na 2ᵃ sessão da 5ᵃ legislatura* (Rio de Janeiro, 1843).

60 Sturz, p. 22.

61 Souza Franco´s publications include: *Os bancos do Brasil; sua história, defeitos da organização atual e reforma do sistema bancáRio de Janeiro* (Rio de Janeiro, 1848); *A SITUAÇÃO econômica e financeira do Brasil. Biblioteca Brasileira*, Rio de Janeiro, I, 1/2 (1863) (a monthly magazine published by the Associação de Homens de Letras) and the 1857–1858 budget proposal and report, *Proposta e relatório apresentados à Assembléia Geral Legislativa* (Rio de Janeiro, Tipografia Nacional, 1857–1858).

62 Carneiro Leão is author of the 1854–1856 budget proposals: *Propostas e relatórios apresentados à Assembléia Geral Legislativa* (Rio de Janeiro: Tipografia Nacional, 1854–1856).

63 On Mauá, see: Barman, Roderick J. 'Business and Government in Imperial Brazil: The Experience of Viscount Mauá'. *Journal of Latin American Studies*, 13 (1981); Marchant, A. *Viscount Mauá and the Empire of Brazil* (Berkeley: University of Califórnia Press, 1965) and Besouochet, Lídia. *Mauá e seu Tempo* (São Paulo: Editora Anchieta, 1942).

64 'Paraná´s voice dissolved in the uproar: Fascinated with an illusion of prosperity and progress, we understood that by the magic power of Bank of Brazil issues we would be able to advance to wherever we wanted. We destroyed believing we were building, inciting more and more issues, ignoring the fact that if the floating capital made available to bill holders was used up, thereby becoming a toxic instrument to the normal state of circulation, we would clog up its channels, becoming seRio de Janeirously and gravely compromised, given that regardless of the shock or disappointment, one would expect the real nature of things to happen very quickly'.

65 Report of the Commission of Inquiry of 1859: 'There was a speculative frenzy. To feed it . . . there was no wavering in the face of the abuse of credit, stimulated by easy money from the issues, abuse that mainly took the shape of the endorsement and acceptance of patronage drafts and other bonds, a plague which has wrought sad results'.

66 Vieira, p. 124.

67 Recovery of investor and market confidence during 1858 took an unexpected turn with disagreement between the Banco do Brasil directorate and the Finance Ministry, leaving foreign exchange positions in London uncovered during early 1858. While Banco do Brasil directors refused to sell pounds from bank reserves to support the faltering conto in London, a collapse of the currency was averted by Maua & Cia purchases at 27 pence, an unusual development involving a private commercial bank intervening in times of financial crisis that remind one of purchases by JP Morgan in financial markets during 1896 to avert a run on the US dollar.

68 Salles Torres Homem founded the magazine *Jornal de Debates Políticos e LiteráRio de Janeiros* (published 1837–1838); *Sociedade em comandita e bancos de circulação* (Rio de Janeiro, 1853); *Questões sobre impostos* (Rio de Janeiro, 1856); *Proposta e relatório apresentados à Assembléia Geral Legislativa na 3ᵃ sessão da 10ᵃ legislatura* (Rio de Janeiro: Tipografia Nacional, 1859) and *Relatório apresentado à Assembléia Geral dos Acionistas do Banco do Brasil (1867, 1868, 1869)* (Rio de Janeiro, 1867–1869).

69 Silva Ferraz authored *Proposta e relatório do Ministro da Fazenda* (Rio de Janeiro, 1860); *Regulamento do Imposto do Selo e sua arrecadação* (Rio de Janeiro, 1860); *Regulamento das Alfândegas e das Mesas de Rendas* (Rio de Janeiro, 1860) and *A Tarifa das Alfândegas do Império do Brasil* (Rio de Janeiro, 1860).

70 Paranhos published *Discurso do Ministro da Fazenda* (Rio de Janeiro, 1861); *Relatórios* (Rio de Janeiro, Tipografia Nacional, 1861–1862); *Proposta do governo sobre a reforma*

do estado servil (Rio de Janeiro, 1871) and *Propostas e relatórios apresentados à Assembléia Geral Legislativa* (Rio de Janeiro: Tipografia Nacional, 1873–1874).

71 As president of Council of Ministers and Finance Minster from 1871 to 1875, Paranhos would unify weights and measures, regulate taxes on property sales, industry and liberal professions and create new notes to assist deposit-taking banks guaranteed by public debt and other bonds.

72 Failures calculated by Calogeras are the following: A.J.A. Souto (41.2), Comes & Filhos (20.2), Montenegro Luna (11.8), Oliveira & Bello (4.0), Amaral & Pinto (0.6) and 90 other financial firms (32.5) totalling 110.5 contos, not counting 115 firms that failed during the months after the crisis. On the 1864 crisis, see the government inquiry report: Brazil, Ministry of Justice. *Commissão de Inquérito sobre as causas da crise na praça do Rio de Janeiro. Relatório da commissão encarregada pelo governo imperial por avisos do 1º de outubro a 28 de dezembro de 1864 de preceder a um inquerito sobre as causas principaes e acidentaes da crise do mês de setembro de 1864* (Rio de Janeiro: Typografia Nacional, 1865). Also, Soares, Sebastião F. *Esboço ou primeiros traços da crise commercial da cidade do Rio de Janeiro em 10 de setembro de 1864* (Rio de Janeiro: Ed. Laemmert, 1864); Andrade, Ana M. R. 'Souto & Cia', in Maria B. Levy (ed.), *Anais da 1ªConferência Internacional de História de Empresas* (Rio de Janeiro: Div. Gráfica da UFRJ, 1991); Guimarães, Carlos G. 'Bancos, Economia e Poder no Segundo Reinado: o caso da Sociedade Bancária Mauá, MacGregor & Cia., 1854/1866' (São Paulo: Universidade de São Paulo, Department of History, Doctoral Thesis, 1997); Pelaez, Carlos M. and Suzigan, Wilson. *História Monetária do Brasil* (Brasília: Editora UNB, 1981) and Vilela, André A. 'The Political Economy of Money and Banking in Imperial Brazil, 1850/1870' (London: London School of Economics and Political Science, Doctorate in Economic History, 1999).

73 On war with Paraguay, see: Costa, Wilma P. *A espada de Dâmocles: o exército, a Guerra do Paraguai e a crise do Império* (São Paulo: Hucitec/Unicamp, 1996); Marques, Maria E.C.M. (ed.). *A Guerra do Paraguai: 130 anos depois* (Rio de Janeiro: Relume Dumará, 1995); Sales, Ricardo. *A guerra do Paraguai: escravidão e cidadania na formação do exército* (Rio de Janeiro: Paz e Terra, 1990); Leuchars, Chris. *To the Bitter End: Paraguay and the War of the Triple Alliance* (Westport, CT: Greenwood Press, 2002) and Whigham, Thomas. *The Paraguayan War* (Lincoln, NE: University of Nebraska Press, 2002).

74 *A crise comercial de setembro de 1864, seguida dos atos do Ministério da Fazenda que lhe são relativos* (Rio de Janeiro: Tipografia Nacional, 1865).

75 Góes e Vasconcelos authored: *Propostas e Relatórios apresentados à Assembléia Geral Legislativa pelo Ministro da Fazenda, Zacaraias de Góes e Vasconcelos* (Rio de Janeiro, 1867–1868), 2 vols; *Proposta para Aprovação de Créditos Abertos pelo Governo no Intervalo da Sessão da Assembléia Geral de 1867–1868* (Rio de Janeiro, 1868) and 19 other manuscripts on law and politics, in addition to speeches compiled in parliamentary annals. See: Cecila H. S. Oliveira (ed.). *Zacaraias de Góes e Vasconcelos* (São Paulo: Editora 34, 2002).

76 Once markets devalued the mil-réis to 28 3/8 in 1875, the government anticipated shipments of funds to Europe, 50 contos to meet obligations and 40 contos to speculate on valuation of the mil-réis.

77 Standard histories of the end of empire and emergence of republic include: Barman, Roderick J. (1999). *Citizen Emperor: Pedro II and the Making of Brazil, 1825–1891* (Stanford: Stanford University Press); Bethell, Leslie. *Brazil: Empire and Republic, 1822–1930* (Cambridge: Cambridge University Press); Carvalho, José Murilo de (in Portuguese). *Os Bestializados: o Rio de Janeiro e a República que não foi* (3rd ed.) (São Paulo: Companhia das Letras, 2002); Graham, Richard. *Patronage and Politics in Nineteenth-Century Brazil* (Stanford: Stanford University Press, 1994) and Viotti, Emília da. *Da Monarquia à República: Momentos Decisivos* (São Paulo: Unesp, 1999).

78 Temporarily replacing the Banco do Brasil with regional banks as discussed in the following chapter.

79 Abreu, Marcelo de Paiva. 'Os Funding Loans Brasileiros – 1889–1931'. *Pesquisa e Planejamento Econômico,* 32/3 (2002): 515–540.

80 Note the optimism of member of parliament Albuquerque in 1888 a year before the end of the empire: 'One can say that this year has been golden for Brazil; free labour, extraordinary coffee harvest, exchange at 27 pence, business optimistic and all social classes more or less satisfied'.

81 Estimates from Mouro, *Ensaios Econômicos,* and Besouchet, p. 242.

82 Decree 10.336 of September 6, 1889.

83 Vieira, p. 177.

84 Silveira Martins published a defense of charges leveled by the Barão de Cotegipe, *Um ministro negociante; discursos* (Rio de Janeiro, 1877).

85 Assis Figueiredo contributed to the magazine *A Reforma*, founded and edited the newspaper *O Progressista*, contributed to the *Ensaio Filosófico e Correio Paulistano* and published: *As finanças do Império* (Rio de Janeiro, 1876); *As finanças da regeneração* (Rio de Janeiro, 1877); *Discurso pronunciado em sessão da câmara quatrienal de 18.04.1879* (Rio de Janeiro, 1879); *Proposta e relatório apresentados à Assembléia Geral Legislativa na 2ª sessão da 17ª legislatura* (Rio de Janeiro: Tipografia Nacional, 1879) and *Relatório (exercício de 1879–80)* (Rio de Janeiro: Tipografia Nacional, 1880).

86 *Proposta e relatório apresentados à Assembléia Geral Legislativa na 3ª sessão da 17ª legislatura* (Rio de Janeiro: Tipografia Nacional, 1880); *Proposta e relatório apresentados à Assembléia Geral Legislativa na 1ª sessão da 18ª legislatura* (Rio de Janeiro: Tipografia Nacional, 1882) and *Proposta e relatório apresentados à Assembléia Geral Legislativa na 1ª sessão da 19ª legislatura* (Rio de Janeiro: Imprensa Nacional, 1885).

87 Souza, Soares de. *Ministério da Fazenda. Proposta e Relatório apresentados à Assembléia Geral Legislativa na 20ª Sessão* (Rio de Janeiro, 1887) and *Discursos proferidos na Câmara dos Deputados e no Senado* (Rio de Janeiro, 1887).

88 On emergence and consolidation of the imperial party system, see Beiguelman, Paula. *Pequenos Estudos de Ciência Política* (São Paulo: Pioneira, 1973).

3 National liberalism and Kemmerer coalitions

The Old Republic (1889–1930)

> *The financial history of the Republic presents several interesting phases for the*
> *scholar of economic laws and their practical application.*
> —Carvalho, *Estudos de Economia e Finanças,* p. 63

Monetary statecraft from 1889 to the 1930 revolution turned on a federalist pact of regional banks, experiments with currency boards (and other institutions) designed to manage foreign accounts, the adaptation of orthodox theories to the realities of an agricultural export economy on the periphery of the world system, and alternating policies of national liberalism countered by Kemmerer coalitions that imposed orthodox adjustment. This chapter reviews the creation of regional banks amidst the provisional republican government, periods of monetary and fiscal austerity imposed by funding loans from London, *three* experiments with currency boards designed to buffer foreign capital flows, and, finally, further policies designed to counter volatile export prices and foreign exchange fluctuations. The politics of monetary policy from 1889 to 1930 provide further evidence of how Brazilian policy makers, now a new republican generation, reacted to circumstances, adapted ideas from abroad, muddled through, satisficed amidst imperfect information and limited rationality and attempted to reconcile political imperatives and market confidence by regulating money, credit, banking and foreign currency markets.

Monetary statecraft from 1889 to 1930 can be divided into five periods. The first period involves the organization of a new regional bank system by finance minister Rui Barbosa in 1890 modelled on federal arrangements in the United States and Germany. The provisional government installed by military coup in November 1889 respected the debts inherited from the empire and retained bank regulations and monetary policies set in 1888 reforms. However, partial (and controlled) concession of monetary authority to regional banks in 1890 was necessary to sustain a pact with regional elites for a federal republican constitution.

After financial crisis and recovery during the 1890s, the politics of monetary policy shifted in 1898 to a second period involving tight money and fiscal austerity designed to reduce inflation and repay funding loans to foreign creditors. Quantitative theories of money led governments to cut spending, reduce credit, and recall and burn paper currency – policies that were introduced as clauses in funding loans from London banks.

From 1906 to 1914, a third period of monetary statecraft involved a return to national-liberal policies with the creation of a currency board and massive amounts of directed government credit to stock excess coffee in order to support world prices, stabilize foreign accounts and move toward a gold standard.

The fourth period of monetary statecraft involves adjustment to trade and investment shocks caused by World War I, followed by a post-war boom in foreign investment. During this period, a second (republican) currency board in the Banco do Brasil was created in 1920, while the national bank was designated as the central bank in 1923.

Finally, after 1924, monetary statecraft involved another cycle of adjustment through austerity, the creation of a third currency board (1926), a new coffee finance scheme run by the São Paulo state government bank; all this amidst another boom in foreign investment. This cycle ended with crisis abroad in 1929 producing a run on currency board reserves as revolutionaries entered Rio de Janeiro in 1930 to end the Old Republic.

The politics of monetary policy from 1889 to 1930 reflect the consolidation of single-state party machines run by governors. This chapter traces monetary policy making in these five periods to demonstrate the complexity and diversity of interests, the emergence of new actors during republican rule and the variety of policy experiments that belie economic or sociological theories of central banking and monetary policy. Neither specific interests (whether agricultural, industrial or financial) nor importation of orthodoxy explain how monetary policy ideas defined problems, how policy alternatives were formulated, how the agenda for policy was set by the financial press, public and congressional debate, and how executive agencies implemented, in fact, policies for money, interest rates and foreign exchange transactions.

The epistemic communities of monetary policy making in the Old Republic include a wide variety of ideas about money, banking, credit and foreign exchange management were taken from abroad and adapted to Brazil from 1889 to 1930. Errors, illusions, and excesses led Celso Furtado to describe this period as a series of attempts to 'subject the economic system to the monetary rules prevailing in Europe'.[1] Two episodes of orthodoxy (1898 and 1924), are indeed marked, however, the record also suggests that policy makers from 1889 to 1930 adapted other, non-orthodox ideas from abroad. And policies frequently combined national-liberal measures of intervention alongside orthodox policies. Orthodox policies were, in fact, modelled on currency reforms in Eastern Europe and other Latin American countries.[2] However, many national-liberals saw imposition from bankers and foreign financial missions to balance government budgets and adopt a gold standard as fundamentally misplaced. As Finance Minister Cincinato Braga summed it up in parliament: 'we have no gold'.[3] Moreover, monetarism was far from hegemonic. National liberals in the Old Republic drew from other experiences in Europe and North America with cycles of national-liberalism, protectionism, imperial expansion, competition between states (culminating in World War I) and business cycles marked by booms, financial crises and serious downturns.

Matters of money, credit and foreign exchange also remained at the centre of political economy from 1889 to 1930 because of continued dependence on agricultural exports (largely coffee) and foreign capital flows. Doctrines of economic liberalism predominated during three of the five periods examined in this chapter. However, governments of all stripes introduced decidedly non-liberal mechanisms to reduce the vulnerability of Brazil to shocks from international markets and finance flows, both on the upside and downside of business cycles. Policies often combined the imposition of orthodoxy *alongside* national-liberal policies to sustain world coffee prices and adjust foreign accounts without freezing domestic credit. National liberal policies to deepen domestic financial markets, modernize industry, and increase consumption and savings were seen as urgent and necessary responses based on the realization that Brazil had remained starkly underdeveloped compared to industrialized economies in the North Atlantic.

Secondary and primary sources delineate a variety of positions, proposals, debates, and policies that sought to reconcile pressures from domestic groups with realities of international markets and foreign credit. Comparative historical analysis and process tracing of monetary policy during five periods from 1889 to 1930 reveal muddling through, recursive causal relations, heterodox adaptation of ideas from abroad, and a wide variety of attempts to reconcile market confidence with imperatives of domestic political support.

1890–1891: regional bank pact for federal constitution

The monetary policies of provisional republican government begin with emergency decrees in late 1889 and broader reforms in January 1890 designed by Finance Minister Rui Barbosa.[4] Baleeiro identifies six core ideas behind Barbosa's reforms:

> Only industrialization could project the country into a position of international leadership; free trade rather than tariffs and protectionism were the means to industrialize; tax modernization could increase public investment and economic growth; fiduciary currency emissions often led to excess but were necessary counter-cyclical measures to maintain resource flows to the government and private sector; central monetary authority was better in principle, but the framework of multiple banks inherited from the empire should be retained; and, finally, government finance was necessary to accelerate economic growth.[5]

These ideas of liberal-nationalism confronted difficult conditions upon Barbosa's confirmation as Finance Minister in November 1891. Pragmatism and gradualism were used by Barbosa to arbitrate pressures; provide credit for domestic agriculture and commerce in dire straits; cut spending and credit from foreign

Table 3.1 Foreign accounts (1889–1891)

	Coffee Exports (million sacks)	*Exchange Rate (mil-réis/pence)*	*Export Revenue (contos)*
1889	159.7	26.7	365.0
1890	110.2	22.6	212.0
1891	65.8	7.2	48.0

Source: Aguiar, Pinto de. *Rui e a Economia Brasileira* (Rio de Janeiro: Fundação da Casa Rui Barbosa, 1971), p. 73.

bankers so as to reverse foreign exchange devaluation (exacerbated by a collapse of coffee exports); and delegate credit and banking to regional and state governments to demobilize the regional military elites that had just deposed the emperor. Dramatic economic developments also arose from abroad, with steep declines in coffee exports and the exchange rate soon followed by the suspension of foreign finance (see Table 3.1).

Finance Minister Barbosa assumed office in the face of a severe liquidity shortage that threatened to bankrupt financial institutions and push the economy into deep recession. The financial boom that preceded the republic presented the provisional government with the same political dilemma faced by the imperial government it sought to replace: if the market was allowed to correct, the dramatic consequences of depression would endanger completion of a federal pact;[6] if, on the other hand, the government were to use emergency legislation to extend credit and temporarily increase paper emissions, this would pressure already increasing prices and accelerate currency devaluation. Political necessity prevailed. Barbosa extended emergency credits to the Banco do Brasil and other private banks (under 1885 legislation) to avert bankruptcies, while restoring the rural credit program designed during the last year of imperial government to compensate farmers for abolition.[7] However, not all emergency measures simply increased credit and paper money. Barbosa also suspended the Banco de São Paulo's concession to emit notes and reduced limits to Banco Nacional emissions by one-third in late 1889.

In January 1890, reforms delegated monetary authority to three regional banks[8] in the north, centre, and south authorized to emit currency tied to treasury notes, gold and currency reserves.[9] Banks were allowed to print currency up to the face value of treasury notes in reserve and to purchase additional notes from either the treasury or market. Both the redeemable value and interest rates of treasury bills were to decline to zero in five years, a scheme designed to reduce federal government debt and shift regional currency emissions toward convertibility. Much ado has been made of these reforms as ideologically driven designs to encourage paper currency emissions.[10] To the contrary, evidence suggests that this scheme of regional banks was a result of political compromise with regional republican leaders. Moreover, Finance Ministry reports are adamant that these were *temporary* mechanisms to address the critical situation provincial businesses, such that policies would later be transferred to a central bank in Rio. Guidelines for currency reserves and credit limits were also designed to avert abuses by state governments.[11] Republican designs were also incremental and gradualist in the sense that they built on the imperial money and credit policies of November 1888.[12]

Early republican reforms under Finance Minister Rui Barbosa in 1890 created two national banks able to emit currency (Banco Nacional and Banco do Brasil, merged in December 1890) and six regional banks able to emit currency anchored on reserves of treasury bills (Banco dos Estados Unidos do Brasil, Banco Emissor do Sul, Banco União de São Paulo, Banco Sul-Americano, Banco Emissor da Bahia, Banco Emissor do Norte). Table 3.2 presents the sum of paper currency emissions from these regional banks through year-end 1890 (Barbosa resigned from the Finance Ministry on 20 January 1891).

The total amount of currency emissions printed and circulated by the regional banks designed during the first months of federal republic appear insufficient to be responsible for the cycle of high inflation that ensued in the early 1890s. Even Barbosa's critics such as Calogeras argue that his system of regional banks did not

Table 3.2 Currency emissions and bonds emitted by regional banks (1890–1892, contos)

	1890	1892	1892
	Currency	*Currency*	*Gov Bonds*
Banco do Brasil	52,336		
Banco Nacional	49,763	277,042*	74,514
Banco dos Estados Unidos do Brasil	62,655		
Banco União de São Paulo	9,500	10,001	
Banco Emissor do Sul	3,500		
Banco Emissor da Bahia	2,000	9,500	
Banco da Bahia		4,000	2,000
Banco Emissor de Pernambuco	4,559	15,558	7,779
Banco Emissor do Norte	1,000	1,000	
Banco de Crédito Popular	4,500	29,014	11,557
Treasury Emission		167,611	
Total Emissions	191,813	513,726	95,850

Source: Aguiar, Pinto de. *Rui e a Economia Brasileira* (Rio de Janeiro: Fundação da Casa Rui Barbosa, 1971), p. 116; Calogeras, J. P. *La Politique Monétaire du Brésil* (Rio de Janeiro: Imprimerie Nationale, 1910), p. 245.

* The Banco do Brasil, Banco Nacional and Banco dos Estados Unidos do Brasil were, by 1892, merged into the Banco da República.

immediately produce a cycle of uncontrolled currency emissions and lax credit to the extent that could have caused inflation and the financial bubble commonly described as the *encilhamento*.[13] Barbosa proposed plural bank emissions tied to government bonds as a temporary solution necessary to accomodate revolutionary and imperial elites in states and refinance debts inherited from the empire. Finance Minister Barbosa argued for regional banks as a political necessity at the outset of the republic. However, by 1890, he argued that a single monetary authority was preferable to plural emissions, even in federal republics.[14] These claims are not just rhetoric or distortions in the memoirs of a Finance Minister. Barbosa's policies attempted to gradually increase government control over monetary flows. For example, a decree in December 1890 merged the Banco dos Estados Unidos do Brasil and Banco Nacional do Brasil and recalled 171,000 contos of treasury bills to reduce emissions by regional banks.[15]

Data from the period of Barbosa in Finance Ministry are also incompatible with claims that he was an ideological advocate of paper currency issues. Vieira estimates that paper money increased 39 percent from 1888 through 1891, while prices increased 62 percent.[16] Moreover, historians suggest that inflation early in the republic was not caused by excessive currency emissions but, instead, from increased demand caused by population increases, the impact of abolition on domestic demand, and the flow of immigrant labour into Brazil.[17] Indeed, the stock of paper money in Brazil upon Barbosa's resignation in 1891 is estimated at 180 contos, up only two contos from the 178 contos of paper money at year-end 1888 (the last full year of empire). Excess paper was inherited from the last months of empire. From the May 1888 reforms to the November 15 coup that deposed the emperor, new banks emitted an estimated *324 contos*, twice 1888 levels and sufficient to drive the stock market bubble. For Topik, the centralization of money, banking and credit in Rio fed this process of financial speculation and crisis; 95 percent of bank notes circulated in Rio de Janeiro.

In terms of ideas from abroad, events suggest neither hegemony of orthodoxy nor correlations between federalism and excessive paper. During the first three years of republican government, Barbosa looks not only to English liberalism but also to American protectionism and German national-liberalism as models for Brazilian policies.[18] Plans for gradual transition to a central bank were inspired more by the Big Five system in England than the federalist system of national banks then in place in the United States.[19] The turn to protectionism exemplified by the McKinley Act passed by the US Congress in 1890 was also noted by Finance Minister Barbosa. Indeed, as Polany, Meier, Gershenkron and others note, belief in the capacity of markets to self-regulate gives way in the late 19th century to patterns of state-led development, corporatist arrangements, trade barriers, and nationalism a cycle inexorably linked to causes of World War I.

By using federal treasury notes as transitional reserves for regional banks and devising means to reduce the impact of exchange devaluation on the treasury, Finance Minister Barbosa combined monetary theories from opposing camps with the long-range goal of reaching currency convertibility. The 1890 reforms were designed to reduce government debt through transfer (and devaluation to zero) of treasury bills to regional banks that served as anchor on emissions. Taxes on gold imports were also seen to create conditions for currency convertibility. These measures at the onset of the republic have been widely debated. However, they surely qualify as examples of monetary statecraft: pragmatic policies designed to raise capital and reduce the deleterious consequences of volatile parameters for policy making.

A variety of pressures led Barbosa to resign in 1891 after nearly three years as finance minister. Political pressures came from São Paulo governor Campos Sales and other representatives from rural areas who resented suspension of credit policies under the empire. Pressures came from international banks concerned about the introduction of currency controls in the January 1890 reforms and tariff increases that sought to encourage domestic production of 300 goods. Correspondence between Finance Minister Barbosa, the Brazilian government representative in London, and Rothschild Bank describe bankers unwilling to extend further loans because they were unable to convince clients to increase exposure in Latin America, especially after declaration of moratoria on foreign obligations by Argentina. On the remarkably better terms of finance for Brazil and other developing countries a century ago, see: Paulo, Mauro, Sussman, Nathan, and Yishay, Yafeh. *Emerging Markets and Financial Globalization Sovereign Bond Spreads in 1870–1913 and Today.* (Oxford: Oxford University Press, 2006).

After Barbosa's resignation, the increased pace of paper emissions under Finance Ministers Araripe and Lucena and the mismanagement of regional banks ensued. The merger of the two largest domestic banks into the Banco da República – originally designed to increase government authority over money and credit – was soon seen to have caused fraud, financial mismanagement and imperial conspiracy in the republican press and opposition groups.[20] Under (republican) President Marshal Deodoro, Finance Minister Baron Lucena loaned over 2 million pound sterling to four regional banks, gathering the wrath of republicans who perceived banks as institutions designed to sustain forces of empire and monarchy. On 23 November 1891, an army and navy revolt deposed the first elected republican president; in good part because of these perceptions of abuses in regional banks. Topik argues that inflation, currency devaluation and fraud 'end the experiment of encouraging private investment banks through issue of abundant inconvertible currency'.[21]

However, the policy pendulum does not swing directly to orthodoxy. Instead, President Floriano Peixoto pursued state-led development policies along the lines of liberal-nationalism. Emergency credits were extended to save commercial banks from failure in 1892, congress approved 'aid to industry bonds', and the two largest banks were merged in 1893 to form the Banco da República with a monopoly over currency emissions. Topik describes this merger as 'a seizure of financial power by the state' with presidential appointment of bank president, vice president and director. The new bank also received concession to manage treasury surpluses, the right to extend credits on future treasury revenue, and other measures that expanded state authority over money, credit, and financial markets.

And when it came, the shift to conservative monetary policies was due less to foreign ideas than domestic perceptions that financial speculation and conservative forces left over from the empire were deeply intertwined.[22] Peixoto's Finance Ministers (Rodrigues Alves, Inocência Correia, Felisbelo Freire) combined belief in necessity of balanced budget, tight money and a return to a gold standard with this view of imperial conspiracy in financial markets during the *encilhamento*. Monetary austerity gained political legitimacy because anitspeculation rhetoric drove electoral campaigns, inflation was eroding salaries, and currency devaluation had reduced domestic consumption and export revenues. The turn to orthodoxy was shaped by this new domestic consensus against financial speculation and abuse of regional banks by imperial elites. The implementation of austerity also delayed to meet the extraordinary expenses of war in Rio Grande do Sul state from 1892 to 1895, the shortfall arising from the shift of tax revenue to state governments in 1892, and the cost of repressing the 1892 naval revolt in Rio.

The 1893 financial crisis in Europe and North America further reduced foreign investment and demand for exports.[23] And rather than an immediate shift to orthodox policies of nonintervention, the Treasury reassumed a monopoly of currency emissions while the government intervened in the Banco da República, assuming assets such as shares of Lloyd Brasileiro and Sorocaba railway company to assure against a run on deposits. However, President-elect Campos Sales' inquiry about the consequences of a moratorium on payments of foreign debt brought a chilling response from Rothschild Bank: 'besides the complete loss of the country's credit the measure could greatly affect Brazil's sovereignty, provoking reactions that could arrive at the extreme of foreign invasion'.[24] Negotiation of a funding loan in 1898 and direct supervision of domestic policies by foreign banks mark the dramatic reduction of monetary policy discretion enjoyed since founding of the republic in 1889.

1898: conditional foreign finance and the new monetary orthodoxy

In 1898, monetary policies shifted to the adoption of severe monetary and fiscal austerity designed to reduce inflation, restore fiscal surpluses, and regain the confidence of foreign investors. The 'financial Darwinism' of Finance Minister Joaquim Murtinho (1898–1902) came to symbolize this turn to orthodoxy with stark interpretations of monetarist theories as justification for draconian policies.[25] The June 1898 funding loan included clauses requiring recall and incineration of mil-réis for government bonds (in lieu of interest payments from 1898–1901), pledge of Rio customs house receipts toward repayment, and supervision of government policies by foreign banks. Adjustment was soon followed by growth, but the recovery of international finance in 1897 also contributed to the success of these policies, with imports remaining 14 percent below historic levels and new investments providing foreign account surpluses. Finance Minister Bulhões (1902–1906) continued this policy of short money and fiscal, such that President Campos Sales' shift to orthodox policies became vindicated. Government accounts produced surpluses for two of his four years in office; the mil-réis rose from near 7 to 14 pence; and a sixfold increase in exports combined with capital inflows made it possible to meet foreign currency obligations while inflation declined at home.[26]

Once again, the turn to orthodoxy was neither linear nor complete. The 1900 domestic bank crisis led the government to first support the Banco da República, then to intervene and reorganize the bank into the fourth Banco do Brasil. Finance Minister Murtinho (notoriously indisposed to intervene in markets) attempted to stem the run on deposits by swapping 186 contos of bank debts due the Treasury for 50 contos new treasury notes, then through emergency loans of 900,000 pounds sterling and 10 contos. After intervening in September 1900, the government created this fourth national Banco do Brasil by converting Banco da República liabilities to Treasury into one-third of new bank shares; allocating one-third of new shares to existing stockholders, and selling the final third. The capitalization of share from 49 mil-réis in 1905, 155 mil-réis in 1906, and 250 mil-réis in 1908[27] enabled the government to redefine public policies on money, credit and banking. The new Banco do Brasil remained exclusive agent for foreign exchange and deposits and lending to Treasury. However, new rules prohibited both loans over six months and any purchase of company stock in capital markets. The Rio financial paper, *Jornal do Comercio*, greeted the new Banco do Brasil as 'able to exercise the functions of a central bank, having available abundant capital to rediscount the paper of other banks, make advances to other banks and finally aid them in moments of crisis'.[28] In sum, even during Murtinho's term as Finance Minister, domestic policy was not just the imposition of austerity and monetary orthodoxy; tariffs and taxes also increased during the Rodrigues Alves administration under Murtinho.

1906: the end of orthodoxy – currency board, gold standard and coffee price support

The third period of monetary statecraft during the Old Republic shifts away from fiscal and monetary orthodoxy in 1906 with President Afonso Pena from Minas Gerais state. New policies sought to support world coffee prices, stabilize foreign exchange rates, and provide domestic credit to avert bankruptcies during periods of adjustment. Influenced by the successful organization of a currency board and gold standard in Argentina, the Caixa de Conversão was created in 1906 with authority to manage money anchored to gold reserves and a fixed exchange rate.[29] This currency board coincided with the 1906 Taubaté Accord, two institutions that mark the end of conservative insistence on fiscal and monetary austerity and non-intervention. Instead, government policies reached beyond Brazilian borders to stabilize world coffee prices and more effectively allocate of export receipts to domestic producers during booms and socialize costs during adjustment.[30] Coffee stocks were financed in 1906 by credits from importers in foreign markets underwritten by the São Paulo state government. Fritsch argues that the federal government soon overcame its reluctance to underwrite coffee stocks in 1907 when financial crisis in London led to the (temporary) suspension of coffee credits. Without credits to stock coffee, both coffee prices and export revenue could have depleted the newly founded currency board and wreck plans to reach currency convertibility under a gold standard.

The international context for Brazilian policy also changed in 1906. Instead of severe conditionality imposed by foreign bankers, a new round of direct foreign investment in the periphery emerged. Brazilian rubber exports boomed until production in Asian colonies came online to reduce world prices in 1910.[31] Abandoning liberal principles of non-intervention, the Brazilian government led public–private investments in ports, railways and other improvements in infrastructure to eliminate bottlenecks, increase productivity, and encourage domestic commerce.[32] Although the 1907 financial crisis shook confidence, recovery of international financial markets during 1908 provided (ironically, for liberal theory) strong political legitimacy to the interventionist combination of coffee price support and currency board in Brazil. These developments were not caused by capital flows, but instead by government policies designed to ensure more effective allocation. A look inside the currency board evidences these cyclical pressures.

Large trade and capital account surpluses at first produced a substantial influx of gold and hard currency reserves into the currency board (see Table 3.3). Deposits increased from just over 37 contos in 1906, to over 63,000 in 1907, rising to 493,000 at peak inflow of capital in 1908. The monetary reforms of 1906 funnelled these reserves directly into credit through the domestic banking system.[33] Furthermore, the Caixa de Conversão increased the capacity of the government to influence domestic

Table 3.3 Currency board (1906–1910, contos)

	1906	1907	1908	1909	1910*
Deposits	37,282	63,796	493,686	141,737	98,641
Withdrawals	—	1,037	11,139	5,850	3,935
Year-end total	37,282	100,041	582,488	718,275	812,981

Source: Calogeras, J.P. *La Politique Monétaire du Brésil* (Rio de Janeiro: Imprimerie Nationale, 1910), pp. 486–487.

* Through May 1910 when closed temporarily.

financial markets through issue of convertible notes for foreign currencies and sale of pounds from reserves to keep the mil-réis below official par. After closing temporarily in 1910, the currency board reopened until a run on its hard currencies led to closure again in 1914.

São Paulo representative and former finance minister Braga reminded congress that the deposits accumulated in the currency board were primarily due to capital inflows and included the principal due on government loans from abroad acquired during a period of international optimism. The trend in Brazilian foreign accounts since the 1898 funding loan suggested the accumulation of large obligations in foreign currency, not the 812 million mil-réis surplus indicated by the sum of foreign inflows into the currency board. The average trade balance from 1899 through 1910 of 15 million pounds ran well below the average debt service of 24 million pounds during the same decade. At a foreign exchange rate of 15 pence per mil-réis, the approximately 20 million pounds surplus in the Caixa de Conversão dominated in the accounting of foreign debt alongside trade and capital flows.

At year-end 1898, Brazilian foreign debt stood at 34.7 million pounds. By 1910, it had increased to over 88.0 million pounds. And while direct investment drove the economy as well, almost half of total foreign debt, over 42 million pounds, was acquired by states and municipalities in overseas bond markets. The cycle of foreign investment appeared to have been state and municipalled, not in Gershenkron's sense but in terms of chronology. Private capital investments summed over 13 million pounds during 1909 alone and totalled a minimum of 30 million pounds of officially registered investments in 1910. In sum, all this hard currency and gold was not foreign reserves and gold in the sense of Brazilian national reserves able to stabilize the currency. On the contrary, these sums represented a (not total) sum of principal owed and foreign capital owned in the country during a period of booming international investments.

Fritsch, Topik and others argue that this first experience with a currency board in Brazil coincided with a period of positive international and domestic developments to produce strong domestic growth and adjust government, national and foreign accounts. By 1912, Topik estimates that a full 40 percent of total domestic money supply was convertible to gold. And liquidity permitted institutional and market advances, with the Banco do Brasil controlling foreign currency exchange markets in Rio, while new regulations required that import taxes be partially paid in gold. Finance Minister Bulhões defended these measures as necessary to avert abuses of monopoly power in foreign exchange markets by foreign banks.

The gold standard and currency board exceeded the expectations of theory and practice on the upside. However, these new institutions also produced unexpectedly perverse consequences on the downside. The accumulation of gold reserves in the accounts of the currency board during good times permitted the expansion of credit through the domestic banking system. However, bad times demanded a threefold reduction of credit to bring bank portfolios into accord with lower gold reserves. In monetary theory, this may be good for adjustment, but in practice, money and credit evaporated when foreign accounts reduced gold reserves. Deterioration in foreign accounts, whether due to trade, finance or investment, led to abrupt reductions in domestic credit. Instead of providing counter-cyclical liquidity, banks were forced to reduce credit. This slowed economic activity which further reduced the creditworthiness of portfolios which further reduced the liquidity of banks. This vicious cycle produced declines in domestic activity well beyond the levels assumed necessary in economic theory to adjust foreign accounts, regardless of whether the government retained a gold standard or flexible exchange rate. Fritsch argues that the trade balance passed this fulcrum during 1912, coinciding with a separate trend toward government deficits that led foreign creditors to refuse new loans. In addition, world rubber prices had declined dramatically after 1910 due to new exports from Asian colonies, while coffee prices fell steeply after judicial orders released stocks in New York under antitrust legislation.

By 1912, the international context that had sustained growth now pressured for adjustment. The government maintained the currency board and gold standard during 1913 in the expectation of new loans from foreign creditors. However, the continued decline in credit, money, bank liquidity and economic activity during 1914 led the government to declare a prolonged bank holiday in August, a moratorium on foreign and domestic debt payments and to print treasury bills to avert widespread bank failures.[34] While the government appeared to face rapidly decreasing policy options, the geopolitical realities of war led to an unexpected shift among foreign creditors. Despite declaring moratoria in August 1914, by October the Brazilian government secured a 15 million pound funding loan that suspended interest payments until 1917 and principal payments until 1927.[35] Unfortunately, whatever advantages the government had gained in the terms of the 1914 funding loan were countered by the deterioration of credit after the war. After 1918, premiums and interest rates on loans to Brazil remained 2 percent and 10 points above levels secured in pre-war loans.

The First World War was another turning point for Brazilian development that required dramatic measures to manage domestic credit and money.[36] The decline of imports and exports led the government to cut spending, increase consumer taxes and emit both short-term treasury bills and long-term government bonds. Once again, the decision to float government paper was driven by political necessity not ideological design. Government paper was issued to meet past due obligations, while the Banco do Brasil was used to alleviate the shortage of liquidity and credit during adjustment to foreign accounts.

On August 24, 1914, an executive decree freed the Treasury to emit an additional 250,000 contos, 150,000 going to meet treasury obligations and 100,000 for credit through banking system. In 1915, the Treasury released an additional 350,000 contos. The consequences of this trade and investment shock were to deepen levels of international and domestic debt.[37] In addition to the trade and investment shock, the impact of war on the Brazilian economy was felt in terms of dramatic increases in costs of shipping, insurance and domestic labour, the latter due to widespread emigration for wartime service in Europe.

The collapse of exports and foreign investment produced a domestic state of economic emergency. Given the unwillingness of domestic markets to purchase government bonds and international finance on hold, paper emissions were the only viable mechanism for the deeply indebted Brazilian government in 1915. In this respect, Cincinato Braga argued that both timing and target of paper emissions were critical. Past paper emissions had indeed involved waste and loss during financial crisis, but if paper emissions provided liquidity for investment in agriculture, then this emergency instrument could serve to avert widespread bankruptcy and invest in exportable goods. According to Braga, paper emissions during 1890 and 1894 were positive examples, given that these issues escaped losses incurred upon collapse of Rio financial markets, the *encilhamento* and did not dissipate as war expenses, but produced, instead, a dramatic expansion of coffee production and exports. Paper emissions permitted the expansion of coffee production from 1890–1894 average production of 2.7 million sacks to 1901–1904 average production of 8.0 million sacks. Indeed, payment of first instalments of 1898 funding loan were made possible by new coffee cycle coming on line in terms of exports and foreign exchange.

Again, paper emissions are justified as political necessity and best possible option, not as an economic doctrine. Hunger and drought had produced an exodus from the countryside to cities. Debate in congress emphasized the psychological dimensions of economic cycles, specifically the need to avert radical solutions and panic. Reference to the economic cycles in German *Konjunctur* theory – those of depression, recovery, fever and crisis – was used to suggest that countercyclical measures to stimulate recovery were needed. Braga argues:

> It is much easier to recover from a crisis of excess currency applied to agriculture than from a crisis of lack of currency that causes bankruptcies and recession. (Saliba, p. 135)

Wartime measures throughout Europe and North America were designed to protect the convertibility and gold standards of major currencies. However, Braga notes that the difference is not one of theory but of circumstance and necessity, indeed a fundamental difference between centre and periphery:

> They only issue gold . . . because they have gold, whose investment has always been zealously defended, now even dictatorially. With us, it is the opposite. We do not have gold, nor do we have the means to acquire it now to underwrite our issue.[38]

Braga rejected the validity of quantitative theories linking domestic money supply directly to foreign exchange rates. The mil-réis foreign exchange rate was determined less by levels of the domestic money supply and more by the trade and investment flows that determined foreign accounts. During periods of export surpluses and or foreign investment, the value of the mil-réis in foreign exchange markets remained stable. During periods of trade deficits or reduced foreign investments, the mil-réis declined in foreign currency exchange markets, irrespective of the domestic management of money supply. The recall and burning of currency during periods of negative flows in foreign accounts had no impact on valuation of the currency and simply pushed the domestic economy into deep recession.

The counter intuitive conclusion of Braga was counter-cyclical monetary statecraft. Government investments were needed to counter the economic and financial factors reducing domestic economic activity. Not cuts in government spending, but real increases in government credits and investments were necessary: 'To reorganize the economy, we need to spend money. We shall do so courageously' (Braga, p. 204). Beyond his rhetoric lies a tradition of Brazilian money management. To reverse the cyclical downturns in the Brazilian economy, it was necessary for the government to lead recovery through credits and investments. This implied rejection of doctrines of non-intervention and adoption of state-led policies used by governments in the advanced economies. This maxim was even more valid in times of government debt. The only way to generate foreign exchange earnings to pay future debt obligations was to reduce government expenditures *and* invest to export.

These doctrines of national liberalism and developmentalism during the Old Republic reflect an underlying shift in Brazilian economy. Compared to the stark dependence on foreign trade and capital flows, and the control of foreign exchange markets by select foreign banks, the Brazilian government and domestic banks appear to have thereby obtained greater autonomy for anticyclical policies. Despite abandoning the gold standard and emitting fiduciary paper during the war years, the foreign exchange rate remained relative stable. Unlike the dramatic declines of the exchange rate during the empire and beginning of the Old Republic, monetary policies from 1914 through 1918 resulted in the devaluation of the mil-réis against the pound by 20 percent.

World War I led to increased Brazilian government control in foreign exchange markets and reduced the presence of international banks in the country. Coffee and foreign exchange markets in London used to be controlled by two banks. The critical juncture of war and the development of new government regulations over foreign currency exchange in Rio suggest that international forces were brought under increasing national control; this being the fundamental shift pointed to by Cardoso and Falleto in their sequence of dependent development. Cardoso, Fernando H. and Falleto, Enzo. Dependency and Development in Latin America. (Berkeley, CA: University of California Press, 1979). Furthermore, the retraction of foreign banks from domestic credit and investments during the war left Brazilian banks in a preferential position. Topik argues that during 1914 domestic banks advanced over foreign banks, from 56 to 74 percent of discount market and from 49 to 57 percent of domestic loans. In sum, foreign exchange devaluation and the adjustment of the Brazilian economy to the trade shock caused by the outbreak of war in 1914 improved confidence in the banking system and led to a 'national-liberal' assertion of domestic finance over international creditors and banks.

Another positive cycle ensued after the war. The postwar boom in Europe and North America soon led to another period of export led growth in Brazil and new cycle of domestic investments in infrastructure. The end of European conflict in 1918 and frost damage in Brazil temporarily eliminated the need to finance coffee stocks, with world prices increasing from 10.8 cents a pound in June 1918 to 22 cents a pound by year-end. The Epitácio Pessoa administration tapped renewed international interest in the periphery to mobilize foreign financial and direct investment in Brazilian infrastructure. However, these developments in the post-war period once again led to downward pressures on coffee prices and the deterioration of foreign accounts. And like movements in 1905, coffee producers and other domestic groups sought to create new mechanisms to support prices and avert declines in export revenue.

1920: currency board II – the Banco do Brasil emissions and exchange account

The fourth period of monetary statecraft during the Old Republic involves the creation of the Carteira de Emissão e Redesconto with discretionary accounts for currency emissions and exchange of commercial paper for treasury notes. These accounts were designed alongside commercial operations in the national bank to reduce the exposure of domestic money and credit to fluctuations in international trade, finance and investment – a vulnerability confirmed by the 1920 financial crisis abroad.[39] The Carteira de Emissão ee Redesconto functioned as a currency board to clear foreign accounts, but because presidential orders could emit treasury notes for Banco do Brasil purchase of commercial paper, the national bank also became a discretionary lender of last resort. Once again, the Banco do Brasil became central to the politics of monetary politics, forced to reconcile pressures from coffee producers for credit, prudent management of its commercial portfolio, and responsibility for both currency reserves and the money supply.[40]

The discretionary design of the Caixa de Conversão increased government control over the domestic money supply and credit and financial markets in the short term, but ballooning government debt and devaluation of the mil-réis led to its abandonment in favour of redesigning the Banco do Brasil as Banco Central Emissor in 1923. This second currency board freed commercial banks to offer an estimated 400,000 contos during 1921.[41] Legislation first prohibited trade of government paper and set emission limits at 100,000 contos. However, in 1922 the bank was freed to buy and sell government notes, while increased emissions were approved three years consecutively.[42] Table 3.4 reports the trajectory of currency emissions and foreign exchange rate from 1920 through 1923.

Because market prices for treasury notes fell and terms shortened, the Banco do Brasil increasingly assumed greater quantities of government debt in its portfolio. In 1921, congress authorized exchange of 500 contos of treasury bills – equivalent to one half the total value of notes held by the bank, a development that alleviated the government deficit but dramatically expanded the monetary base during the last quarter of 1921. This monetization of the fiscal deficit added to the inflationary pressures of exchange devaluation

Table 3.4 Currency emissions and exchange rate (1920–1923)

Year	Emission Limits	Exchange Rate (mil-réis yr. average)
1920	100,000	
1921	200,000	8.4
1922	300,000	7.1
1923	400,000	5.3

Source: Falcão, Waldemar. *O Empirismo Monetário no Brasil* (Rio de Janeiro: Companhia Editoria Nacional), p. 32.

during 1920–1921 and threatened to paralyze the Banco do Brasil's commercial operations.

Recourse to foreign finance temporarily averted collapse of the system. Fritsch argues that financial recovery in London made new banks eager to extend credits to Brazil and compete with traditional lenders. Given the recovery of coffee prices in August 1922 and estimates for a small crop,[43] foreign bankers lent sufficient amounts to maintain reserves in the currency board and permit the continuation of domestic credit, finance, and domestic money management, despite such operations being built on foreign loans. Fritsch explains such an apparent lack of banking prudence by competition between banks in London. In any case, short-term credits were consolidated in May 1922 through the lead of merchant banks traditionally associated with Brazilian government. Signs of economic recovery during 1922 reinforced the flow of foreign finance to Brazil and temporarily improved the conditions for domestic monetary policy. Coffee prices recovered to improve the trade balance, while another cycle of public works programs and domestic industry also increased domestic activity.

This shift to optimism during 1922 also led the Bernardes administration to develop new reforms designed to transform the Banco do Brasil into a central bank and create a separate institution for coffee price supports, the Instituto do Café.[44] In 1923, Banco do Brasil president Cincinato Braga proposed and congress approved new regulations to limit rediscount operations and clarify its role as lender of last resort.[45] Falcão argues that the nomination of Braga and presentation of reforms to congress on 8 January 1923 led to further pressures on the mil-réis in foreign exchange markets, with value of the domestic currency falling from 7.5 mil-réis a pence during first quarter 1922 to reach 4.6 mil-réis a pence at bottom on 7 November 1923.

Debate in congress and the financial press turned on opposition to the use of government notes as bank reserves versus defence of these measures by the government as necessary to sustain domestic credit and growth. Those defending principles of new monetary theory such as Calogeras, Brandt, Freire and Murtinho argued that a lack of confidence in Finance Minister Sampaio Vidal and Banco do Brasil president Cincinato Braga's defense of paper emissions had led to the excessive devaluation of the mil-réis that endangered progress toward economic stability and currency convertibility. The dramatic increase of liquid government debt and devaluation of the mil-réis during 1922 reinforced conservative criticisms of Vidal and Braga's monetary management, exemplified by Mario Brandt, federal representative and former finance secretary of Minas Gerais state.[46] The 1922 congressional finance committee report signed by Anibal Freire condemned this permissive relation between a discretionary currency board and national bank and led to the resignation of Finance Minister Whitaker in December 1922.

During this period, the political legitimacy of the government and the course of debates and realities of monetary policy appear to run separate, parallel courses. Since the first revolts against the Old Republic led by socialist and labour movements in 1917, military cadets in 1918, and the 'municipal' movement (that denounced widespread fraud in the 1919 municipal elections), opposition to the exclusive system of single-state parties increased dramatically during the 1920s. After widespread revolts during 1924, São Paulo state was governed under state of emergency decrees with few interruptions until revolutionary movements ended the Old Republic in May 1930. This trajectory of political challenges to the exclusive single-state party system inaugurated by Campos Sales in 1891 would meet up with the credit shock after the 1929 crash overseas to produce a run on the gold deposits of the currency board.

Cincinato Braga's 1924 report as president of the Banco do Brasil contains several arguments central to understanding the politics that led to the end of the national bank's prerogatives to emit currency. Braga emphasizes the impact of insufficient trade surpluses and government deficits and debt, factors that made the assertion of the Banco do Brasil as the central bank extremely difficult, while the mil-réis reached an historic low of 4 and 21/32 pence on foreign exchange markets. Braga argued that the trade and investment shock from World War I, a flight to German marks, French francs, and Italian lira because of their respective devaluations and politics at home (the outbreak of civil war in Rio Grande do Sul and declaration of a state of emergency by federal government in 1924) had eroded the confidence of investors necessary to stabilize the currency and pursue monetary policy.

The 1924 Banco do Brasil annual report includes the stark prospect of 5.571 million pounds in foreign currency obligations above and beyond national sources of revenue. However, in an address to congress, Braga argued that the worst was over and that it was necessary and possible to invest in transportation improvements to reduce bottlenecks and ensure higher levels of economic growth. Given the prospects for peace in Rio Grande do Sul and the apparent end of revolts in Bahia and Rio, plans to reduce sending and produce real reductions in government deficits could be presented to investors for new government issues at home and credits abroad. Federal government deficits had declined from peaks of 424 and 453 contos in 1921 and 1922, to 223 contos in 1923, with 80 contos of a one-time payment of high-interest government paper during 1923, suggesting for national bank president Braga, that government accounts during 1924 would improve. Furthermore, international markets were once again favourable to Brazil, not just because of underlying indicators but because the government arranged early payment of 9.0 million pounds to liquidate a 30-year loan in three years. Braga reminded congress of the shift in mood and markets following the 1898 funding loan that consolidated foreign debt, increased foreign investment and produced a period of strong economic growth that put government and foreign accounts back on track.

The positive perceptions of Brazil abroad were reinforced by recovery of trade surpluses, the valuation of the mil-réis from just over 4.0 to 5.1 during 1923, and coffee futures market predicting another strong harvest while world demand surged to avert excess supply. Braga also reported two institutional developments that enabled the Banco do Brasil to reduce the volatile fluctuations of foreign exchange rates that had wracked international transactions. By stocking coffee in warehouses before reaching Brazilian ports, the government was able to avert dramatic price declines without foreign currency risks and costs in London markets controlled by foreign banks. Furthermore, the Banco do Brasil had opened offices in London to reduce the cost and volatility of coffee and foreign exchange transactions, while creating daily liquidation of import tax revenues in Rio to further help reduce the volatility of foreign exchange transactions. New legislation was being prepared to create a National Mortgage Bank with guarantee of the Treasury, an institution that could increase credit without directly pressuring stocks of government debt.

Given that currency convertibility was not possible in these circumstances, Braga emphasized the prudence of short-term credits by bank to avert the accumulation of arrears and portfolio deterioration.[47] While the demand for credit was beyond the bank's capacity, especially in the interior, Braga notes that no currency emissions were approved during the first months of his term during May and June 1923. However, given that the government was unable to float additional paper in the domestic market, paper currency emissions began during second semester 1923 and early 1924. Two bank policies attempted to reduce the inflationary impact of paper emissions, limits on commercial bank rediscounting at the Banco do Brasil and the recall of over 62 contos in paper money.[48] This combination of policies had increased Banco do Brasil reserves and reduced obligations during 1923. Braga notes that reserves had increased from 40 contos at year-end 1922 to over 90 contos at year-end 1923, with the bank on schedule to reach the target for July 1924 of 100 contos in reserves.[49]

In sum, the 1924 annual report of the Banco do Brasil reveals gradual institutional innovations that sought to reduce the volatility of foreign exchange and export prices, while seeking to channel renewed financial interest in Brazil abroad more effectively through domestic credit and state-led investments in infrastructure. This document serves as an example of liberal-nationalist and developmentalist doctrines. However, it also registers the nonlinearity of monetary statecraft and the different logics and timing of economic and political change. After authoring the report, Braga was forced to resign from the Banco do Brasil presidency along with Finance Minister Sampaio Vidal, signalling a return to orthodox measures of money management.

1924: the return to orthodoxy

After finance committee inquires in congress led to the resignation of Braga in late 1924, the government shifted to tight money policies more in accord with orthodoxy. By May 1925, President Bernardes argued for the need to recall currency to revert excessive emissions and revalue the mil-réis against foreign currencies. The new policy called for recall of 98 contos through the Banco do Brasil and Caixa de Amortização. Recalls exceeded these levels.[50] The rapid recovery of the foreign exchange rate vindicated this turn to orthodoxy and coincided with another boom of foreign investment into Brazil. Once again, a wave of direct foreign and financial investment from Europe and North America into Brazil created an influx of capital into the currency board, stabilized foreign exchange rates, and changed economic conditions. This sequence involving orthodox policies of tight money, the valuation of the mil-réis against foreign currencies, a boom in foreign financial and direct investment culminating in strong economy growth provided strong political legitimacy for conservative theories of money management and non-interventionism.

However, the apparent success of tight money and quantitative theories led, once again, to their continuation well after recovery of economic activity generated trade surpluses, capital inflows, and growth. The shifting fortunes of foreign investment, the negotiation of new loans from foreign banks eager to compete with traditional lenders to Brazil, and state-led development policies drove the period of economic growth between 1924 and 1928. Events in Brazil seem insufficient to warrant the dramatic influx of foreign capital after 1923. Indeed, political realities conspired against investor confidence. Again, it deserves note that, after 1924, civil war in Rio Grande do Sul, regional revolts in São Paulo and Bahia, and military revolts in Rio had led state and federal governments to declare states of emergency.

The single-state parties that dominated the Old Republic elected Washington Luis to the presidency in 1926. However, this level of political risk and high foreign and domestic debt normally produce caution. In this respect, foreign finance seems to have acquired a dynamic of its own. Once foreign banks signed loans, their eagerness to outbid other banks appears to have overridden rational considerations. This drove another cycle of growth in Brazil between 1926 and 1929 before the October crash in North America and Europe.

Moreover, pressures from organized interests led to adoption of measures outside orthodoxy, especially after signs of economic recovery and yet another boom in international investment became apparent. Rio commercial organizations specialized in such lobbying; and textile producers apparently achieved relief in the form of emergency credit. These perceptions matter because design of another currency board would automatically channel foreign funds into board reserves and thereby increase levels of credit that domestic commercial bank could extend. Fritsch emphasizes the legitimacy of the currency board precisely because it provided rules for domestic allocation of foreign capital flows. This was seen as necessary to avert the excesses of discretionary lending through the national bank under Cincinato Braga.

The development of another scheme to stock coffee and support producers through Banespa, the São Paulo state government bank, also suggests that the last years of the Old Republic were far from a linear shift toward orthodox monetary and credit policies. Furthermore, Fritsch emphasizes the eagerness of London banks without previous experience in Brazil to finance this new fund to transform

Banespa in to the major lender of last resort in São Paulo state. Indeed, the São Paulo program reproduced preceding federal experiences by first participating in a period of rapid foreign financial investment to Brazil, followed by successive record harvests and sudden reversals in international coffee markets that, all too soon, liquidated funds designed to support coffee prices and producers.

In sum, although perceptions of adjustment and recovery vindicated conservative theories of monetary policy, this last growth cycle under the Old Republic had more to do with foreign capital flows and state-directed investments. Federal and state government initiatives attempted to reduce bottlenecks in infrastructure and transportation to increase growth during booms. And boom it did. After remaining stagnant in 1925, real gross domestic product (GDP) increased from 5.2 percent in 1926, 10.8 percent in 1927 and 11.5 percent in 1928. And unlike past growth cycles that immediately pressured domestic prices and devalued foreign exchange, this cycle ended only because the inflows of foreign capital dried up by mid-1928. The boom thus ended *before* crisis. Fritsch argues that the end of the Old Republic reflected the end of another cycle driven by foreign capital flows, with the sudden stop occurring a year before the October 1929 crisis on Wall Street.

In terms of ideas from abroad, these cyclical shifts to more orthodox monetary policies sustained by 'Kemmerer coalitions' in Brazil reflected a global movement in the 1920s to design independent central banks and adopt quantitative theories of money, credit, and economic policy.[51] The modern currency reform movement was associated with the stabilization of currencies and domestic prices during the 1920s, first in the United Kingdom, then the United States, followed by a variety of countries in Scandinavia and Eastern Europe. Moreover, Mexico, Bolivia, and other Latin American countries founded central banks during this decade.[52]

Brazilian policy makers widely debated adoption of orthodoxy. Far from doctrinaire advocates of new theories, the financial weekly columns of Carvalho and debates in the congressional finance commission suggest careful consideration of a variety of experiences with reforms, and an emphasis on the need for gradualism and proper sequencing of reforms.[53] Policy makers shared an underlying agreement about the need to shift toward a convertible currency and gold standard.[54] But, as Finance Minister Bernardino de Campos notes in his 1898 report to congress, 'a gold standard is not for those who want it but for those who can have it'.[55] The conclusion of most Finance Ministers, members of congressional finance committees and writers in the financial press was that gradual adoption of fiscal, foreign exchange, banking, financial, credit and monetary reforms would be necessary to create conditions for currency convertibility.[56]

Moreover, experiences in Eastern Europe, Latin America, and India were examined by Brazilian policy makers (the latter as early as 1900), because of the similar challenges of adapting modern currency reforms to an agrarian export economy. For Carvalho, the Czech experience with valuation of domestic currency despite paper emissions suggests that quantitative theories required consideration of the trade balance, foreign investment levels, and general confidence. Given the intense return of Western European investments to Czechoslovakia during the 1920s, international matters were critical. The Belgian experience also provided an important reference in terms of sequencing reforms to regain confidence in domestic currency and economy. Consolidating government debt, creating a currency board, and increasing fiscal control were preconditions for money managememt. Hungary combined international supervision through the League of Nations and dispensing of 25,000 public servants. The stabilization of the zloty in Poland under supervision of a US advisor involving central bank independence and foreign loans to manage money seemed particularly relevant to Carvalho.[57]

Carvalho and Falcão therefore criticized legislation of 18 December 1926 for combining all together measures that required time and sequencing to work. Moreover, creation of a new currency (cruzeiro) alongside the mil-réis and setting legal parity at below-market levels made the transition to a stable and convertible currency more difficult. Debate in congress on monetary policy and currency stabilization revolved around three groups; those that opposed designs to reach currency convertibility, those that defended government policies, and those that disagreed with the methods employed by the government that failed to sequence properly and proceed gradually.[58]

The turn to modern currency theories began during the Bernardes administration in 1924. This approach culminated with approval by congress of a package of reforms soon after inauguration of Washington Luis in 1926. President Washington Luis was determined to adapt stabilization programs from Europe to stabilize the economy and reach currency convertibility under a gold standard. By December 1926, congress approved a package of monetary and currency policies designed to stabilize a new gold backed currency, the cruzeiro. Campaign speeches and his first presidential address to congress recognized the need to prepare the terrain for currency reforms. However, instead of gradual measures, Washington Luis rushed a package of reforms to a floor vote in December 1926, including the following: (1) gold standard, (2) cruzeiro as new currency fixed against gold at $1 = 200$ mg gold and the pound at 900 mil-réis to 5.9 pence, (3) creation of a currency board to avert foreign exchange volatility, (4) authorization to operate in foreign exchange markets to avert devaluation and (5) transformation of the Banco do Brasil into an independent central bank. Congress approved these measures, and implementation proceeded at different paces until the crash of 1929 overtook events.[59]

Several matters captured the attention of representatives and the financial press during this last cycle of domestic growth and crisis 1926–1929. First, domestic factors were seen to have preceded the impact of the 1929 crisis from abroad, making adjustments in some respects more dramatic, in other respects easier. Second, critics argued that President Washington Luis' currency reform failed to tighten the money supply in accord with Cassel's standard of 3 percent. Instead, currency recalls were suspended. Falcão reports 250 percent growth of paper money between 1914 and 1926; far above the 36 percent increase in GDP.[60] And contrary to Cassel's prescriptions, the currency board continued to emit an estimated 800 contos into the domestic economy as required by the influx of capital during this period.

Finally, new cruzeiros were anchored by gold reserves but created a situation of dual currencies. Moreover, in the haste to create currency convertibility to gold the bizarre alchemic measure was taken of *melting gold* into coins to ensure their value, rather than retaining gold in the currency board as reserve for the new monetary unit. Parities for the new cruzeiro were also skewed. The formula to set the exchange rate at 5,115/128 pence per cruzeiro looked to averages from 1921 to 1926, years of mil-réis devaluation (average foreign exchange rates between 1914 and 1925 being 10.5 – almost double the 5.3 rate used in 1926 reforms).

In retrospect, perhaps the most bizarre aspect of the 1926 reforms was the melting of gold into the new cruzeiro in the expectation that this would ensure stabilization. Foreign loans financed gold to mint new cruzeiro coins – not credits, bonds, funding loans or other traditional mechanisms of foreign finance, but brut gold. Rothschild & Sons and Dillon Read and Co. coordinated loans of 8.75 million pounds and 41.5 million pounds, respectively, at 91.5 percent of face value and 6.5 percent interest rates to underwrite reforms that combined quantitative currency theory and alchemy. Gold not melted into coin was deposited at a third currency board organized during the Old Republic. As with previous experiences (the Caixa de Conversão, 1906–1914, and Caixa de Emissão e Redesconto, 1920–1923), international capital flows drove a domestic cycle of boom and bust. Foreign investment flows deposited in the currency board increased the liquidity of banks and domestic credit.[61] However, once foreign capital and trade revenues declined during 1928, the inverse ensued and credit evaporated well before the October 1929 crash.

When crisis hit in 1929, previous outflows of foreign capital and trade deficits had already threatened to empty the currency board. Whatever progress had been made in terms of monetary reform and stabilization, the reality is that the Brazilian economy was left in a situation of dual currencies without capital controls. This contributed to the flight to gold beginning in late 1929. The currency reforms of 1926 had created a new cruzeiro, convertible and backed by gold in the currency board, alongside the old mil-réis notes, a fiduciary currency backed by only by treasury bills in the currency board and Banco do Brasil (see Table 3.5).

Dual currencies are notoriously unstable. When the October 1929 crash on Wall Street produced a crisis of confidence in the domestic Brazilian banking system,

Table 3.5 Dual currencies (1928)

Mil-Réis Denominated Reserves	
Banco do Brasil*	592,000
Treasury Notes	1,997,304
Stabilization Account Notes	744,284
Sub-total Mil-Réis Reserves	3,313,580
Cruzeiro denominated reserves	
Stabilization Account	744,284
Banco do Brasil	406,801
Sub-total Gold Reserves	1,151,085

*Law No 5.108, 18 December 1926, defined the Treasury as responsible for Banco do Brasil reserves denominated in mil-réis.

Table 3.6 Run on gold and hard currency reserves (*Caixa de Estabilização*, 1930)

January	796,331
February	695,331
March	651,085
April	343,978
May	345,288
June	342,676
July	260,598
August	167,698
September	134,125

Source: Falcão, Waldemar. *O Empirismo Monetário no Brasil* (Rio de Janeiro: Companhia Editoria Nacional), p. 104.

the immediate result was a run on the gold reserves of the currency board. Foreign exchange rates and reserve levels in the currency board remained stable through the first nine months of 1929. However, Table 3.6 reports the run on gold in the currency board during 1930.

Braga alerted the consequences of this run on gold deposits. Designers of monetary reforms were so determined to use reserves of gold and hard currency to reach convertibility of the cruzeiro that the run on gold not only depleted the currency board, but the *entire stock* of treasury reserves. Once domestic and foreign investers began to refuse funds for government, this meant that the country was literally defenceless.

Paradoxically, the transfer of hard currency and gold reserves from the Banco do Brasil into the currency board occurred during Getulio Vargas' term as Finance Minister in 1927. The total sum of foreign currency and gold reserves in the national bank – 10 million pounds – that provided guarantee for 592 contos of mil-réis circulating in the domestic economy were simply transferred from the Banco do Brasil to Treasury. Vargas then ignored the clause calling for compensation of the national bank for these 10 million pounds. He also transferred the remaining 11.2 million pounds of treasury reserves into the currency board where they too were subject to market fluctuations. The flight of an estimated 11.2 million pounds from the currency board during the months of revolution would leave Brazil without reserves of foreign currency or precious metals or recourse to finance at home or abroad.

Conclusion

The politics of monetary policy between 1889 and 1930 reveal a variety of lessons about monetary statecraft. Policies at times reflected insistence on orthodox austerity inspired by quantitative theories of money and currency stabilization. However, search for alternative policies during cycles of boom and bust, the history of debates involving Finance Ministers, Banco do Brasil presidents, congressional finance committees and the financial press such as *O Economista Brasileiro*, *Jornal do Comércio* and *Wileman's Brazilian Review* suggest that Brazilian monetary policy was not simply misplaced orthodoxy. To the contrary, primary and secondary sources reveal cumulative experiences with policies of money, credit, banking, currency boards, foreign capital flows, external shocks, export finance, exchange markets, and problems associated with the accountability and independence of monetary authorities. Indeed, the politics of finance, money and credit in Brazil from 1889 to 1930 provide striking similarities to problems in the 21st century caused by the liberalization of finance and capital. Perhaps the most sobering conclusion about the politics of monetary policy during the Old Republic is that crisis abroad in 1929 overshadowed institutional advances.

Policy makers continued to adapt ideas from abroad to shape domestic development between 1889 and 1930. Reforms pursued during the first years of republican government sought to create regional banks that could build on the financial institutions of the old regime to reverse the notorious lack of credit and money in the interior, while recalling fiduciary paper money when necessary. The idea of using (gradually devalued) federal treasury notes for regional bank reserves sought to reduce the debt of central government, while bank mergers and additional mechanisms sought to increase federal government control over currency emissions. Reforms of Finance Minister Barbosa (1889–1891) thereby attempted to solidify the federal political pact, expanding banking services to states while gradually reasserting central government control over credit, money and paper emissions.

After Barbosa's resignation, excesses of federalism and fiduciary paper during the 1890s produced a shift to orthodox adjustment underwritten by London banks, epitomized by the 1898 funding loan. Tight money and government spending cuts through 1900 were strongly legitimized by foreign capital inflows that produced the first of several boom and bust cycles channelled through a currency board (after 1906). Problems associated with dependence on primary exports and foreign capital flows worsened with the outbreak of World War I. A second funding loan in 1914 and adjustment during wartime gave way to recovery and organization of another discretionary currency board in 1920 within the Banco do Brasil. This second currency board channelled foreign capital into another cycle of expansion, briefly interrupted by adjustment during 1924–1925, to produce growth that ended at the same time crisis hit in 1929. In 1930, a run on gold and hard currency reserves held in a third currency board (created in 1926) ended these dynamics of liberal-nationalism and foreign capital flows that defined the politics of monetary policy during the Old Republic between 1889 and 1930.

Primary and secondary materials from this period reveal several characteristics of monetary statecraft in Brazil. Fritsch argues that cycles of growth during the Old Republic were driven by waves of foreign investment and capital flight.[62] Furtado, Pelaez and others note that conservative Finance Ministers perceived bankruptcies during economic contractions as necessary for modernization and often remained unwilling to provide countercyclical measures. During periods of growth, maintenance of short money after elimination of government deficits and inflationary pressures also slowed the economy. Finance Ministers often insisted on monetary and fiscal austerity because they believed that the independence of Treasury from political pressures threatened prospects for reaching currency convertibility.

Conservative insistence on short money and non-intervention also failed to address export problems during good times. A classic observation about Latin American economies is that import of finished goods constrains growth. This is due to deteriorating terms of trade between primary exports and finished imports. For Brazil, the inelasticity of world coffee prices and volatility of foreign exchange were equally important. Good coffee harvests reduced prices on world markets and valued the mil-réis against foreign currencies to reduce the margins of coffee producers. In theories of international trade, these shifts should signal reallocation of resources. In reality, the mil-réis increased a full 70 percent against the pound from 1898 to early 1905. This eroded support for liberal policies. Instead, coffee producers sought price support and credit and banking policies capable of channelling trade surpluses to domestic growth.

Orthodox monetarism in the Old Republic was thus far from monolithic. Policies of money, credit, banking and foreign exchange between 1889 and 1930 reveal institutional innovations during hard times and policies that attempted to allocate capital inflows during good times more effectively. The concept of monetary statecraft describes this more pragmatic, gradualist trajectory of Brazlian monetary policies during the old republic. In addition to internal differences among advocates of orthodoxy, liberal-nationalism and state-led development, the day-to-day challenges of volatile money, credit, foreign exchange, export markets and stop-and-go foreign investment produced shared searching for viable policies to socialize losses, allocate surpluses, reduce the costs of speculation, and take advantage of opportunities.

Policy makers in the Old Republic conceived monetary policy broadly in relation to a wide variety of matters of credit, finance, foreign investment, foreign exchange rates and economic adjustment. One need not approve of paper emissions to agree with Cincinato Braga: 'Let us not be misled, what we have before us is not just a minimal detail of exchange rates. Rather, in all its complexity, it is the monetary problem of Brazil' (Braga, 14 December 1910, Address to Congress, p. 101).

The 'complex problem' of monetary policy in Brazil has to do with foreign capital flows and adjustment through the domestic financial system. Monetary statecraft during the Old Republic focused on ameliorating the consequences of an open, export-oriented economy and changing capital flows from abroad. Policy makers created currency boards, contracted funding loans and, alternatively, sought to protect and subsidize national production and modernize by Darwinian measures of selection amidst downturns. These polar approaches of national liberalism and orthodox monetarism anticipate many policy making approaches in later periods of Brazilian history.

Debates also reveal fundamental differences about domestic business cycles. For example, the mil-réis often ended well below par against foreign currencies. Former Finance Minister Serzedelo Correia and member of the Congressional Finance

Committee, argued, in 1906, that this was due to the absentee character of capital ownership and consequent obligation to remit profits abroad:

> We are a country where absenteeism or the sending of profits abroad is enormous. About 85% of the profits from our trade are not ours: building rents, interest on shares, bank and company dividends, in fact most of the productive capital is not Brazilian in its profits, and all this emigrates.
>
> And thus in the four-year period of Campos Sales, with an annual trade balance of about 20 million Sterling in our favor, it was never possible to achieve a rate of more than 12. (Saliba, 1983, p. 119)

This does not imply a bias against foreign finance in the Old Republic. Although a national liberal, Cincinato Braga supported the 1914 funding loan for reasons of geopolitics and finance. For Braga, foreign finance had saved France from the loss of sovereignty to Germany in 1870. However, Egypt and Turkey had lost their sovereignty through excessive foreign debt. Braga also argues that the 1898 funding loan to Brazil made possible counter-cyclical investments and recovery of coffee exports able to pay off loans and sustain growth.

The impact of foreign finance thus depends on domestic policy making institutions and procedures. Unfortunately, three-fourths of the 1914 funding loan either returned abroad to pay past-due obligations of state and municipal governments or was used to pay the salary of government employees in arrears. Neither provided significant counter-cyclical effect or helped the modernization of infrastructure or productivity. The government also spent funds from foreign finance on the acquisition of destroyers and torpedoes, thereby remitting funds back to Europe. Foreign finance of infrastructure and transportation in Brazil made special sense because of the severe bottlenecks that constrained export capacity and impeded the generation of foreign exchange to repay debt. Braga also warned that benefits from infrastructure investments accrue only in the long term. The reality of severe imbalance in foreign accounts seemed to define a dark future for Brazil in the short term.

The question of foreign finance was not ideological. Instead, it made a variety of constraints in Brazil apparent, such as poorly organized taxation, poor resource allocation, transportation bottlenecks, lack of rural credit, irrational tariffs and persistent government deficits and debt. These matters made the inflationary printing of fiduciary currency more perverse, with cycles of inflation, speculation and the misallocation of resources resulting from desperate measures or designs by organized groups to receive emergency credits. Perhaps the greatest problem with excessive paper emissions was its devaluation of the mil-réis against foreign currencies and the impact devaluation had on trade surpluses necessary to meet foreign obligations.

A broader conclusion that appears from the 1889–1930 period is that the deepening of financial crisis increases the need for broader coalitions and the conciliation of domestic and international investors. These are moments of monetary statecraft that combine dramatic adjustment and broad domestic political coalitions to pass legislation and legitimate new institutions and regulations of money, credit and finance. This requires more than the sum of interested parties. Design of monetary institutions requires the redefinition of national interests and the reorganization of the state in its relation to domestic and international economic forces. Amidst the volatile business cycles and their devastating domestic consequences from 1889–1930 in Brazil, these moments were unexpectedly frequent.

The former finance secretary of Minas Gerais state is understated when he notes that the history of the Old Republic reveals several interesting phases for those who study economic laws and their practical application. This chapter has reported a wide range of evidence that suggests that the practical application of economic laws in the sub-optimal situations of the Old Republic provide lessons that remain relevant for understanding politics and monetary policy. Government policies and institutions of finance, credit, money and trade during the Old Republic faced not just hard times, but very bad and very good times in rapid succession. This volatility of an export economy on the periphery of the world system also created a greater train of debates and policy experiments designed to reduce the impact of business cycles on domestic development. Until the October 1929 crash, illusions, mistakes, errors and misplaced assumptions accompanied gradual change, while patronage, single-state parties and social exclusion overshadowed doctrines of political liberalism. After 1930, adjustment and growth would continue to take unexpected turns, as a variety of political new ideas from not only liberals, but communists, fascists, and corporatists mixed to produce another regime and policy framework, that of national populism and income substitution industrialization.

Notes

1 Furtado, Celso. *The Economic Growth of Brazil: A Survey from Colonial to Modern Times* (Berkeley, CA: University of California Press, 1959), p. 177. On the persistence of orthodoxy, see: Pelaez, Carlos M. 'As conseqûencias econômicas da ortodoxia cambial e fiscal noBrasil entre 1889–1945'. *Revista Brasileira de Economia,* 25(3), (1971), 5–82 and Fritsch, Winston. *External Constraints on Economic Policy in Brazil* (London: Macmillan, 1988).

2 On the concept and analysis of Kemmerer coalitions, see: Drake, Paul. *The Money Doctor in the Andes: The Kemmerer Missions, 1923–1933* (Durham, NC: Duke University Press, 1989).

3 Braga notes that the gold in the Caixa de Conversão was the *principal* of debts owed to British banks.

4 Barbosa apparently was nominated by military leaders because of his *Diario de Notícias* newspaper columns criticizing imperial policies. He took office without any parliamentary, financial or administrative experience to become a central figure in provisional government, especially in economic policy and writing a federal constitution.

5 Baleeiro, Aliomar. *Rui, um Estadista no Ministério da Fazenda* (Rio de Janeiro: Casa da Rui Barbosa, 1952), pp. 37–38.

6 Besouchet claims that, in 1890, 726 of 773 farms in São Paulo, Rio de Janeiro and Espírito Santo states were bankrupt, with debts summing to 42 contos.

7 From 26 November to 27 December 1889, decrees 13, 19, 20, 23, 24, 33, 50-b,c,d,e granted permission to emit currency to Banco Mercantil de Santos, Crédito Real do Brasil, Banco Comercial do Rio, Banco Mercantil da Bahia, Banco de Pernambuco, Banco Comerical Pelotense, Banco União da Bahia and Banco Sociedade Comércio da Bahia.

8 Barbosa discusses the US experience at length as reference for policies, especially the necessity for plural paper emissions by Lincoln to reinforce the union during civil war. 'The metal issuing banks fell back, discouraging their circulation. The aid from the paper currency, authorized by the Law of July 18, fell on an eager market, like a frosty drop in the ocean, notwithstanding having surpassed the limit of the amount permitted. A vast inflow of companies and transactions, which the revolution had taken by surprise, ran the imminent risk of collapsing in a huge catastrophe, signaling the start of the Republic with a dire stock market crash, under the pressure from an invincible currency famine. It was in the midst of those perplexities and spurred by those dangers, that I turned to the only possible salvation in a similar state of affairs, as the United States had done in similar circumstances and in the face of identical needs, to guarantee the currency with the backing of the national debt' (Barbosa, Rui. *Obras Completas*. Vol. XVIII, 1891 – T.II, *Relatório do Ministério da Fazenda*, p. 53).

9 After Finance Minister Barbosa threatened to resign in the face of resistance to reforms, the leader of the provisional government, General Deodoro Fonseca, called an emergency cabinet meeting. Debate between finance minister, war minister and provisional president reflects the difficulty of reconciling macroeconomic realities and regional interests. 'Campos Sales sees an instrument of partisan action in the São Paulo issuing bank, "a power even in politics". He says the banks established by Ouro Preto gave him the elections. This meeting leads to additional decree: Deodoro Fonseca, February 1: Article 1: for the issue on policies, the State of São Paulo shall constitute a regional bank with the State of Goias. Article 2: The total issue on the policies by the four issuing banks is set at two hundred contos, with one hundred contos for the central region and one hundred contos for the others. Article 3: Any provisions to the contrary are revoked'. Aguiar, Pinto de. *Rui e a Economia Brasileira* (Rio de Janeiro: Fundação da Casa Rui Barbosa, 1971), p. 89.

10 Franco, Gustavo H. B. *Reforma monetária e estabilidade durante a transição republicana* (Rio de e Janeiro: BNDES, 1983), p. 89; Calogeras, J. P. *La Politique Monétaire du Brésil* (Rio de Janeiro: Imprimerie Nationale, 1910), p. 10.

11 'Banking plurality in the issue of non-convertible paper is an invention that economists had never discussed in theory. It could be conceived as a temporary transition, when, as in the first months of the Republic, we were under pressure from the needs imposed on the incipient dictatorship by the claims of a domestic nature' (Barbosa, *Obras*, p. 55).

12 These reforms built on similar system implemented by the last finance minister of the empire in 1888, reforms that set interest rates at 4.5 percent. Significant problems arose due to bank strategies to buy gold instead of treasury bills. As long as banks had access to loans of gold bullion in London at low interest rates, the ability to loan three times this capital was preferred. This led to demands from banks to equalize terms, conceded in May through June 1890, permitting paper emissions based on anchor of treasury bills.

13 'The strict demands of Decree No.165 of January 17, 1890 for the implementation of the issue of public debt bonds impeded credit institutions from exaggerating' (Calogeras, p. 221).

14 'On that matter, I always thought it to be a question of advantages, never of principles. Thus, in the weighing of the advantages, so great is their weight in favor of the banking sector, that federalism itself, in countries such as Switzerland where it is most characteristically personified, has already sacrificed the logic of its system, heading rapidly towards centralization. In a nation such as Brazil, in beginning with the federalist experiment in the organization of the republic, I believe that that the most evident political needs prescribe an essential bond of Union, against the centrifugal movement, which the exaggeration of claims of local autonomy could impress on the country; the concentration of issues into one large establishment of national credit' (Barbosa, Rui. *Finanças e Política da Republica* [Rio de Janeiro: Companhia Impressora, 1892], pp. 156–157).

'From the loan of 1889, I set aside 90.000 *contos*, thanks in part to the deposits from the issuing banks, and in part to the operation prescribed in decree No. 823B of

October 6, 1890. If to these amounts we add the portion from the policies put into the Treasury by the circulation banks, this amounts to more than 100.000 *contos*. But, since the December 7 Decree provided for the redemption of paper currency within a five-year period, with these various funds, we would achieve a reduction of somewhere in the region of 280,000 *contos* in the national debt' (Barbosa, p. 197).

15 Barbosa argues that as of the second quarter of 1890, policies were designed to recall currency and shift towards a single monetary reference: 'in which two solutions were encompassed: the subordination of our currency regime to a progressively uniform system and the redemption of paper currency' (Barbosa, *Obras*, p. 122).

16 Vieira, Dorival T. *Evolução do Sistema Monetário Brasileiro* (São Paulo: Gráfica da FFCL, 1962), p. 191.

17 The current exaggeration of prices is explained in good part by a single cause, which no financial measure could avoid or modify: the enormous growth in population and within said population, the enormous increase in consumption (Barbosa, *Finanças e Política*, p. 263).

18 Topik emphasizes the importance of Germany as the primary reference adopted by Mayrink, the principal financial advisor to Barbosa and later president of the Banco do Brasil. Subsequent Finance Ministers would shift back to the monetary orthodoxy of the currency school and doctrines of economic liberalism, embodied by Joaquim Murtinho's strange economic interpretation of Darwin.

19 'The evolution of the banking system carried out gradually by the Ministry of Finance over an eleven-month period, culminated in the setting up of an apparatus that would lead to the unification of the issuing power' (Aguiar, p. 165).

20 Afonso Pena: 'The center of all financial fraud in the Banco da República, which wants to impose itself … as the incarnation of the new republic' (Topik, Steven. *The Political Economy of the Brazilian State, 1889–1930* (Austin, TX: University of Texas Press, 1987), p. 136.

21 Topik, p. 31.

22 Peixoto promptly dismissed Mayrink, associated with Barbosa and imperial elites.

23 The foreign trade shock led to a two-third collapse of coffee prices and devaluation of mil-réis from above 12 to 7.2 pence. Domestic and foreign debt soon thereafter summed to half of the government budget, while deficits tripled and inflation is estimated to have pushed domestic prices up 60 percent from 1985 to 1898.

24 Da propaganda a presidência, p. 186 in Topik.

25 Vilela, Nícia L. (ed.). *Idéias Econômicas de Joaquim Murtinho* (Brasília: Senado Federal/Fundação Rui Barbosa, 1980).

26 Paper money decreased from Rs785.941:758$000 in 1898 to Rs664.792:960$000 in 1906, suggesting the extent of monetary contraction. The consequences appeared to strongly support these policies of austerity, with the exchange rate increasing from 7.375 reis per pence in 1898 to 16.45 reis per pence in 1906.

27 Shareholders recovered losses when bank reopened at 30 percent of pre-crisis.

28 Topik, p. 40.

29 The Caixa de Conversão attempted to stabilize the foreign exchange rate at 15 pence per mil-réis by receiving gold coin and printing only currency convertible to gold.

30 Furtado describes coffee support programs in these terms of socialization of costs.

31 On the end of the rubber cycle, see: Weinstein, Barbara. *The Amazon Rubber Boom, 1850–1920* (Stanford, CA: Stanford University Press, 1983).

32 From 1902 to 1914, British investment in Brazil increased from 660 million to 1.1 billion USD, while French investment increased from 140 to 780 million USD.

33 Banks were required to maintain their portfolio below three times gold reserves in the currency board. Falcão argues: '*Caixa de Conversão* (currency board), the strange apparatus set up in 1906 to stabilize the exchange rate and due to its independent function, would have a spate of paper currency to meet the upswings in the exchange rate, that,

although convertible, would be poured into markets by the board' (Falcão, Waldemar. *O Empirismo Monetário no Brasil* [Rio de Janeiro: Companhia Editoria Nacional], p. 15).

34 At the start of 1913, the financial crisis which had alarmed the public entered its acute period.

35 Foreign policy conflicts included German refusal to remit payment for coffee stocks confiscated upon capture of Belgium and compensation sought from Brazil for 40 commercial ships detained in Brazilian ports. Both matters terminated once the Brazilian government declared support for the allied war effort in 1917, with ships commissioned to Lloyds Brazil.

36 On import substitution industrialization, see Fishlow, Albert. 'Origins and consequences of import substitution in Brazil,' in Di Marco, Luis E. (ed.). *International Economics and Development: Essays in Honor of Raúl Prebisch* (New York: Academic Press, 1972), pp. 311–365. Villela, Anibal V. and Suzigan, Wilson. *Política do Governo e Crescimento da Economia Basileira, 1889–1945* (Rio de Janeiro: IPEA/INPES, 1973).

37 By 1915, federal government debt totalled 105,570,380 pounds, state government debt summed to 49,453,940 pounds and municipal governments had contracted 12,783,650 pounds in foreign obligations. If one assumes obligations (temporarily suspended) of 1 percent principal and 5 percent interest on total government debt of 167,807,970 pounds, this sums to foreign debt obligations of 10 million per year. Foreign currency obligations on direct foreign investments were estimated at 12 million per year, totalling 22 million pounds per year. In terms of domestic government debt, the total liquid debt of the federal government in 1915 was estimated at 1,314 contos, state government debt at 378 contos and municipal government debt at 156 contos, summing to 1,800 contos, or 7.2 million pounds sterling at 16 pence exchange rate.

38 Saliba, Elias T. (ed). *Idéias Econômicas de Cincinato Braga* (Brasilia: Senado Federal, 1983), p. 136.

39 The abrupt decline of world coffee prices in 1920 led producers to appeal for both emergency credits and the creation of new mechanisms to stock coffee along the lines of the 1906 accord. After congress refused to purchase coffee stocks through emission of treasury bills, the creation of the Carteira de Emissão in October 1920 responded to these pressures for liquidity.

40 Topik argues that Issue bonds to 100,000 contos to rediscount notes from other banks. 'Permanent defense of national production' goal means transform Banco do Brasil into the central bank.

41 Domestic banks favoured by domestic capital requirements for rediscount operations increased market share of financial transactions from 50 percent to 70 percent.

42 The Treasury supplied the bank with notes, payed over 40 contos in interest rates on those notes and permitted trading all the while taking loans out from the bank. Receipts from these operations were distributed 30 percent to the bank, 20 percent to the Treasury, 30 percent to Carteira de Redescontos reserves and 20 percent to purchase gold reserves for paper money.

43 Abreu notes the early emergence of coffee futures markets because of the ability to accurately predict crop yields almost a year ahead of harvest on the basis of flowering, barring frost damage.

44 The institute shifted from previous stocks accumulated abroad to a new series of depots located along railways in Brazil. These warehouses could stockpile excess production to avert the dramatic declines in world prices that had wracked the Brazilian economy since the empire, but without the foreign exchange obligations incurred by maintaining stocks abroad. Deposit guarantees could be issued directly by the warehouses to coffee producers, who then deposited these credits with regional banks. These developments were driven by necessity, given the unwillingness of foreign banks to finance price-support schemes and the sustained opposition to coffee price support in Washington and New York (see Brandes, 1962, p. 130). Indeed, the 1922 loan included a clause that

prohibited the federal government from using funds to support the price of coffee in international markets. A record coffee crop in 1923 brought these matters to a head, with declining prices forcing the government to begin stocking coffee before formal founding of the Coffee Institute.

45 Cincinato Braga: 'Plan to Set Up the Issuing Bank, grounds: 1) the function of issuing money should not belong to the National Treasury, but rather to an issuing bank that would become the center of the country's banking system; 2) no bank note should be put into circulation, without its issue being made by the issuing bank with a signed underwriting guarantee, for its effective redemption' (p. 46).

46 See: Brandt, Mario. *As ilusões Financeiras.*

47 Bank policy: avert speculation, limit loans to 30-, 60- and 90-day loans at 9 percent, 10 percent and 11 percent interest.

48 Braga presents the following figures in the 1924 report: 389,000 contos (2nd semester 1923 emissions), 439,000 contos (January 1924 emissions), 62,794 to be recalled in 1924 equals 377,156 total monetary impact. Regarding discounting, Braga also warned congress: 'Banks understood they could permanently fall back on rediscounting as a means of carrying out their normal operations, making the BB almost like a silent partner of those institutions. However, that can not be the function of rediscounting, but rather that of a safety valve to be used as an exception in the event of accidental difficulties' (p. 345).

49 100,000 target to be met for 7/30/1924 by law 6635 1/8/1923 to recall 1,856,590.

50 Falcão, *O Problema Monetário*, p. 72.

51 Comparison with stabilization of Indian ruple in 1900 that served as referent for currency stabilization in Philippines, Greece, Checkoslovakia (1923), Austria (1924), Poland (1924), Belgium (1925) and Hungary (1927), the latter substituting paper currency for pengo at standard of 0.263157 grams of fine gold. Chile also implemented monetary reforms under consultancy of Kemmerer, author of *Modern Currency Reforms*, responsible for implementation of currency reforms in 10 countries.

52 Carneiro, J.A.B. *As recentes reformas monetárias na Europa central* (Rio de Janeiro, 1927).

53 Carvalho adds that attempts to implement monetary reforms without the necessary conditions 'will be nothing more than a sterile contrivance with harmful results, bringing no lasting benefit and will lead to a burden' (p. 14).

54 Carvalho notes: ' . . . since independence, all Brazilian statesmen have sought to provide us with a stable currency with an intrinsic, universal value, to replace the non-convertible paper currency' (p. 88).

55 Ministério da Fazenda, Relatório Anual (Rio de Janeiro: Imprensa Nacional, 1898), p. 1.

56 'Circulation on a gold standard cannot be decreed, but its advent can be prepared for' (Carvalho, p. 88).

57 Finally, a British financial mission to Brazil led by Lord D'Abernon, author of *German Currency: Its Collapse and Recovery, 1920–26*, visited Brazil precisely during the implementation of monetary reforms by the Washington Luis administration that attempted to combine the elements used in Eastern Europe to stabilize currencies during the 1920s.

58 Carvalho lists those opposed to stabilization policies as Leopoldo de Bulhões, Carlos de Figueiredo, Mario Brandt, Epitácio Pessoa, Luis Adolfo, Muniz Sodré and Barbosa Lima. Supporting the government in congress were Senators Sampaio Correia, Paulo Frontin and João Lira and Federal Deputies Lindolfo Color, Manuel Vilaboim and Julio Prestes. Those critical of excessive pace included José Carlos de Macedo Soares and representatives Paulo de Morais Barros, Mario de Andrade Ramos, Eugenio Gudin and Castro Maia.

59 Debates in congress also registered difficulties presented by existing levels of government debt, estimated by Braga to surpass 1 million contos. Trade surpluses averaged 15 million pounds, far from the 30 million pounds needed to service foreign debt.

60 Falcão, p. 86.
61 Carvalho: 'Washington Luis [was judged] naively for having taken a great step toward the obtaining of our metal currency backed by the gold locked in the vaults of the Stabilization Fund: that gold, as it arrived, was being placed in the Stabilization Fund, and then being exchanged for convertible bills, which were deposited in the current account and trading account at the Bank of Brazil for payment of the floating debt, has moved the market, in the rightful needs of trade, industry, farming and stock raising' (p. 97).
62 Thus a long cycle of recovery and growth proceeds a period of rupture due to world war in 1914, while another cycle of recovery and growth is followed by problems and collapse by 1929. Opposition to orthodoxy emerged during both times of boom and bust. Fritsch, Winston. 'Apogeu e Crise na Primeira República: 1906–30', in Marcelo de P. Abreu (ed.), *A Ordem do Progresso: Cem Anos de Política Econômica Republicana, 1889–89* (Rio de Janeiro: Campus, 1990), pp. 31–72.

4 From national populism to financial repression under military rule and delayed transition (1930–1993)

From 1930 to 1993, monetary statecraft shaped Brazilian development first by adjusting to global crisis through national populist strategies of import substitution industrialization (1930–1945), then as disputes between developmentalists and monetarists during postwar democracy that ended in military coup (1945–1964), then as orthodox adjustment and state-led finance under military rule (1964–1982) and, finally, by monetary chaos, inertial inflation and anti-inflation packages during the decade of transition from military rule (1983–1993). From 1930 to 1945, the Banco do Brasil remained the central agent for government policies of money, credit, finance, and foreign exchange designed to mobilize savings and channel resources toward industrialization and other development challenges. From 1945 to 1964, the politics of monetary policy embody the macroeconomics of populism controlled by a coalition centred in the Banco do Brasil that maintained prerogatives over money, credit and banking.[1] After the breakdown of democracy and military coup in 1964, orthodox reforms were first imposed (1964–1967), but soon ceded to state-led development financed by foreign capital inflows (1968–1982). From 1983 to 1993, foreign debt and fiscal crisis were exacerbated by a 'last dance syndrome' during the political void caused by protracted transition whereby regional elites mismanaged state government banks and accelerated inertial inflation. Six heterodox plans from 1986–1993 froze prices and wages but failed to control inflation.

1930–1945 politics and monetary policy under Vargas' Estado Novo

The 1930 revolution is a watershed in Brazilian history. In 1930, the core structures of the Old Republic (single-state parties, the hegemony of governors, regional oligarchs, and dependence on coffee exports) gave way to provisional revolutionary government, a variety of failed attempts to create new political institutions during the early 1930s and a drift toward authoritarianism ending in the corporatist - inspired Estado Novo under Getulio Vargas. The combination of domestic revolution and global crisis shifted policies toward import substitution industrialization, the devaluation of the mil-réis, controls over foreign exchange and imports and switching of credit toward domestic production and consumption.[2] This section explores the politics of these new policies from 1930 to 1945.

Since Fausto (1970), the collapse of the Old Republic is seen as caused more by the exclusive character of single-state parties and the emergence of political opposition within municipalities than the impact of the 1929 crash and depression abroad. Brazil instead, the economy pressured incoming revolutionaries for cyclical reasons of coffee production and a severe contraction of the money supply underway since late 1928. Abreu estimates that the monetary base fell 14 percent from late 1928 through 1930, while bumper coffee crops and collapse of foreign demand cut prices from 11 to 4 pence per sack in the period 1929–1931. Provisional government was thereby confronted with economic crisis and shortage of foreign currency reserves soon after taking power in November 1930.

The first Finance Minister of the provisional government, José Maria Whitaker, hoped to secure a funding loan from abroad to complete adjustment. Orthodox policy recommendations are exemplified by the British mission under Otto Niemeyer that called, in a July 1931 report, for the gradual elimination of coffee price support policies, greater fiscal discipline, reduced prerogatives for state and municipal governments to secure foreign finance and creation of an independent central bank to lead Brazil to a gold standard for currency. However, abandonment of the gold standard by the United Kingdom in September 1931 reinforced scepticism about orthodoxy and quickened the search for alternatives amidst depression abroad. After the São Paulo state government failed to secure foreign finance to continue stocking coffee supplies, and the federal government in Rio de Janeiro refused provide support, bankruptcies spread through the sector. Crisis deepened as the monetary base contracted, moratoria on foreign debts were declared by states and municipalities, the cruzeiro lost value abroad, foreign currency reserves fell and exporters were forced to barter. In September 1931, the government suspended payments on foreign debt and granted monopoly of foreign exchange transactions to the Banco do Brasil.

In November 1931, the resignation of Whitaker and nomination of Oswald Aranha led policies further away from orthodoxy. However, change was gradual and caused by reaction to circumstances and muddling through rather than ideological design. Aranha continued both negotiations with foreign creditors toward another funding loan, and Whitaker's policies limiting state and municipal debt. He also increased interest rates and reserve requirements of commercial banks held at the Banco do Brasil, burned 400 million cruzeiros acquired in sale of treasury notes, and created a Bank Mobilization Account at the Banco do Brasil to save private banks. By 1934, an agreement with foreign creditors reduced foreign debt payments by two-thirds.[3] Some of these policies are orthodox. Coffee policies were not. Abreu estimates that 70 million sacks of coffee were incinerated between 1933 and 1937 (equal to three years' world consumption). The Economic Readjustment package of 1933 forgave half of coffee debts and introduced new coffee subsidies under the National Department of Coffee.[4] Finance Minister Aranha also saved domestic banks, first through the Banco do Brasil Rediscount Facility (Carteira de Redescontos) then, after 1932, through a new Bank Mobilization Fund (Caixa de Mobilização Bancária).

Strong recovery of the economy during the mid-1930s legitimized these new monetary policies at the Banco do Brasil. Indeed, while depression continued abroad, positive circumstances in Brazil converged to produce strong and sustained growth that would last through the 1950s. Centralization of finance and monetary policy in the Banco do Brasil, price supports for coffee and the mobilization of domestic savings directed toward import substitution became pillars of policy making in Brazil until the early 1980s.[5]

The provisional government hoped that reserves in the Banco do Brasil and its Currency Board (Caixa de Estabilização) would be sufficient to cover foreign exchange requirements. Nonetheless, like previous experiments during the 19th century discussed in the previous chapter (and the Conversion Fund [Caixa de Conversão] in 1914), the Currency Board was also liquidated in 1929. These failures of currency boards led Brazilian policy makers to conclude that conversion of foreign capital into domestic currency during times of crisis was not viable. After liquidation in 1929, the functions of the currency board were transferred to the Banco do Brasil in November 1931.[6] The government thereafter sought to rebuild the credibility of the Banco do Brasil overseas as demands for payments increased from foreign investors. This placed the Banco do Brasil once again in the role of supervisor of the banking system. Before resigning, Finance Minister Whitaker also settled accounts between the Banco do Brasil and Treasury, leaving the bank with a large sum of foreign currencies to cover withdrawals abroad.

A centrepiece of monetary policy under Finance Minister Aranha was the creation of a Bank Mobilization Fund (Caixa de Mobilização Bancária) in 1932.[7] This fund set reserve requirements for commercial banks to be held at the Banco do Brasil and, in practice, helped reverse the domestic credit crunch by helping banks to meet obligations and increase loans.[8] This fund rebuilt the confidence of depositors in commercial banks and increased the capacity of the Banco do Brasil to serve as lender of last resort to private banks. The Fund also financed price support programs through Treasury and the National Department of Coffee (Departamento Nacional do Café). This combination of orthodox adjustment and proto-central bank policies at the national bank suggest that monetary policy making after 1930 was conducted as statecraft, that is to say; reacting to circumstances, building on existing institutions, and attempting to reconcile domestic political support while regaining confidence of international investors.

In 1833, the Banco do Brasil also funded the Departamento Nacional do Café (National Department of Coffee, NDC), to replace the Conselho Nacional do Café. Rotating credits (créditos rotativos) from the national bank were to be reimbursed through coffee export tax receipts. After 1937, policies attempted to reduce subsidies to coffee production, but when the Department could not meet payments to

Table 4.1 Commercial bank deposits at the Banco do Brasil (1932–1944, million cruzeiros and percent total bank deposits)

	Cz	*% Bank Deposits*
1932	858.0	20.1%
1933	644.0	15.4%
1934	310.0	6.4%
1935	592.0	12.4%
1936	601.0	11.6%
1937	798.0	13.5%
1938	902.0	11.5%
1939	1,094.0	15.4%
1940	1,291.0	18.3%
1941	1,118.0	12.6%
1942	2,272.0	20.0%
1943	2,497.0	13.6%
1944	3,421.0	15.6%

Source: Central Bank of Brazil, *Gerência de Operações Bancárias*. 'Relatório de 1965.' (Brasilia: Central Bank of Brazil, 1965) Available on https://www.bcb.gov.br/? DOCHIST1965 report, 1965, p. 11

the Banco do Brasil, the Treasury took out a loan from the Banco do Brasil Rediscount Facility and simply credited the balance to the Department.

The Banco do Brasil also financed government expenses incurred during defeat of the 1932 Constitutionalist revolt in São Paulo and drought in the northeast region. State and municipal governments unable to repay foreign investors also appealed to the Banco do Brasil to cover debts. The bank did so by direct financing with the National Treasury as guarantor. This placed monetary policy and the Banco do Brasil at the vortex of politics and economics. As Vieira notes:

> With the increasingly fragile state of the economy and of the monetary system, there was fertile ground for the loss of confidence in the public sector, this favoured changes and revolutions, which, as they were new expenses, made the situation even worse.
>
> (Vieira, 1981, p. 272)

The Foreign Exchange Facility of the Banco do Brasil excluded the private sector from foreign exchange operations.[9] The bank gained monopoly over import permits (letras) and used receipts to pay remittances and duties owed by federal, state and municipal government entities (and for payment of imports, also duly certified by staff at the Banco do Brasil). The Banco do Brasil thereby remained the operational arm of various types of foreign exchange rate policies adopted during the following 15 years. The extent to which bank deposits outpace paper money after the 1929 revolution suggest the importance of these bank-related monetary policies (see Figure 4.1).

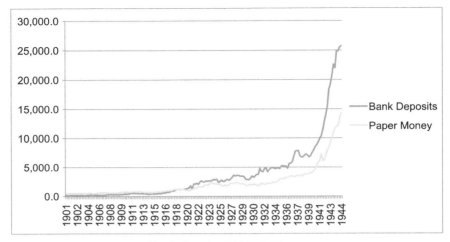

Figure 4.1 Paper money and bank deposits (1901–1941)
Source: Ipeadata

Global crisis, domestic recovery and sustained growth from 1930 to 1945 provided political support and legitimacy for the concentration of monetary policies in the Banco do Brasil. Credit expanded by an average of 20 percent per year, but the accumulation of gold and foreign currency reserves kept apace, reinforcing confidence and undercutting orthodox economists and critics that feared inflation.

During the 1940s, debate raged between Eugenio Gudin and Roberto Simonsen about economic planning that revealed fundamentally different views of government policies for money, credit and finance. However, monetarists such as Gudin remained on the defensive; unorthodox policies were perceived to have produced a period of strong and sustained growth. The events of national populism and import substitution industrialization are still debated. However, one conclusion seems warranted: rather than ideological design, evidence from policy tracing and historical accounts suggest that the unorthodox policies and institutions that emerged after the 1930 revolution confirm the importance of monetary statecraft and the particular configuration of domestic policies. Given the stark underdevelopment of Brazil before 1930, the turn inward during the 1930s amidst global depression and wartime differ from policies pursued in advanced economies at the centre of the world economy. This difference has long been recognized in standard conceptions of Brazilian development. What is less recognized is the importance of monetary and finance policy communities during the 1930s and 1940s. These conflicts between monetarist and developmentalist epistemic communities and policy coalitions became central to broader conflicts that led to crisis, confrontation and the breakdown of democracy by 1964.

The politics of monetary policy (1945–1964)

The unorthodox monetary policies introduced from 1930 to 1945 were sustained after transition to democracy in 1945 until military coup ended national populism and developmentalism in 1964. An epistemic community of economists and policy advisors linked to domestic industrial and agricultural groups and politicians repeatedly vetoed legislation designed to reform the Brazilian monetary system. Most Latin American countries created central banks early in the 20th century. An advisory entity, the Superintendancy of Money and Credit (SUMOC), was created in 1946 The Central Bank of Brazil was created in *1965* after the breakdown of democracy under military rule. The political theory of veto coalitions explains the delay of central banking in Brazil. The national-developmentalist coalition at the Banco do Brasil vetoed independent central banking and monetary policy until after the breakdown of democracy in 1964.

Monetary statecraft from 1945 to 1964 in Brazil turns on an increasing split between groups advocating reform toward more orthodox liberal and monetarist economic policy and, in opposition, the national-developmentalist tradition. Developmentalists found support from the United Nations Economic Commission on Latin America, the National Development Bank (Banco Nacional de Desenvolvimento Econômico, BNDE) founded in 1952, and the Banco do Brasil.[10] Foreign monetary policy sought to deepen collaboration with the United States, but failed, because of geopolitics, to secure a southern hemisphere Marshall Plan. In general, US policy sought to free market forces and encourage the Brazilian government to adopt orthodox policies to increase confidence among foreign investors. However, US–Brazilian working committees on money and finance during the 1940s also proposed, and indeed led to creation of the National Bank for Economic Development. Moreover, policies in the 1950s shifted away from orthodoxy in favour of recommendations from the UN Economic Commission on Latin America (ECLA).

The national-developmentalist coalition centred in the Banco do Brasil included broad sectors in industry, labour, commerce, and agriculture. This coalition systematically defeated attempts to slow growth, reduce credit, control monetary expansion, and liberalize domestic banking and finance. The period of sustained post-war economic growth further legitimacy of this national-developmental coalition. How these unorthodox policies worked for over two decades requires a closer look, given the contested interpretations of this period. For orthodox theories of money and finance, the Brazilian experience from 1945 to 1964 is a classic case of the macroeconomics of populism. For Dornbusch, Cardoso, Gudin, and Nóbrega and Loyola, state-led policies of directed credit exacerbated income inequality and caused fiscal imbalances and economic disequilibria. However, for developmentalists, the policies of the post-war period provide a positive legacy and domestic policy tradition that increased economic growth amidst underdevelopment.

Unlike the uncontrolled lending and finance through state government banks during the transition from military rule in the 1980s discussed below, the transition from Vargas' Estado Novo in 1945 to competitive electoral politics did not produce a wave of easy money. Bulhões argues that neither credit policies at the Banco do Brasil nor overall credit supply were excessive.[11] Abreu suggests that credit shrank in the period 1945–1950 by 25 percent. In sum, monetary policies after transition from the authoritarian Estado Novo under Getulio Vargas to competitive elections and democracy did not produce a credit bubble or increased financial transactions on the part of monetary authorities (Banco do Brasil, Rediscount Facility, Bank Mobilization Facility). This counters economic theories that see democratization as endangering monetary policy.

Moreover, after the 1950 election returned Getulio Vargas to the presidency, conservative policies were imposed by Finance Minister Horácio Lafer.[12] The approach of the 1950 elections appears to have weakened Finance Minister Correia e Castro, leading to his replacement by Guilherme de Silveira in 1949 in order to shift policies toward more generous credit policies. Lobbies of industrial, agricultural and populist electoral machines appealed for increased lending during the election year. However, Finance Minister Lafer imposed spending reductions during 1951–1952 to generate federal government surpluses of 0.9 and 0.6 percent of gross domestic product (GDP). Meanwhile, Banco do Brasil president Ricardo Jafet pursued expansionary policies, increasing the value of credit from the national bank in real terms by 66 percent in 1951 and another 40 percent in 1952. This tension between adjustment policies pursued by the Finance Minister and expansionary monetary policies pursued by the Banco do Brasil would continue during the period of post-war democracy. Tensions between the Finance Ministry and Banco do Brasil overshadowed other designs and reforms of monetary policy.

In 1946, a new Superintendancy for Money and Credit (Superintendência de Moeda e Crédito, SUMOC) gained prerogative to set interest rates for rediscount operations and compulsory deposits of commercial bank reserves, foreign exchange policies, registry of foreign investment and domestic bank supervision. However, the Banco do Brasil retained its Rediscount Facility and Bank Mobilization Facility that let the bank provide lending of last resort and exercise de facto control of the supply of credit. The National Treasury (at the Finance Ministry) also retained an Amortization Facility (Caixa de Amortização) with prerogative to print or amortize money, but Treasury could not directly place or remove money from circulation without operating through the Banco do Brasil Rediscount Facility. This meant that the Banco do Brasil could generate cash by rediscounting commercial paper at its Rediscount Facility covered by a loan for the value discounted from Treasury to the Banco do Brasil. Upon maturing, the Banco do Brasil would return commercial paper to Treasury for incineration at the Amortization Facility. In 1942, regulations capped Treasury rediscounting to 25 percent of foreign reserves. However, Congress averted this limit by simply canceling debts across the Rediscount

Facility, Treasury and the Banco do Brasil. Foreign currency trading also remained under control of the Banco do Brasil. Indeed, the Banco do Brasil also managed foreign trade policy through a Foreign Trade Portfolio – Carteira de Comércio Exterior, CACEX, created in 1953 to authorize exports and imports.[13]

The primary monetary authority from 1930 to 1964 thereby remained the national bank. From 1945 to 1961, the Bank Operations Division (Gerência de Operações Bancárias, DEBAN) of the Banco do Brasil reports an increase of compulsory deposits for banks at the national bank from 1.8 to 54.0 billion cruzeiros in cash and from 0.4 to 22.8 billion cruzeiros in government bonds for total of 1.8 to 76.8 billion cruzeiros (5.9–11.5 percent of bank deposits in the country).

Instead of creating a central bank in the 1940s, a gradual, minimalist strategy for monetary reforms was pursued. Given the veto coalition of developmentalists centred at the Banco do Brasil, a new generation of monetarist economists such as Gudin and Bulhões focused on the training of personnel and the development of independent monetary data that could support subsequent policy initiatives. Despite the creation of SUMOC, the Banco do Brasil retained core functions of central banking and finance ministries such as supervision of banks, monopoly on foreign exchange operations, regulation of bank reserves, discretion to rediscount to banks, and management of the money supply. SUMOC became an agency responsible for the creation of economic data and research in monetary economics.

Table 4.2 Compulsory deposits at Banco do Brasil (1945–1961, Cr$billion)

	Cash	*Govt*		*Percent*
		Bonds	*Total*	*Total Bank Deposits*
1945	1.8			5.9
1946	1.6	0.4	1.8	6.0
1947	1.4	0.6	2.0	5.8
1948	1.6	0.6	2.0	5.8
1949	1.6	0.6	2.2	4.9
1950	1.7	0.6	2.3	3.8
1951	1.7	0.9	2.6	3.8
1952	1.7	0.9	2.6	3.4
1953	2.1	1.2	3.3	3.7
1954	2.7	1.4	4.1	3.9
1955	2.9	1.6	4.5	3.7
1956	4.1	2.2	6.3	4.3
1957	12.6	1.9	14.5	7.2
1958	14.3	9.9	24.2	10.0
1959	21.7	15.7	37.8	10.7
1960	35.3	21.2	56.5	11.6
1961	54.0	22.8	76.8	13.5

Source: Central Bank of Brazil, *Gerência de Operações Bancárias, Relatório de Atividades,* 1965, pp. 11, 13.

From 1950 to 1954, broader conflicts between the Vargas administration and the US government (and foreign investors) overshadowed monetary policy. Political and economic impasse led to power vacuum and policy paralysis. Announcement of a 100 percent increase in the minimum wage served to escalate confrontation, culminating in the suicide of Vargas and swearing in of his Vice-President, Café Filho. Ricardo Jafet was dismissed from the presidency of the Banco do Brasil in 1953 under charges of abusing linked operations at the bank. However, the Banco do Brasil continued to increase lending contrary to Ministry of Finance policies of adjustment. Café Filho brought a more orthodox financial and economic policy team led by Eugenio Gudin to government. However, unable to implement broad measures of monetary reform (because prerogatives remained at the national bank), Gudin issued a series of SUMOC instructions designed to increase discipline over currency. Caps were set for interest rate payments on deposits, while both discounting rates and commercial bank reserve requirements were increased. Although these reforms sought to reduce the role of the Banco do Brasil in money management, they were soon were abandoned under political pressure, and Gudin resigned after seven months at the Finance Ministry.

In 1955, Whitaker returned as Finance Minister, arguing that three adverse developments required adjustment policies.[14] The first was a trade conflict with the United States over Brazilian coffee exports that had, for Brazil, cut export prices and volumes. The second problem arose from the May 1954 increase of the minimum wage by 100 percent, roughly 60 percent over retail price increases for the same period. According to Whitaker, the third problem arose from excess credit from the Banco do Brasil and financial assistance to commercial banks (via the Banco do Brasil, rediscount operations and the Bank Mobilization Account). Banco do Brasil lending increased from Cz14.9–55.5 billion 1950–1954, while financial assistance increased Cz5.0–13.66 billion.[15]

The resignation of Gudin and the return of Whitaker occurred amidst the escalation of opposition to President Vargas from groups allied to US foreign policies, new foreign investments and the liberal União Democrática Nacional (National Democratic Union, (UDN)). The suicide of Vargas in August 1954 averted military intervention and secured conditions for election of Juscelino Kubitschek and a PSD-PTB alliance in the 1956 elections. President Kubitschek then produced another period of strong economic growth driven by expansionary money, credit, and banking policies. His audacious Target Plan (Plano de Metas) was designed to achieve 50 years of development in five. Remarkably, plans lacked consideration of the financial sources able to underwrite the targets for infrastructure and import substitution. For Abreu, President Kubitschek retained an 'utter disregard for macroeconomic constraints,' such that severe disequilibria were left by the development programs pursued during his administration.[16] Once again, monetary reforms paled against the veto coalition in the Banco do Brasil.

Lucas Lopes and Roberto Campos proposed a program of monetary stabilization in 1957. However, Kubitschek refused to slow investments and programs underway that were seen as necessary to reach development targets. Substitution of Finance Minister Lucas Lopes in July 1958 for Paes de Almeida (former president of the Banco do

Brasil) signaled a further return to developmentalist policies that sought to guarantee generous money through credit from banks.

Monetarists also lost to developmentalists when President Kubitschek refused to adopt adjustment policies proposed by the International Monetary Fund (IMF). Epistemic communities differed about the causes of inflation. Monetarist economists such as Roberto Campos and Lucas Lopes argued that the overheating of the economy and excessive money and credit had driven inflation to record levels (40 percent) by 1959. In opposition, structural economists trained at the United Nations Economic Commission on Latin America (ECLA) argued that inflation was not due to excess money and credit but, instead, because of the inability of the Brazilian economy to keep pace with demand inflation. It followed that more, rather than less, credit and money were required. Confrontation with the IMF also increased President Kubitschek's popularity, which was already considerable given the average GDP growth of 8.1 percent from 1955 to 1960 and the clear signs of success (despite shortfalls) in achieving the audacious development goals during his administration.

In sum, monopoly over monetary policy at the national bank generated opposition from orthodox economists and policy circles, an opposition that would soon come to advance reforms under military rule in the 1960s. Conflicts between developmentalists and liberals deteriorated in the early 1960s and contributed to the breakdown of democracy and military intervention on 31 March 1964. Policies at the beginning of the Quadros administration (1960–1961) briefly pursued austerity in response to increasing inflation, foreign debt, and imbalances inherited from the 1950s. However, policies of adjustment betrayed populist promises of his campaign.[17] After the resignation of Quadros (seven months after taking office) in August 1961, political instability intensified and further exacerbated macroeconomic problems, especially inflation and balance of payments shortfalls. A Three-Year Plan (Plano Trienal) was launched in December 1962 by Celso Furtado, Minister of Planning (Ministro do Planejamento) of President João Goulart, with the aim of combining stabilization with a return of industrial growth.[18] Once imbalances were resolved, public planning was expected by Furtado to accelerate growth. However, the plan faced obstacles in the renegotiation of the foreign debt and was criticized by national-developmental and political leaders of the left close to the president. Inflation persisted and a recession marked the end of the expansionary cycle of the Plano de Metas under the Plano Trienal; restrictive monetary policy would further brake the economy.

Evidence from 1945 to 1964 suggests both unusual arrangements of Brazilian monetary policy institutions and the late development of specialized agencies for government money, credit and bank supervision policies. The escalation of conflict between national populist groups associated with the Goulart presidency from 1962 to 1964 and internationalist groups associated with military and US alliances led to the breakdown of democracy and military intervention on 31 March 1964. The breakdown of democracy has been widely debated. Economic mismanagement and lax monetary policy can be cited as part of problems leading to the escalation of conflicts. However, viable monetary policy reforms appear very late in the process of polarization, such that policies proposed by Furtado and Dantas under the Goulart presidency were endorsed by the IMF and US government under President Kennedy. However, monetary policy fades into the background as political confrontation escalated in late 1963 and early 1964. Monetary reforms would be implemented only after military coup on 31 March 1964.

The politics of monetary policy under military rule (1964–1982)

Economists under the new military government believed that inflation was responsible for financial disintermediation, reduced savings and the disorganization of values and prices. Their views were diametrically opposed to structuralist theories and developmentalist policies that had predominated for much of the 20th century. Instead, adjustment was required before pursuing development. Consensus emerged in favour of gradual stabilization strategies to avert further shocks or distortions in income distribution.[19] New policies embodied by the 1965 PAEG increased greater control over currency issues and reduced inflation through 1967. Further institutional reforms were characterized by the centralization of policy, fiscal reform, financial reforms, the creation of the Central Bank of Brazil, new exchange rate and industrial development policies and the implementation of adjustment under agreement with the IMF.[20] Perhaps the most important reform was the establishment of monetary correction over fiscal deficits with the intent of eliminating the common practice of delaying government payments under accelerating inflation.[21] Reforms were designed to create financial institutions with clearly defined roles able to tap new savings channels and operate under rules for monetary correction, a practice that spread rapidly through the financial sector.

At year-end 1965, SUMOC was replaced with a National Monetary Council (Conselho Monetário Nacional, CMN) charged with elaborating monetary, financial, budget and government debt management policies. These reforms marked the beginning of a profound change for the Banco do Brasil and the politics of monetary policy. The Banco do Brasil retained its hybrid character as executor of government policy and largest commercial bank in the country. However, it increasingly ceded prerogatives of credit, banking and monetary policy to specialized agencies and the Central Bank of Brazil. The functions of SUMOC were redistributed in ways that indicate this separation of monetary policy from Banco do Brasil. The Central Bank of Brazil was designed to assume functions associated with monetary authority such as the regulation and supervision of credit and financial institutions; monitor and control of foreign capital and foreign currency reserves; and the control of money supply and currency issues according to recommendations set by the National Monetary Council.

Hermann argues that the PAEG reforms led to an increase in the number of domestic banks, deepening of financial intermediation and increased growth under military rule.[22] However, reforms during the 1960s also led to the concentration of the Brazilian domestic financial system in a select number of banks, while government paper indexed against inflation became the focal point of domestic finance instead of long-term investments. Welch and Studart also emphasize that the trend away from long-term liabilities and widespread use of indexed financial instruments produced unexpected consequences.[23] Contrary to reforms designed to encourage stock market capitalization, the crash of equity prices in 1971 delegitimized stock market finance and reinforced bank-centred operations in Brazil. Monetary reforms under military government led to the consolidation of a select number of private and public financial institutions.[24]

1965: Central Bank of Brazil

Under military rule, congress approved legislation in September 1964 submitted by representative Ulysses Guimarães to create a National Monetary Council and retain SUMOC. However, the Senate amended the bill to replace SUMOC with a central bank; and the Chamber approved the Senate version; over opposition from the Banco do Brasil and rural caucuses such that presidential sanction by General Castelo Branco was granted by year-end 1964. The Banco do Brasil caucus nonetheless inserted provisions that assured continued autonomy within the national bank while core functions of rediscounting, foreign exchange operations, bank supervision and money supply management were officially ceded to the Central Bank.

The Central Bank of Brazil was also granted control over agricultural development funds and directed credit. Moreover, 'The Central Bank, created independently, later became a subservient organization. From a severe sheriff became a depraved money printer'.[25] Two developments stand out: Creation of a separate 'monetary budget' in government accounts; and a 'movement account' between the national bank and Treasury. Regarding the monetary budget, Sola and Marques note that funds in this separate budget soon outpaced the 'fiscal budget' approved by congress and would only be controlled after the 1988 Constitution ended this dual-budget system that left monetary authorities with substantial prerogatives and policy discretion under military rule. Regarding the creation of the 'movement account' that would impede central bank control over the money supply for two decades, Nóbrega and Loyola note:

> The preservation of Banco do Brasil as the depositary of the voluntary commercial bank reserves and the executor of decisions of the Central Bank generated the necessity for the creation of a special account to register the transactions between the two institutions. This account, which also became known as 'movement account' supposedly would be in balance every week, but this rarely happened, with Banco do Brasil becoming systematically in debt, with rising negative balances. The vices of the old system – monetary budget and the open 'movement account' – had survived'.
>
> (Nóbrega and Loyola, 2006, p. 64)

Nóbrega and Loyola note two further unorthodox sources for revenue and monetary policy in the central bank. First, the Central Bank of Brazil received tax revenues directly from taxes on financial operations and exports introduced in 1965, revenue that became part of the monetary budget independent of legislative or executive policy making. Second, involvement of the Central Bank of Brazil in agricultural finance and development banking placed the central bank very far from traditional monetary policies. After 1965, central bank officials became responsible for negotiating program finance with the Inter-American Development Bank and World Bank as well as the creation of internal department for analysis and approval of agricultural and agro-industry credits and development finance. Nóbrega and Loyola also note that over 90 percent of staff hired at the Central Bank of Brazil during the 1960s were, or remained, employees of the Banco do Brasil on leave.

Creation of the Central Bank of Brazil was nonetheless central to reforms under Planning Minister Roberto Campos and Finance Minister Bulhões during the Castelo Branco presidency and did indeed embody orthodox monetarist conceptions. For example, from 1964 to 1967, the Brazilian Central Bank refused financial assistance to banks and liquidated private banks.[26] However, a clear shift away from orthodoxy after 1967 under military president Costa e Silva and Planning Minister Delfim Netto reversed the intentions of reformers. Adjustment ceded to period of rapid economic growth spurred by foreign financial investment, a stock market rally (that collapsed in 1971) and state-led finance and investment policies driven by substantial foreign capital inflows. These state-led policies would continue under military presidents Medici (1969–1973) and Geisel (1974–1979), despite two oil price shocks, rising international interest rates and increasing foreign debt levels.

The influence of private banks and firms on monetary policy in Brazil also increased under military rule. Finance Minister Delfim Netto increased membership on the National Monetary Council to include members from the private industry and finance.[27] However, instead of imposition of orthodoxy, a shift toward state-led development occurs as embodied in the 1967 Program of Strategy and Development (Programa de Estratégia e Desenvolvimento, PED) that sought to both spur development and control inflation. Credit policy targeted consumer durables and real estate. To stimulate internal demand and recovery, the government channeled foreign capital flows by investing heavily in infrastructure through state-owned enterprises, while industrial policy subsidized private sector investments and projects. Direct foreign investment also accelerated economic growth. Moreover, instead of adjusting the global oil shock, military president Geisel launched the Programa Nacional de Desenvolvimento (National Development Program, PND II) in 1974. This plan contained ambitious goals for 10 percent GDP growth with priority toward heavy industry and capital goods in an attempt to complete import substitution industrialization. As a complementary measure, imports were made more expensive by tariffs and financial policies. The public sector focused on long-term investments such as infrastructure, oil exploration and hydroelectric dams. The PND II was based on the assumption that foreign finance inflows made targets feasible. Foreign finance seemed attractive, given the shallow domestic credit market, and the collapse of the stock market, and the existence of global liquidity that promised cheap money.

Other reforms that sought to deepen private credit markets during the 1960s also produced unexpected consequences. In 1965–1966,[28] private investment banks were created with the aim of providing long-term finance. State government development banks also received new regulations by the end of the 1960s.[29] The BNDE consolidated its activity as the main agent for government investments and source of special lines of credit to the private sector via intermediary banks and BNDE subsidiaries. The bulk of long-term credit came from the BNDE. In 1965, the Law of Capital Markets (Lei de Mercado de Capitais, Law nº. 4.728, 14 July 1965) also attempted to deepen capital markets and provide longer-term financing. Bond issues did indeed become important during the 1970s, but neither bonds nor equity markets became central for public or private finance. Instead, the collapse of the stock market in 1971 and the emergence of secondary markets for short-term government paper indexed against inflation reinforced both the bank-centred character of the Brazilian financial system and the Banco do Brasil as largest domestic financial institution.

The reforms of the mid-1960s did increase the financial sector in Brazil. However, instead of indicating financial development, the indexation of assets against inflation and the increasing importance of short-term government paper ensued. According to Zini, the percentage of financial investment/GDP increases from approximately 25 percent in 1955 to 44 percent in 1975. However, the market share of government banks increases during this period, suggesting a greater role of the state in the allocation of resources under military rule. State involvement was particularly marked in terms of directed credits, lending for long-term investments, and use of government bonds to manage money in a widely traded new open market. The open market for government paper indexed against inflation involved a variety of transactions across financial institutions, companies, and individuals that transformed these bonds into de facto currency.

The Central Bank increasingly used this open market for government bonds to implement monetary policy. By selling bonds, it would withdraw means of payment from circulation, reduce liquidity and increase interest rates. The Central Bank, Treasury and federal government banks remained the largest participants in the market for short-term government bonds. During the 1970s, this open market for indexed government bonds became a focal point for Brazilian political economy.

These financial developments were also critical because tax receipts declined and expenditures on subsidies and transfers increased during this period. Loans thereby became the main source of revenue for the public sector. Under military rule, both foreign capital inflows and the domestic market for government paper increased substantially. Conceição Tavares argues that this implied a shift away from government bank lending, at least while capital flowed from abroad:

In the boom, of 1970 to 1973, the Banco do Brasil and BNDE markedly decreased the rhythm of their loans, since the relative demand by public funds for investment dropped considerably. The private sector, in the full euphoria of the boom, received considerable profits; the rates of self-financing of large companies grew and even small and medium firms found themselves in enviably lucrative positions with easy credit from the private banking sector. . . . The period 1970–73 was the only one, in the post-war period, in which there was a joint sense of euphoria across all segments of private capital: national and international, large and small, agricultural, industrial and mercantile.[30]

However, once rates of growth began to fall, the tendency inverted. The government intervened to stop a cyclical downturn in the economy, especially using the BNDE to maintain the level of investments in heavy industry. The scarcity of credit became increased after 1975, as a consequence of the contractionary monetary policy to combat inflation, as well due to speculation in government bond markets.

As indexed government bonds became used as money in public and private transactions, the government was forced to print official paper money for their liquidation. This became the core problem for monetary policy that drove inertial inflation. While prices and volumes in secondary markets for government paper increased, the *de jure* currency continued to lose value.

The Government Economic Action Plan (PAEG) and agreement between the military government and International Monetary Fund exemplify the ascendance of orthodoxy. However, the details of institutional design and state-centred trends after 1967 suggest substantial divergence from traditional institutions of central banking and monetary policy. Instead of stock market-centred financial system and economy driven by private investments, loopholes of reforms and foreign capital inflows produced a period of state-led development under increasingly hardline military rule. The declaration of a moratorium on foreign debt payments by Mexico in August 1982 marked the beginning of the end of this cycle of strong economic growth underwritten by the government and foreign investment. Indeed, dual foreign debt and fiscal crises persisted throughout the 1980s in Brazil, while a series of heterodox anti-inflation policy experiments after 1985 marked the transition from military rule to democracy.

The politics of monetary policy during fiscal and foreign debt crises in the 1980s also involved delayed transition and capture by oligarchs. Given the political stalemate between federal military government and newly elected governors, the political economy of transition focused on state government autonomy over fiscal, monetary and credit policies. State governments became central motors of debt, moral hazard, and lack of control over money management.[31] Brazil descended once again into monetary chaos.

Recognition of institutional dysfunctions and the writing of new policy proposals emerged gradually within the specialized agencies of the federal government. The National Monetary Council commissioned studies and the preparation of reforms, encouraged by international financial institutions aghast at government accounts and accounting procedures, and deeply concerned about the cost of foreign debt and fiscal deficits under inflation that breached 100 percent per year in 1982. Nóbrega and Loyola report that National Monetary Council reforms toward rationalizing government accounts, closing the movement account, eliminating rural lending by the Central Bank, and reinforcing the independence of the central bank were overturned by the courts in 1984. Once again, a veto coalition centred in the Banco do Brasil was able to delay monetary and fiscal reforms. The politics of monetary policy in Brazil came to be determined by the sequence of heterodox anti-inflation packages from 1986 to 1993 that sought to unify markets for government paper and *de jure* currencies.

The last dance syndrome (1985–1993): capture during transition to democracy

The politics of monetary policy after transition from military rule was shaped by the disruptions of heterodox anti-inflation packages (in 1986, 1987, 1989, 1990 and 1992) and the centripetal pull of federal government monetary authorities over state and municipal government policies that ballooned public debt. This dual track of anti-inflation packages and gradual institutional reforms defines the politics and monetary policy until the Real Plan stabilized prices in 1993. From 1985 to 1993, central banking and the politics of money, credit and banking have to do with repeated attempts by teams of economic policy makers to coordinate price and wage freezes designed to shock inflationary expectations. Officials at the Central Bank of Brazil, Ministry of Finance and other economic policy making ministries attempted to coordinate policies amidst rapidly changing circumstances. The politics of monetary policy became that of coordinating policy-among small teams of economists reporting directly to presidents that staked their prestige on bringing and keeping inflation down.

The Cruzado Plan (1986) under President José Sarney replaced the cruzeiro, froze prices and wages, ended monetary correction of government paper, introduced unemployment insurance and a wage trigger to protect salaries and, finally, declared a moratorium on payment of foreign debt.[32] The plan inaugurated a period of experimentation with heterodox policies that, temporarily, reduced inflation while accelerating growth and real income gains among salary and wage earners. The strong growth experience in the months following the Cruzado Plan transformed the 1986 national elections into a strong plebiscitary vote in favour of President Sarney and the PMDB that won 22 of 23 governorships and increased its share of state and federal assemblies.

The unraveling of the Cruzado Plan led to adoption of the Bresser Plan in 1987.[33] The Bresser Plan attempted to maintain the price and wage freeze and moratorium while eliminating the trigger that automatically adjusted salaries. Finance Minister Bresser argues that the technical faults of the plan paled in comparison to the lack of political support for further fiscal policies and renegotiation of foreign debt: 'The lack of political support for my economic program was clearly the central problem'.[34] Given the predominance of national developmentalism in the PMDB, opposition of organized labour to the elimination of the wage trigger clause and opposition in the coalition government of President Sarney to fiscal and foreign debt policies led to the resignation of Bresser Pereira on 20 December 1987.

In 1989, months before the end of the Sarney administration, the Summer Plan (Plano Verão) declared another price and wage freeze, while attempting to impose fiscal discipline and set an agenda for the privatization of state-owned enterprises and the elimination of indexation clauses in government paper and private contracts. Once again, politics undercut the implementation of policies. Elections in October 1989 reduced the ability of President Sarney to sustain public opinion in favour of anti-inflation policies. Upon inauguration on 15 March 1990, President Collor reasserted executive authority and shocked investors with another package of policies designed to reduce inflation, lower the government deficit, liberalize trade and modernize the economy. Despite his party's controlling only 5 percent of the Federal Chamber, President Collor confiscated an estimated 80 percent of Brazil's liquid financial assets. Moreover, the Collor administration soon achieved many of its short-term economic policy goals, producing government surpluses, reducing interest rates, extending the terms for government paper and stabilizing the exchange rate. Meanwhile, markets and the political opposition remained dazed as the new administration received support from the media and public (confiscated savings were returned) and faced surprisingly little opposition from congress and governors, many of whom appeared more concerned with organizing for the 1990 elections than national policies at the end of their terms in office. The Collor Plan thereby deepened monetary disorder, produced a recession and damaged confidence in the banking system.

From 1986 to 1993, a series of more gradual institutional (and constitutional) developments occurred alongside the more dramatic efforts of monetary authorities to accompany the volatile impacts of anti-inflation policy packages and their consequences on prices, wages, government accounts, the money supply, credit and banks. This dual trajectory of monetary and financial policies can be reconstructed, in retrospect, by comparing the gradual institutional changes and legal framework for central banking and financial policies, alongside the sequence of seven anti-inflation packages and several intermediate measures designed to reinforce these plans. This final section of the report provides a brief overview of this dual trajectory of dramatic economic packages and gradual institutional reforms.

Gradual initiatives sought to end the monetary loopholes inherited from the period of military rule. In 1986, the Banco do Brasil lost prerogative to balance accounts through the movement account. Development and agricultural lending was also transferred from the Central Bank of Brazil to Treasury, while the 1988 Constitution prohibited further lending directly from Treasury. These reforms reflect a broader process of the separation of powers since transition from military government. Instead of the centralization of policies and politics in select economic superministries, policy making increasingly became delegated to specialized agencies responsible for management of the money supply and bank supervision, while subsidized and directed credit, fiscal policy and development programs were delegated to other federal government ministries and agencies.

Moreover, Nóbrega and Loyola argue that measures designed to create institutional advances were inserted into policy packages:

> During the Cruzado and Bresser plans, there was a list of legal changes prepared by the staff of the Central Bank to improve the performance of the institution and financial markets. The majority of the changes were introduced in legislation associated with the plans, although they were not directly related to the stabilization process. This technique became known within the Central Bank as 'smuggling'.
>
> Nobrega and Loyola, 2006, p. 83, n12

Reforms also eliminated the separate monetary budget, while management of public debt was transferred from the Central Bank to the Ministry of Finance. Thereafter, the Finance Ministry was required to seek congressional approval for issue of government debt.

In 1988, a Single Account (Conta Única) of the Treasury at the Central Bank also attempted to control the movement of resources between federal banks and the National Treasury. This was carried out by the substitution of the movement account of the government at the Banco do Brasil. The Single Account eliminated more than 5,000 government bank accounts, permitting a more efficient control of the flow of deposits of the government. The National Treasury also assumed administration of activities related to the Programs of Support for Agriculture and Exports, transferred from the Central Bank, as well as the management of the portfolio of problematic housing loans from the period of military rule.

However important these gradual improvements of monetary policy and central banking were, they also coincided with the escalation of inertial inflation and the emergence of a peculiar type of politics described by Sola and Kugelmas as *brinksmanship*.[35] The foreign debt and fiscal crises during the 1980s have been treated from a variety of perspectives. For most observers, the persistence of high inflation during the late 1980s and early 1990s brought the country repeatedly to the brink of hyperinflation.[36] However, once again, the relation between economic crisis and politics is not linear. The concept of enabling constraints, as well as brinkmanship, describe how the escalation of crisis may increase the autonomy of politics in the sense of opening windows of opportunity for reforms.

Anti-inflation plans during the 1980s were often accompanied by liberalization policies. In 1987, the National Securities Commission began to open Brazilian financial markets to foreign investors.[37] In 1991, tax exemption was granted to foreign investment in domestic capital markets and privatization funds were opened to foreign investors. In 1992 Brazilian firms were authorized to float shares on the New York Stock Exchange as American depositary receipts.

Sola and Marques also argue that the Central Bank of Brazil exerted control over state banks in an incremental process that tightened with each state banking crisis. Crises were caused both by mismanagement of state banks (often towards to winning elections) and by adjustment to stabilization programs which tended to briefly control inflation and produce boom and bust consumer driven cycles. State government banking crises therefore coincided with the electoral calendar (1982, 1986 and 1990) and stabilization plans (1986, 1989–1990).[38] Sola and Marques emphasize four further political uses of state government banks: (1) direct loans to state governments, (2) finance of state-owned enterprises, (3) holding of state government bonds not absorbed by financial markets and (4) extending Revenue Anticipation Grants (Antecipação de Receita Orçamentária). For Sola and Marques, the rounds of state and municipal government debt rescheduling during the 1980s and early 1990s reflect a gradual assertion of monetary authority on the part of the federal government over state governments. For example, following the state bank crisis of 1987, the Central Bank gained the ability to assume temporary control over insolvent state banks and introduced legal accountability of state administrators for banking abuses. While state banks placed under federal intervention in 1987 were eventually returned to their respective state governments with no significant judicial action taken against their managers, the Central Bank gained a new tool to discipline state banks. In 1990, the National Monetary Council imposed new limits on state bank loans to the public sector. In 1992, legislation to hold administrators in state enterprises were also increased and the Senate further limited the ability of subnational governments to contract new debt.[39]

In sum, from 1985 to 1993, heterodox anti-inflation packages temporarily froze prices and wages, briefly increased real wages, and reduced the losses of non-indexed asset holders and wage earners (i.e. the poor). This produced a political-electoral cycle involving attempts to end inflation and sustain political coalitions. The politics of monetary policy from 1985 to 1993 also a last dance syndrome whereby local political machines built under military rule in states and municipalities abused state government banks and enterprises in the expectation that central government would assume their debts. This increased domestic government debt dramatically and led to the privatization of over 23 state government banks during the 1990s. Gradual institutional reforms were also pursued during this period, often accompanying anti-inflation packages. Thus, the politics of monetary policy from 1985 to 1993 involves complex interactions between a sequence of heterodox shocks designed to reduce inertial inflation, a centrifugal pull against central bank and federal government monetary authority and, nonetheless, gradual reforms of financial and monetary policy in terms of the specialization and separation of powers and policies.

Conclusion

This chapter has examined the politics of monetary policy in Brazil from 1930 to 1993. First, inward-oriented policies after the 1930 revolution generated a period of domestic mobilization of savings, capital, and investment. Second, the period of competitive electoral politics from 1945 to 1964 produced a series of increasingly unsustainable macroeconomic policies described by Dornbusch as the macroeconomics of populism. Third, monetary, financial, and banking reforms after military intervention in 1964 produced unexpected consequences. Instead of generating a more open liberal market economy and private banking, reforms under military rule were soon overshadowed by a period of state-led growth funded by foreign capital inflows. In Brazil, financial repression under military government (whereby subsidized credit and government policies crowded out market forces) proved very different from experiences with neo-liberal policies under military government in Chile, Argentina, and Uruguay during the 1970s.

Fourth, from 1982 to 1993, foreign debt and fiscal crises severely constrained monetary policies in Brazil. Furthermore, the protracted transition from military rule produced a perverse political cycle we describe as a 'last dance syndrome' that exacerbated already severe problems of money, credit and finance. So rather than a consequence of democracy, the bankrupting of state government banks by regional political elites and the loss of control over credit, money and spending occurred under military rule and during the unusual political void of delayed transition to democracy in Brazil. Traditional regional elites recast their political machines during a decade of protracted transition to usurp central government prerogatives over monetary policy.

The politics of monetary policy from 1930 to 1993 suggests the incremental institutional advances behind the construction of monetary authority in Brazil, the importance of critical junctures for initiatives of reform, and the veto coalition against orthodox policies centred in the Banco do Brasil. For most of the 1930–1993 period, the Banco do Brasil retained a monopoly or preeminent market shares and/or control of policies and funds for credit, finance, foreign exchange, trade, industry, agriculture and prerogative to print money and rediscount to banks. This produced strong returns at the bank and reinforced developmentalist ideas and favour of state-led development.

These findings are consistent with core ideas in comparative political economy; that the construction of monetary authority involves path dependent sequences and particular configurations of markets and institutions. The gradual specialization and differentiation of monetary policy agencies in Brazil suggests processes typical of economic statecraft and the importance of the separation of powers for democracy. Scholars of Brazilian political institutions have emphasized the simultaneous empowerment of legislative, judiciary and executive since the 1988 Constitution. This chapter suggests that increased executive capacity and the emergence of an epistemic community of monetary policy specialists are also essential aspects of development and democratization. Review of the politics of monetary policy from 1930 to 1993 suggests increasingly complex interactions between increasingly separate and specialized agencies and branches of federal government. The politics of monetary policy from 1930 to 1993 in Brazil confirm core ideas in the theory of monetary statecraft about how politics shapes monetary policy and development.

Notes

1 On the veto coalition centred in the Banco do Brasil, see: Nóbrega, Mailson and Loyola, Gustavo. 'The Long and Simultaneous Construction of Monetary and Fiscal Institutions', in Sola, Lourdes and Laurence Whitehead (eds.). *Statecrafting Monetary Authority: Democracy and Financial Order in Brazil* (Oxford: Centre for Brazilian Studies, 2006). On veto coalitions, see: Tsibelis, George. *Veto Players* (Princeton, NJ: Princeton University Press, 2002).

2 For an overview of the economy and economic policy making, from 1930 to 1945, see: Abreu, Marcelo P. 'The Brazilian Economy, 1928–45', in Leslie Bethell (ed.), *Cambridge History of Latin America* (Vol. IX) (Cambridge: Cambridge University Press, 2002).

3 See: Fausto, *Història do Brasil* (São Paulo: Edusp, 1994) and Moreira, Regina L. 'Aranha, Osvaldo', in *Dicionário Histórico-Biográfico Brasileiro, Pós-30* (Rio de Janeiro: Editora FGV), pp. 281–310.

4 On the politics of coffee policies, see: Bates, Robert. *Open-economy Politics: The Political Economy of the World Coffee Trade.* (Princeton, NJ: Princeton University Press, 1998).

5 On economic growth in Brazil and Latin America during the 1930s, see: Thorp, Rosemary (ed.), *Latin America in the 1930s.* (London: Palgrave, 1984).

6 Law n°. 19.423.

7 Law n°. 21.499.

8 'The Fund would extend loans to the banks in relation to assets. In turn the loans could not be used for other upcoming bank operations; the resources received from the Fund would only be used for operations linked to the active assets that were shown to the Fund. The loans could be extended for up to 5 years' Villela, Anibal V. and Wilson Suzigan. *Política do Governo e Crescimento da Economia Basileira, 1889–1945* (Rio de Janeiro: IPEA/INPES, 1973), p. 182.

9 Law n°. 20.695, 20 November 1932.

10 On epistemic communities, politics and economic policy making from 1945–1964, see: Loureiro, Maria R. *Os Economistas no Governo* (Rio de Janeiro: Editoria FGV, 1997) and Sola, Lourdes. *Idéias Econômicas, Decisões Políticas* (São Paulo: Edusp, 1998).

11 Bulhões, Octavio G. and Kingston, Jorge. 'A política monetária para 1947'. *Revista Brasileira de Economia*, Rio de Janeiro, 1/1 (1947): 9–50.

12 On Lafer's views of financial policy, see: Lafer, Horácio. *O Crédito e o Sistema Bancário no Brasil* (Rio de Janeiro: Editora Nacional, 1948) (Report submitted to Federal Chamber Finance Committee as Federal Deputy and rappórteur).

13 Founded in December 1953, but closed in response to frequent accusations of corruption and abuse, the government substituted the Cacex with the *Carteira de Exportação e Importação* (Export Import Facility).

14 Whitaker, José M. *Seis Meses, de novo, no Ministério da Fazenda* (Rio de Janeiro: 1956).

15 Op.cit. p. 1.

16 Abreu, op. cit.

17 Abreu, Marcelo P. (ed). (1990). *Ordem do Progresso: Cem Anos de Política Econômica Republicana, 1889–89* (Rio de Janeiro: Campus).

18 The entry of foreign capital as an alternative source of finance also received regulation in the same period. Law n° 4131, 1962, deals with the capture of resources in other countries by Brazilian firms. As a result of this law significant sums of resources came into the country over the following decade. Resolution n° 63 allowed Brazilian banks to raise funds abroad and pass them on to domestic firms.

19 Adjustment policy in the *Plano de Ação Econômica do Governo* (Economic Action Plan of the Government, PAEG) contained cuts in spending and subsidies to reduce the budget deficit and wage and monetary controls. Monetary correction was introduced to

'improve the prestige of the public bonds, in this way to finance government expenditure with resources that were not subject to inflation' (Pelaez, Carlos M. and Suzigan, Wilson. *História Monetária do Brasil: Análise da Política, Comportamento e Instituições Monetárias.* (Rio de Janeiro: IPEA/INPES, 1976), p. 277. See also: Fishlow, Albert. 'Thirty Years of Combating Inflation in Brazil: From the PAEG (1964) to the Plan Real (1994)' (University of Oxford Centre for Brazilian Studies, Working Paper, 2005).

20 On reforms under military government, see: Simonsen, M. H. *Inflação*, 1970, pp. 23–56.

21 Law nº 4357, July 1964, established monetary correction.

22 Hermann, Jennifer. 'Financial system structure and financing models: the Brazilian experience and its perspective (1964/1997).' *Journal of Latin American Studies*, (2002), 34: 71–114., Lees, Francis A., Botts, James M., Cysne, Rubens Penha. Banking and Financial Deepening in Brazil. (London: Palgrave Macmillan, 1990) pp. 242–248; Castro, Antonio B. and Souza, Francisco E. P. *A Economia Brasileira em Marcha Forçada.* (Rio de Janeiro: Paz e Terra, 1985).

23 Studart, Rogerio. Investment Finance in Economic Development, (London: Routledge, 1995), pp. 122–123.

24 Lees *et al.,* 1990, pp. 112–113.

25 Campos, Roberto *A lanterna na popa – Memórias* (Rio de Janeiro: Topbooks, 1997), cited in Nóbrega and Loyola, 2006, p. 64.

26 On bank failures and government policies, see: Lundberg, Eduardo. 'Saneamento do Sistema Financeiro – A Experiência Brasileira dos Últimos 25 Anos' (Central Bank of Brazil, Memo, 2005).

27 Barker, W. J. *Banks and Industry in Contemporary Brazil; Their Organization, Relationship and Leaders* (New Haven, CT: Yale University: 1990).

28 Law nº 4728, 14 July 1965 and Resolution nº 18 of the Central Bank, 18 February 1966.

29 Teixeira (1978): Resolution nº 93, 25 June 1968, Resolution nº 119, 16 July 1969 and Circular nº 128, 16 July 1969 – this legislation was altered in 1976.

30 Tavares, op. cit. p. 121.

31 On governors during the transition to democracy, see: Abrucio, Fernando. *Os Barões da Federação.*

32 See interviews of policy makers in Rego, J. M. and Mantega, G. (eds.), *Conversas com Economistas Brasileiras.* (São Paulo, Editora 34, 2000); Belluzzo, Luiz G. and Almeida, Júlio G. *Depois da Queda: A Economia brasileira da crise da dívida aos impasses do Real* (Rio de Janeiro: Civilização Brasileira, 2002); Bresser, Pereria and Luiz, Carlos. *Economia Brasileira: Uma Introdução Crítica* (3rd ed.) (São Paulo: Editora 34, 1997).

33 On the Bresser Plan, see: Bresser-Pereira, Luiz, C. 'Estabilização em um ambiente adverso: a experiência brasileira de 1987'. *Revista de Economia Política.* Vol. 13 no. 4 (52), Oct./Dec. 1993, p. 1636.

34 Ibid., p. 33 (author's translation).

35 On brinksmanship, see: Sola, Lourdes and Kugelmas, Eduardo. 'Crafting economic stabilisation: Political discretion and technical innovation in the implementation of the real plan, in Sola, Lourdes and Whitehead, Laurence (eds.), *Statecrafting Monetary Authority: Democracy and Financial Order in Brazil* (Oxford: Centre for Brazilian Studies, 2006), pp. 85–116.

36 On the political economy of high-and hyperinflation in Latin America, see: Fanelli J. M., Frenkel, R. and Rozenwurcel, G., 'Growth and Structural Reform in Latin America: Where We Stand' in W. C. Smith, C. H. Acuña and E. A. Gamarra (orgs.) *Latin American Political Economy in the Age of Neoliberal Reform* (Miami: North South Center, 1994) and Giambiagi, F., *Finanças Públicas* (Rio de Janeiro: Campus 1999).

37 Resolution 1289, 1987.

38 Loyola, Gustavo. 'Os bancos públicos estaduais' (Brasília: Central Bank of Brazil, 1992).
39 Sola, Lourdes and Marques, Moisés. 'Central banking, democratic governance, and the quality of democracy.' in Sola, Lourdes and Whitehead, Laurence (eds). Statecrafting Monetary Authority: Democracy and Financial Order in Brazil. (Oxford: Centre for Brazilian Studies, 2006), pp. 143–204.

5 Monetary statecraft and democratization (1994–2014)

Monetary statecraft in Brazil has continued to shape development and democracy after transition from military rule: by ending record levels of inertial inflation; by using emerging market crises as enabling constraints to modernize monetary policy and Central Bank operations; and by tapping monetary channels to accelerate social inclusion and manage consumer-led growth. After a decade of monetary chaos under military rule and transition governments, gradual implementation of heterodox policies restored price stability in 1994 to provide political support for further reforms. During eight years under coalition governments of Fernando Henrique Cardoso (1995–2002), the Central Bank of Brazil was modernized with new staff, divisions, technologies and policies designed to approximate monetary policy with markets and better regulate and supervise banks. From 1995 to 2002, the modernization of the Central Bank was seen as part of new, market-oriented frameworks such as inflation targeting, flexible foreign exchange, fiscal reforms, liberalization of trade and banking and privatization of state-owned enterprises and state government–owned (but not federal government–owned) banks.

Governments formed by the Partido dos Trabalhadores (Worker's Party, PT) under presidents Lula (2003–2010) and Dilma Rousseff (2011–2014) retained most of these market oriented reforms and policy frameworks. This began as a strategic choice seen as necessary to avert currency crisis and adjust the economy. However, inflation targeting, flexible foreign exchange, and delegation of monetary committee and Central Bank decisions were reinforced once new monetary channels proved able to promote consumer-led growth, serve as counter cyclical policy, and accelerate social inclusion from 2004 to 2013. After coming back from the brink of financial crisis during 2003, monetary channels became new policy instruments for managing 'downmarket' consumer-led growth and counter-cyclical measures. Monetary channels also were used to provide basic income grants by the federal government to accelerate financial inclusion based on broader conceptions of citizenship and social justice. This differs, fundamentally, from theories of microfinance based on the private sector, non-governmental organizations and entrepreneurship. The ability of counter-cyclical policies to quickly reverse the credit crunch and economic downturn in Brazil caused by global financial crisis during 2008–2009 further reinforced political support for the broader framework of monetary policy and central banking modernization.

This chapter traces the construction of Central Bank capacity amidst financial crises during the 1990s and early 2000s; the strategic acceptance of market-oriented monetary policies and central banking by an opposition, working-class party; and the adaptation of theories and concepts from monetary economics to accelerate social inclusion and manage downmarket consumer-led growth. These experiences with politics and monetary policy differ both from policies in the Brazilian past of national populism and state-led developmentalism as well as the traditional policy strategies of working-class parties abroad based on Keynesian theories of macroeconomic demand management.

These experiences are at odds with both mainstream and critical theories about politics and monetary policy. First, the construction of Central Bank independence in Brazil *after* price stability occurred in the reverse causal order posited by economic theories. It was only after heterodox theories of inertial inflation and muddling-through policy making reversed inertial inflation during 1994 that the organizational modernization of the Central Bank became possible and monetary reforms were able to increase the independence of the Central Bank. Second, contrary to the dominant views of financial crises, fiscal dominance, and globalization that emphasize constraints on states and government policy, the series of emerging market crises during the 1990s and early 2000s *enabled* rather than constrained initiatives of monetary policy reforms and Central Bank modernization. Third, contrary to sociological theories of private bank capture and biases in microfinance toward the private sector and non-governmental organizations, the use of monetary channels to manage downmarket consumer-driven growth and implement new social policies such as basic income grants through citizenship cards (through a government savings bank) suggest different causal relations in Brazil. Instead of zero-sum relations between politics, democracy and optimal monetary policy, the record from Brazil suggests positive-sum relations between democratization, social inclusion and improved monetary policy making. Indeed, new monetary channels of change in Brazil suggest that longstanding theories of *fiscal constraints* stand in need of revision.

Monetary statecraft in Brazil since 1994 also involved adapting ideas from abroad. Since transition from military rule, new epistemic communities in monetary economics, monetary policy, central banking and financial inclusion adapted ideas from abroad about inflation, inflation targeting, flexible foreign exchange, fiscal control and basic income. For example, the theory of *inertial inflation* produced unprecedented political legitimacy, presidential popularity and allocation of resources to lower classes. This theory was developed by Brazilian (and Latin American) economists that rejected orthodox ideas about slowing the economy to reduce inflation to elaborate, instead, a theory of inertial inflation that identified indexation as the most critical cause of inflation and proposed and implemented policies able to *reduce inflation while redistributing income to the poor*. In Brazil, this provided policy makers with the political support and market confidence necessary to pursue measures designed to modernize central banking and launch new frameworks for monetary policy.

Figure 5.1 introduces this different trajectory of monetary statecraft in Brazil by plotting four interest rates from 2002–2014: first the 'SELIC' interest rate, the

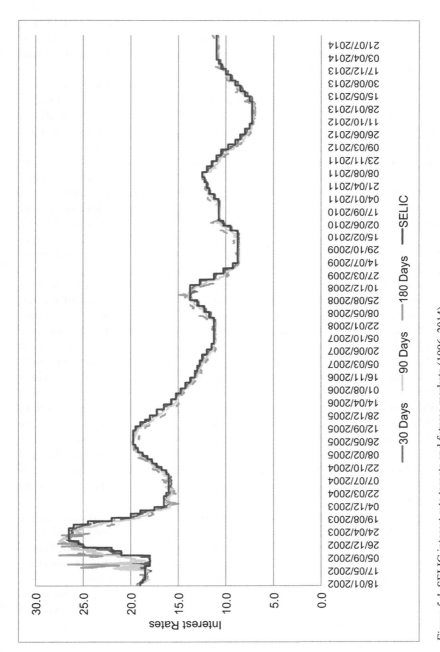

Figure 5.1 SELIC interest rate targets and futures markets (1996–2014)

Source: Instituto de Pesquisas Econômicas Aplicadas (IPEA), Ipeadata, available on http://www.ipeadata.gov.br/

Sistema Especial de Liquidação e de Custódia (Special System for Liquidation and Custody) that is the interbank overnight interest rate target set by the monetary policy commission (Comitê de Politica Monetária, COPOM). Alongside the official SELIC interest rate are plotted three futures market contracts (30, 90 and 180 day) for SELIC interest rates traded on the BMF-Bovespa (Bolsa de Mercadorias e Futuros, Bolsa de Valores de São Paulo, Commodities and Futures Exchange, São Paulo Stock Market).

The time series begins in 2002 when the price for SELIC interest rate futures contracts reached over 25 percent as opposition candidate Luis Inácio Lula da Silva, increased in the polls for the presidential election of October. The divergence of the policy rate and the market rate suggests how the lack of market confidence reached crisis proportions and threatened to undermine inflation targeting. However, during the 2000s, SELIC interest rates set by the monetary policy committee can be seen to increasingly accompany both downward and upward pressures in 30-, 90- and 120- day futures market trading, albeit from record high rates to remain at much higher levels than other developing and emerging countries and far above interest rates in advanced economies through 2012. This trajectory from the brink of crisis to remain among the highest real interest rates in the world increased space for monetary policy making in Brazil.

Notwithstanding high interest rates, large marginal returns (and risks) accrued from advances in monetary policy making in Brazil after the end of inertial inflation amidst the sequence of emerging market currency crises.[1] For politics and monetary policy in Brazil, *worse begot better*. The benefits of monetary policy reforms and Central Bank modernization accrue not despite very high interest rate levels but *because* coming back from the brink of crisis proved a 'blank slate' for recreation of credit, finance and money relations. The previous chapter traces how inertial inflation and six anti-inflation policy packages from 1986–1993 caused credit to fall to nearly 20 percent of gross domestic product (GDP). The present chapter focuses on the recovery of credit and monetary relations after 1994, a process that belies theories of politics and monetary policy from economics and sociology. It follows that, at the end of the time series of Figure 5.1 in 2014, further gains remain possible given that benchmark overnight interbank interest rates remain at 11 percent nominal (5.5 percent real) levels.

Figure 5.1 also introduces how monetary statecraft in Brazil involved policy convergence with market expectations driven by the creation of new divisions at the Central Bank for market relations and communication. The creation of futures markets for interest rates and foreign currency exchange at the BMF-Bovespa are important indications of this convergence. A prior indication of efforts to encourage approximation between monetary policy and markets is the development and refinement of a Central Bank survey of private-sector economic forecasts, the *Focus* survey. Introduced as part of transition to inflation targeting amidst crisis in 1999 (another example of enabling constraints), the *Focus* survey is based on a biweekly questionnaire circulated to the top 120 banks and consulting firms in

Brazil to measure their current forecasts. Results are published anonymously (except for awarding the top five forecasts for accuracy), with average forecasts and standard deviations for two-year time span providing an important source of information for Central Bank and monetary policy committee decisions.[2]

Since adoption of inflation targeting and a flexible foreign currency exchange rate regime in 1999, economic shocks, foreign and domestic, have been buffered through market-driven adjustment rather than policies of command and control or fixing of prices and rates. Under the fixed currency exchange regime from 1994 to 1999 (seen as necessary to sustain the new currency), the Brazilian government was forced to react to three international currency crises (Mexico, 1994–1995; Asia, 1997; Russia, 1998) by increasing SELIC benchmark overnight interbank interest rates to *45 percent*. Since 1999, external shocks to the Brazilian economy have been absorbed primarily through market-driven currency exchange devaluation. And while monetary authorities increased benchmark overnight interest rate targets to over 25 percent in 2002–2003 (and to 20 percent in 2005 and 14 percent in 2008 as the global financial crisis hit Brazil), this trajectory opened new policy alternatives. Despite record high interest rate levels, shallow credit markets and exclusion of the majority of Brazilians from the banking system, the framework of fiscal control, inflation targeting and flexible foreign exchange increased space for domestic credit and income policies.

This chapter examines this trajectory of monetary statecraft and democratization since 1994 as follows. We first review how muddling through implementation of inertial inflation restored price stability and enabled Central Bank modernization amidst currency crises in emerging markets. We then examine the requirement for commercial banks to place consumer deposits at the Central Bank as a critical policy mechanism before reviewing how floating the real and adopting inflation targeting in 1999 set a new context for monetary policy. Analysis of new epistemic communities in monetary policy making and a broader look at the composition of money and national financial accounts in Brazil then clarify why it is essential to reassess core ideas about money, finance and inequality to better understand how monetary channels provide new opportunities and risks for social inclusion and political development.

Muddling through monetary policy: the Real Plan

The Real Plan exemplifies monetary statecraft because of the gradual, incremental strategies used to implement the theory of inertial inflation. Instead of adopting recommendations from abroad to combine reforms in a single big bang, or repeat the 'heterodox shock' strategy to freeze prices and wages that failed six times from 1986 to 1992, the Real Plan was implemented differently, that is to say gradually with a view toward both market perceptions and political support. Indeed, compared to the six preceding anti-inflation plans, the policies of Cardoso as finance minister appear piecemeal, even minor. Fiscal reform began in February 1994 by negotiating legislative support for a 15 percent cut in constitutionally mandated transfers from the federal government to states and municipalities. On 1 March

1994, the Unidade Real de Valor (Real Value Unit, URV) was launched to function as daily reference for Central Bank adjustments to the cruzeiro (basically determined by devaluation of the cruzeiro against the US dollar). The URV helped focus the attention of investors and the public on a single government index. After setting and subsequently meeting fiscal and monetary performance targets, Finance Minister Cardoso announced that the URV would serve as referent for a new currency to be launched on 1 July 1994 (made by his successor Ciro Gomes at Finance). Policy measures were thus announced as trial balloons, well ahead of time, rather than attempting to surprise markets or shock inflation out of the economy through price and wage freezes.

The Real Plan launched Cardoso as presidential candidate because the end of inflation produced significant real gains in income, especially among the poor. As inflation fell, real wages increased an estimated 20 percent during the first six months after the Real Plan (June–December 1994). Moreover, the real income of poor Brazilians increased an estimated 50 percent during this period because inflation no longer eroded salaries.

The Real Plan also resulted from a new generation of economists who adapted ideas from abroad. Theories of inertial inflation emerged in Latin America during the 1980s because the indexation of prices, wages and financial instruments accelerated inflation but rarely resulted in hyperinflation. To avert flight to dollars or other fixed assets, governments increasingly indexed bonds against inflation as described in the preceding chapter. The theory of inertial inflation suggested that the existence of 'dual currencies' (one being the official de jure currency, the other indexed government bonds) could provide a different course for monetary policy, consisting simply in the organization of a transition from the former to the latter. From 1986 to 1992, six anti-inflation packages based on the theory of inertial inflation were implemented in Brazil. This is an example of adapting economic ideas from abroad. However, public policy requires not only problem identification and policy formulation, but also implementation. From 1986 to 1992, the implementation of theories of inertial inflation was conducted as 'shock therapy' through price and wage freezes broke contracts, disorganized markets and further disrupted economic activity. Implementation by shock therapy produced brief periods of strong growth that soon produced shortfalls and inflationary pressures. The theory of monetary statecraft draws attention to this critical difference emphasized in theories of public policy: that muddling through is often required to implement new policy frameworks.

Central Bank modernization after price stability

Price stability opened new horizons for the organizational modernization of the Central Bank. However, change was not linear. Nor were reforms cumulative in the sense that improved economic parameters enabled further reforms. Instead, unexpected consequences ensued, and crises served as enabling constraints to promote further reforms. Two unexpected consequences were caused by price stability: a dramatic increase in government debt and banking crisis. However, instead of impeding change these unexpected consequences proved enabling constraints for new policy initiatives. The dual fiscal and banking crises accelerated the launch of new initiatives, such as deposit insurance (1996), new procedures to monitor credit risk to provide earlier warning of problems and reduce the cost of interventions (1996), new requirements for bank capital reserves and risk monitoring under the Bank for International Settlements Basel II accord (1997) and new reporting standards and central risk information centre (1997). And the sequence of financial and currency crises in emerging markets during this period tended to further increase opportunities to 'smuggle' monetary reforms and measures of Central Bank modernization as part of emergency decrees or legislation.[3]

To retain the confidence of markets, reforms were proposed in dialogue with financial institutions and stakeholders in markets for government debt and foreign exchange. Central Bank reforms sought to provide earlier warnings able to *anticipate* banking problems and permit market-driven solutions to monetary problems. This represented a shift away both from command and control styles of public policy and the reactive policies and informal collaboration that had prevailed during anti-inflation plans in Brazil designed to end monetary chaos from 1986 to 1992. Instead, reforms were designed to enable more specialized functions of monetary policy. This can be seen in terms of organizational change at the Central Bank of Brazil. From 1986 to 1994, policy making at the Central Bank of Brazil involved a small group responsible for implementation of anti-inflation packages. Each plan (Cruzado in 1986; Bresser in 1987; Summer in 1989; Collor I in 1990; Collor II in 1992) *subordinated Central Bank policies* to broader monetary, fiscal and currency targets seen as necessary to sustain price and wage freezes. A lack of trained staff and poor information technology also rendered the Central Bank unable to supervise banks or monitor the money supply and market trends.

Price stability produced another unexpected consequence: banking crisis. Because price stability reduced the income of banks from arbitrage under high inflation, several mid- and large-sized banks failed in 1995. In August 1995, the Central Bank assumed control of the Banco Econômico (eighth largest private domestic bank) and, in November 1995, the Banco Nacional (sixth largest private domestic bank). This quickened the pace of reforms and broadened support for new legislation on government interventions into ailing banks. New rules favoured acquisition of troubled banks by other financial institutions over government intervention, replacing regulations in place since the 1930s that relied on simple decrees from the federal executive. In 1995, the Central Bank received, for the first time, authority to audit financial institutions and pursue policies of prevention based on market operations and capitalization of banks. Instead of reacting to the failure of banks after the fact, this provided a new framework to infuse capital, transfer or acquire bank shares or reorganize financial institutions through merger or acquisition.

Price stability required three different federal government programs for private, state and federal government banks: the Programa de Estímulo à Reestruturação e ao Fortalecimento do Sistema Financeiro Nacional (Program to Stimulate the Restructuring and Strengthening of the National Financial System, PROER) to

Table 5.1 Failed banks and buyers in 1996 banking crisis

Bank Interventions	Buyer
Banco Econômico	Excel e Caixa Econômica Federal
Banco Nacional	Unibanco
Banco Mercantil de Pernambuco	Rural
Banco Banorte	Bandeirantes
Banco Bamerindus	HSBC, Caixa*, Banco do Brasil

Source: Central Bank of Brazil, Department of Bank Operations

* Real-estate portfolio

save and sell failed private banks from 1995 to 1997 (see Table 5.1); a second to privatize bankrupt state government banks, the Programa de Incentivo à Redução do Setor Público Estadual na Atividade Bancária (Program of Incentives to Reduce State Public Sector Banking Activity, PROES) that privatized 27 state government banks from 1997 to 1999; and finally the capitalization and development of reforms for federal government banks, the Programa de Fortalecimento das Instituições Financeiras (Federal Programme to Strengthen Federal Financial Institutions, PROEF) from 1999 to 2001.

The abuse of state government banks under military rule and prolonged transition was one of the major sources of monetary chaos. Crony credit led to record levels of nonperforming loans that were transferred into the money supply by rolling over loans or increasing public debt by transfer of assets or writing off loans.

However, instead of privatization, the Cardoso administration used federal government banks (Caixa Econômica Federal, Banco do Brasil and BNDES) for measures of monetary policy making and central banking.[4] Federal banks were used to split non-performing loans off from private banks and state government banks before their resale or privatization. The Cardoso administration also used federal government banks to monitor state governments along the lines of a 'domestic IMF' to induce fiscal and administrative reform of state and municipal governments. In June 2001, bad credits held at federal banks were transferred to a new asset management entity (Empresa Gestora de Ativos, EMGEA) at the Ministry of Finance, while low-interest-bearing assets were swapped for new paper from Treasury paying market interest rates.[5] Capital was injected into three of four federal government banks to bring these institutions within Basel II Accord capital guidelines (8 percent capital reserves weighted by risk) and tougher requirements set by Brazilian Central Bank resolution 2.682/99 for provisions against risk (11 percent capital reserves weighted by risk).

In 1995, creation of a bank deposit insurance fund was also critical for improving confidence in the banking system (Table 5.2). The Fundo Garantidor de Créditos (Credit Guarantee Fund, FGC) was funded by 0.25 percent of daily balances of bank deposits to be held at the Central Bank to cover up to R$20,000 of individual bank accounts in the case of bank failure. Large payouts ensued during 1996

Table 5.2 Federal government deposit insurance recipients

Year	Number of Recipients
1996	146,841
1997	3,948,698
1998	39,054
1999	7,656
2000	357
2001	7,988
2002	0
2003	419
2004	1,903
2005–2010	0
2011	1,973
2012	2,015
2013	9,921
Total 1996–2013	4,166,825

Source: Central Bank of Brazil, available at http://www.bcb.gov.
br/?id=FGCESTAT&ano=2014

to cover losses from the banking crisis. However, payouts thereafter declined to zero by 2002, and after increasing during 2003 and 2004 remained at zero from 2005 to 2010 such that no deposit insurance payments were necessary during adjustment to the 2007–2008 global financial crisis.

In 1997, the Central Bank adopted new *Core Principles for Effective Bank Supervision*. Based on guidelines from the Bank for International Settlements, the Central Bank of Brazil set capital reserve requirements and new reporting standards for risk analysis of bank portfolios, developed new measures to induce banks to respect these standards and trained and equipped new staff for auditing and supervising banks and credit risk. Amidst crisis in 1999, the Central Bank increased the minimum level of capital reserves from the BIS-recommended guideline of 8 to 11 percent. However, given the conservative policies of banks in Brazil to hold greater levels of capital reserves, the average Basel Index of Brazilian banks since 2000 has remained significantly above the 11 percent limit set by the Central Bank, varying between 15 and 20 percent through 2014.

This higher level of capital reserve requirements reflects the greater caution of the Central Bank and monetary authorities (see Table 5.2). While international monetary institutions such as the Bank for International Settlements and regulatory authorities in advanced economy struggle to increase equity and capital reserves in domestic banks, one of the reasons Brazil was able to escape severe consequences of global crisis in 2008 (credit crunch and capital flight) was the larger cushion provided by higher levels of capital reserves. This is consistent with research on banking that suggests conservative (higher) capital reserve levels are far less costly that the riskier strategies of private banks that led to large capital losses in the 2007–2008 financial crisis.

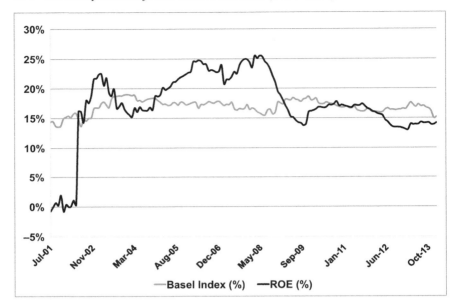

Figure 5.2 Average bank Basel Index and returns on equity (ROE), 2000–2014

Source: Central Bank of Brazil

Another series of reforms that approximated monetary policy and markets in Brazil was the improvement of information on bank credit portfolios and credit risk. In 1997, the Central Bank created a new Centro de Risco de Crédito (Centre for Credit Risk) to manage a new database on credit risk for all loans over R$5,000. This replaced the use of two categories (good and bad loans over 90 days late) with both qualitative evaluation and indexes expanded (in 1999) to nine levels of credit risk, ranging from 'AA' to 'H' with corresponding levels of required coverage. In 2000, data on credit and bank risk were then placed online for consultation by credit institutions. Over 874,000 credit risk consultations were made during first semester 2001; this increased to over 5 million consultations by first semester 2002. Instead of reacting to circumstances once bad loans had eroded the capital of banks and credit portfolios, the Central Bank trained new staff and created new divisions able to better monitor banks. In-person visits to credit institutions were introduced to inspect portfolios and calculate risk exposures with new credit matrices for each bank.

The modernization of Central Bank operations since the late 1990s included the digitalization of documents and internal procedures, automated collection and scheduled public reporting of data from banks, creation of a separate database and supervision procedures for mortgage credits and credit consortia and implementation of the digital Sistema Brasileiro de Pagamentos (Brazilian Payments System, SBP). After 2002, the Brazilian Payments System enabled automated, online, real-time monitoring of bank transactions. This further increased the capacity of the Central Bank to monitor and supervise banks and reduce the risks of liquidity shortages and bank failures. Improved transparency and accuracy of payments procedures during the 2000s was also fundamental for the modernization of government social policy payments and other services that have accelerated financial inclusion discussed below.

Central Bank deposit reserve requirements

The previous chapter traces the importance of bank deposit reserve requirements held by monetary authorities in Brazil since commercial banks began to keep a portion of their deposits at the 'lead' bank, the Banco do Brasil in the 1930s. Made mandatory in 1945, then transferred to the Central Bank of Brazil in 1965, this policy reflects a further cautious buffer for monetary policy. Indeed, instead of full transition to reliance on market-based mechanisms of central banking such as bond issues and the use of benchmark interbank interest rates to manage credit flows, commercial bank deposits held at the Central Bank continue to provide a powerful option for monetary policy. Table 5.3 reports the levels of bank deposit reserve requirements from 1994 to 2014. This differs considerably from the problem encountered by many central banks in advanced economies during and since the global financial crisis of 2007–2008 where zero-bound interest rates and massive injections of liquidity reached the limit of policy options available to monetary authorities.

Gradually releasing commercial bank deposits held at the Central Bank reflects, and reinforced, the low supply (20 percent of GDP in 1990) and high cost of credit in Brazil. During transition to the new currency in July 1994, 100 percent of demand deposits held by commercial banks in Brazil were retained by the Central Bank. Thereafter, the Central Bank used the release of mandatory deposits as a mechanism to increase liquidity at levels compatible with sustaining price stability. Reserve requirements remained at 75 percent in 1999, with reduction to 65 percent in October 1999 and 45 percent in June 2000, suggesting the gradual release of credit over five years. Moreover, the lack of market confidence during transition to the PT government of President Lula in 2002–2003 forced the Central Bank to raise reserve requirements to 60 percent. And rather than abandon the policy of mandatory reserve requirements during the 2000s, the Lula government increased this measure to reduce flows of credit twice: once from 42 to 43 percent in 2009 to allay fears of inflation and, once again, from 43 to 44 percent in July 2010 amidst a second period of concern about excessive credit flows.

Like other policy instruments at very high rates in comparative perspective, the requirement that commercial banks in Brazil maintain over 40 percent of their deposits at the Central Bank is an anomaly.[6] The path from monetary chaos, risks to expanding the supply of credit and conservativism learned from crises in the past may explain this anomaly. However, the trajectory also is marked: during the 2000s, 1 percent changes in reserve requirements are fundamentally different if compared to holding *100 percent of demand deposits* (and 30 percent of savings

Table 5.3 Central Bank deposit reserve requirements (1994–2014)

Date		Deposits		Savings Accounts		Deposits		
		Demand	Time	Housing	Rural	Demand	Time	Savings
< 1994		50%		15%	15%			
1994	Jul	100%	20%	20%	20%			
	Aug		30%	30%	30%			
	Dec	90%	27%					
1995	Apr		30%					
	Jul	83%						
	Aug		20%	15%	15%			
1996	Aug	82%						
	Sep	81%						
	Oct	80%						
	Nov	79%						
	Dec	78%						
1997	Jan	75%						
1999	Mar		30%					
	May		25%					
	Jul		20%					
	Sep		10%					
	Oct	65%	0%					
2000	Mar	55%						
	Jun	45%						
2001	Sep		10%					
2002	Jun		15%					
	Jul			20%	20%			
	Aug					3%	3%	5%
	Oct					8%	8%	10%
2003	Feb	60%						
	Aug	45%						
2008	Oct	42%				5%	5%	
	Nov				15%			
	Jan						4%	
	Sep		14%					
	Mar		15%			8%	8%	
2009	Jun	43%			16%			
	Dec		20%			12%	12%	
2010	Jun				17%			
	Jul	44%				6%		
	Sep					0%		
2011	Oct						11%	
	Jul				18%			

Source: Central Bank of Brazil

deposits) from July to December 1994 to reverse inertial inflation. This suggests both the different magnitude of monetary statecraft in Brazil and the distance from standard practices in advanced economies.

Floating the real (January 1999)

Floating the real in 1999 provides further evidence of how financial crisis proved enabling constraints for monetary reforms in Brazil. After currency crises in Mexico (1994–1995) and Asia (1997), declaration of moratorium on foreign debt by Russia in 1998 produced, once again, runs on currencies, credit crunches and financial crises in developing countries. In Brazil, the Cardoso administration secured a $41.0 billion standby agreement with the International Monetary Fund (IMF) to keep crisis at bay weeks before the October 1998 elections. However, after several attempts failed to implement alternative foreign currency arrangements during January 1999 failed and foreign currency reserves were nearly depleted, the real was floated on foreign currency exchange markets (Figure 5.3).

The Cardoso administration floated the real on 15 January 1999. This ended the fixed (later pegged) exchange rate that had served as central reference since June 1994. After briefly experimenting with schemes of pegs and bands for foreign currency exchange, once the real was floated it devalued from 1.2 against the US dollar to 1.52 in January and 1.91 in February. Devaluation and revaluation thereafter proved increasingly important for monetary policy. Devaluation proved critical for adjustment during subsequent crises: in the wake of moratorium on foreign

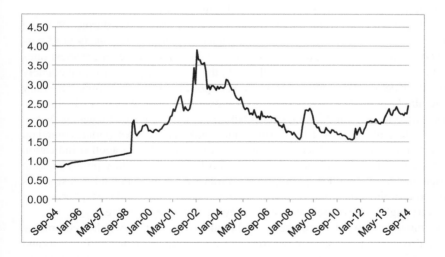

Figure 5.3 Foreign exchange rates (1994–2014; R$/US$)
Source: Ipeadata

debt payments in Argentina and the September 2011 attacks in the United States that produced a credit crunch and capital flight from Brazil and during 2002–2003 as the opposition candidate Luis Inácio da Silva increased in the polls, won the October elections and took office in January 2003. Instead of imposing adjustment through command and control policies or fiscal adjustment, the devaluation of the real after 1999 produced adjustment through market devaluation of the foreign exchange value of the real that reduced imports and increased exports. This process also involved large marginal returns rather than incremental improvement. During 2003, devaluation of the real against the dollar reached 4.0 while, in comparison, subsequent periods of adjustment devalued the real by much smaller increments.

Inflation targeting (April 1999)

Financial crisis also served as enabling constraints for the implementation of inflation targeting in 1999 (see Table 5.4). Inflation targeting was not part of a linear, cumulative progression of reforms but, instead, was introduced amidst crisis and record high levels of interest rates introduced by monetary authorities, once again, to avert capital flight and restore confidence. As means of coming back from the brink of crisis, inflation targeting produced large marginal gains (and costs) on a far different scale than the zero-bound erosion of policy space that has been encountered by many central banks in advanced economies since the global crisis of 2007–2008. Despite extremely high interest rates and crisis, adoption of inflation targeting in Brazil during 1999 signified a commitment toward further market-oriented policies.[7] Instead of imposing costly command and control decisions such as price and wage freezes, inflation targeting sought to align interest rates with expectations (as measured in forecasts and futures markets).

To bring inflation within targets for the consumer price index during 1999, the monetary policy committee increased benchmark interest rates *from 39 to 45 percent* on March 4. The committee also signaled their intent to reduce interest rates by introducing a 'downward bias' clause in the statement published immediately after the meeting. This increased discretion of policy between meetings, necessary to let the Central Bank accompany market overshoot and reduce SELIC interest rates twice (to 42.0 and 39.5 percent) before the next scheduled meeting. More-over, instead of setting SELIC overnight interbank interest rates, policies relied on futures market prices and set *targets* for the SELIC rate. This is another indication of transition away from command and control toward monetary policy making based on market confidence and pricing, a transition implemented because crises proved enabling constraints and with large marginal gains (and costs) because of the very high interest rates necessary to regain market confidence.

Communication policies at the Central Bank and by monetary policy committee have also sought to increase transparency to align policy with market forecasts and expectations. This has involved new Central Bank divisions of research, communication and surveys of investor forecasts designed to tap expectations. Policy modernization thereby involved early and more detailed publication of transcripts of policy meetings and, as mentioned, launch of the *Focus* survey designed to

Table 5.4 Monetary policy committee inflation targets (1999–2016)

Target Year	Date Target Set	Target	Band	Limits	IPCA
1999	30/06/1999	8.0	2.0	6–10	8.9
2000		6.0	2.0	4–8	5.9
2001		4.0	2.0	2–6	7.6
2002	28/06/2000	3.5	2.0	1.5–5.5	12.5
2003	28/06/2001	3.25	2.0	1.25–5.25	9.3
2003	27/06/2002	4.0	2.5	1.5–6.5	
2004	27/06/2002	3.75	2.5	3–8	7.6
2004	25/06/2003	5.5	2.5	2–7	
2005	25/06/2003	4.5	2.5	2.5–6.5	5.7
2006	30/06/2004	'	'	'	3.1
2007	23/06/2005	'	'	'	4.4
2008	29/06/2005	'	'	'	5.9
2009	26/06/2007	'	'	'	4.3
2010	01/07/2008	'	'	'	6.5
2011	30/06/2009	'	'	'	5.8
2012	28/06/2010	'	'	'	5.9
2013	30/06/2011	'	'	'	5.9
2014	28/06/2012	'	'	'	6.4
2015	28/06/2013	'	'	'	6.4*
2016	25/06/2014	'	'	'	

Source: Central Bank of Brazil, 'Histórico de Metas para a Inflação no Brasil', available at www.bcb. gov.br
* = average forecast in Central Bank *Focus* survey.

measure the economic forecasts of the top banks and consulting firms in Brazil. Central Bank and monetary policy committee communication strategies adapted frameworks from abroad to increase transparency and align Central Bank policy with market perceptions.[8] In 1999, the vote tally and minutes of monetary policy committee meetings were provided immediately after announcement of policy decisions rather than 90 days later. Creation of the Central Bank research department also commissioned research on inflation targeting,[9] financial risk and pricing and the microeconomics of banking and convened an international seminar to assess international experiences with inflation targeting held 3–5 May 1999.[10]

Monetary statecraft under inflation targeting and flexible foreign exchange

After 1999, monetary policy making turned primarily on interest rate policies and interventions into foreign exchange markets. By first semester 2001, foreign accounts had improved; government debt fell below 54 percent of GDP and the exposure of public debt to foreign currency devaluation and a better payment schedule had eased government obligations. However, capital flight in the wake of the 11 September attacks on the United States, crisis in neighbouring Argentina,

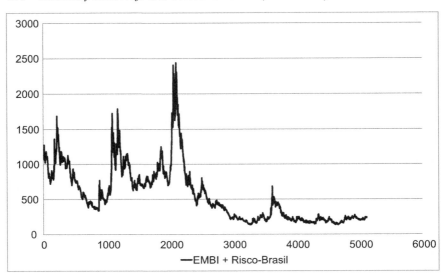

Figure 5.4 Emerging market bond index, Brazil risk (1994–2014)
Source: Ipeadata, JP Morgan

slowdown in the world economy and fear among foreign investors as opposition party PT candidate Luis Inácio da Silva rose in the polls forced monetary authorities to increase SELIC interest rates once again. The Brazilian government met IMF fiscal targets during 2001 and direct foreign investment levels ($20 billion) exceeded market forecasts. However, the Central Bank nonetheless was forced to offer foreign currency indexed treasury bonds as hedge to stem the devaluation of the real. In September 2001, the Cardoso administration also reached a US$15.6 billion stand-by agreement with the IMF to ease concerns of investors.

Political risk perceptions during 2002 increased the premia on Brazilian sovereign issues to historic levels, reaching 24 percent over benchmark US federal reserve issues (see Figure 5.4).[11] To avert crisis, PT presidential candidate Lula issued, in June 2002, a 'carta ao povo brasileiro' (letter to the Brazilian people) that promised to respect foreign and domestic debt contracts. This pre-electoral commitment by presidential candidate Lula is an exemplar of the third (of eight possible) political response to market pressures able to avert financial crisis in emerging markets, as defined by Whitehead.[12] Despite historic opposition to liberalization, privatizations and market-oriented reforms, this pre-electoral commitment was maintained. Upon taking office in 2003, President Lula did, in fact, retain the core economic policies of fiscal control, flexible foreign exchange and inflation targeting. He also nominated Bank of Boston CEO Henrique Meirelles as Central Bank president to regain the confidence of investors. Several legislative proposals were sent to congress as further signals designed to reverse political risk perceptions and record premia on markets at home and abroad.

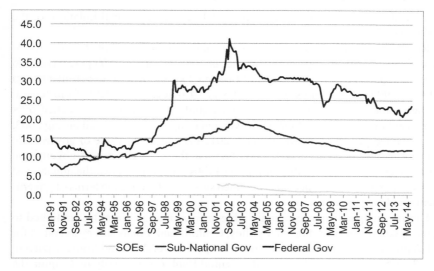

Figure 5.5 Government debt, percent GDP (1991–2014)
Source: Ipeadata

After the unprecedented suspension of export credits during 2002, Brazilian firms began to return to international capital markets, and Cbond prices increased and Brazil country risk ratings declined during fourth quarter 2002. After declining to 48 percent of face value during 2002, Brazilian Cbonds recovered 64 percent of face value at year-end 2003. Brazilian EMBI country risk ratings also fell from peaks of 2,390 and 2,443 during July and August 2002 to trade at 700 points over US benchmark issues by year-end 2003.

Official creditors such as the IMF and World Bank also helped avert a currency crisis by providing support to Brazil during the period of government transition and economic adjustment. In February 2003, the IMF completed the second review of the US$30.0 billion stand-by agreement with Brazil, strongly endorsing the new government's economic policies, especially the maintenance of fiscal and monetary austerity to reverse inflationary pressures due to the devaluation of the real against foreign currencies during 2002.

While markets recovered and international financial institutions supported Brazilian government policies, monetary statecraft at home continued to involve record high interest rates. The COPOM decision to raise benchmark SELIC interest rates to 25.5 percent (January 22) and again to 26.5 percent (February 19) demonstrated the commitment of the Lula administration to the broader policy-making framework. However, to avert further austerity and recession, the new Brazilian Central Bank president, Henrique Meirelles, first increased the 2003 inflation target to 8.5 percent on January 21 (previous outer limit was 6.5 percent), then declared that the target most likely would be met only in 2004. The IMF also set a relatively loose target (outer limit) of 17.5 percent annual inflation for the September 2003 review.

Record high interest rates used to avert capital flight further pressured government debt. The origin of government debt in 2002 was largely (60 percent) due to municipal and state government debt (assumed by the federal government from 1997 to 1999),[13] as well as interest rates (19.4 percent) and debts from federal agencies and firms (15.5 percent). Total liquid government debt reached over 60 percent of GDP during 2002. However, once adjustment occurred during 2003, the sustained period of growth through 2012 decreased the value of government debt to near 30 percent of GDP. And because the average term of government bonds decreased substantially during the 1990s and early 2000s, the annual cost of financing government debt also declined substantially once the terms of government bonds improved.

During this process of economic adjustment, inflation targeting continued to serve as centrepiece for monetary policy. Central Bank *Focus* survey averages for IPCA projections increased from 6.6 to 10.4 percent for 2002 and from 5.2 percent to 9.2 percent for 2003. However, the Central Bank *Focus* survey first captured a reversal of inflationary pressures. During 2002, major bank projections converge in predicting a decline of IGP-ID and IGP-M inflation figures for 2002 to 2003. Average projections for IGP-DI declined from 21.93 percent for 2002 to 16.7 percent in 2003, while IGP-M projections declined from 23.58 in 2002 to 10.0 percent in 2003. Thus, despite breaching the outer levels of inflation targets, the Central Bank survey of bank forecasts for wholesale and retail inflation served as indicators that inflation had peaked and would decline during 2003.

Policies thereafter sought to adjust the economy to this *nucleus* of inflation. Although trading on futures markets were suspended during 2002, data from Central Bank *Focus* surveys for consumer price increases (12.5 percent for 2003 and 8 percent for 2004) provided information to suggest that policies remained consistent with market expectations. The *Focus* survey continued to tap major bank projections that wholesale (IGP-DI and IGP-M) indexes would decline during 2003–2004. Average projections for the IGP-DI index fell from 15.0 to 8.8 percent in 2003–2004, and projections for the IGP-M index fell from 16.0 to 9.0 percent for 2003–2004. These expectations of declining inflation informed average bank forecasts that SELIC interest rates would fall to 22 percent at year-end 2003 and 17.9 percent by year-end 2004.

Litmus tests for recovery: article 192 and reform of social security and taxes

The coalition government of President Lula also pursued initiatives that served as further litmus tests to recover the confidence of markets. The legislative agenda during 2002 included altering Constitutional Article 192 to increase Central Bank independence, regulation of private pension funds for public servants and the extension of the 0.38 percent CPMF tax on financial transactions. Given new rules that placed provisional decrees from the executive first on the legislative calendar,

Congress was forced to vote on decrees that increased the authority of Comissão de Valores Mobiliários (Capital Market Commission, CVM), reschedule agricultural debts and prohibit public employee strikes. Leaders of the PT government in Congress also brought new labour laws, social security reforms and tax reforms to votes.

To sustain market confidence during 2003, the Lula government also pursued revision of regulations on money, credit and finance in Article 192 of the 1988 Constitution. However, instead of pursuing Central Bank independence, the government sought to alter Article 192 to permit discussion of consensual reforms in separate pieces of ordinary legislation. This freed the government to revise rules such as a 12 percent cap on interest rates, limits to foreign capital holdings in financial institutions, legal requirements for credit agencies, commercial banks and investment houses, deposit insurance on personal savings and procedures for bank supervision. Once again, economic theories of Central Bank independence and sociological theories of capture fail to explain the gradualist muddling through strategies designed to recover market confidence evidenced by the legislative agenda of the Lula government during 2003.

Sticky prices during 2003 delayed adjustment. While price indexes declined after January 2003, inflation peaked higher than expected and ceded at a slower pace than most analysts predicted. This led the government to increase the target for inflation in the letter of intent with the IMF to 17.5 percent (outer limit for the IPCA consumer price index target in September 2003). Although the official inflation target of 8.5 percent increase in the IPCA consumer prices remained in place for 2003, Central Bank president Meirelles publicly admitted that a two-digit figure was not out of the question and that, realistically, 8.5 percent target would most likely not be met until 2004. Although domestic factors such as weak demand, unemployment, high interest rates and an abundant harvest suggested downward price pressures, the pass-through of foreign exchange devaluation, increased oil prices because of war in Iraq and uncertainty about foreign investment and finance flows produce large standard deviations in forecasts and volatility in futures markets for foreign exchange.

The second quarter of 2003 brought further news of gradual control over inflation, the recovery of the real against foreign currencies and a variety of positive developments. The core economic policies in place since 1999 (monetary and fiscal rigor, inflation targeting and flexible foreign exchange) were maintained at considerable costs by President Lula during first semester 2003. However, calculations of moratorium have ceded to the calendar and content of structural reforms (tax, social security, financial, bankruptcy) and the timing and pace of recovery. Despite increasing opposition from domestic groups determined to resume growth, the economic team of President Lula has insisted in completing the process of economic adjustment and controlling inflation before reducing interest rates and relaxing fiscal rigor.

President Lula and the new PT coalition government instead emphasized monetary caution to eliminate inflationary pressures early in their four-year mandate. The nomination of three conservative monetary economists as Central Bank directors in May 2003 provided further confirmation of this cautious strategy for monetary policy. The decision by the Brazilian Central Bank and Monetary Committee to reduce benchmark SELIC interest rates by 0.5 percent to 26.0 on June 18 also demonstrated the determination of monetary authorities to complete adjustment to inflationary pressures from exchange devaluation during 2002. During 2003, both forecasts in Central Bank *Focus* surveys and prices in futures markets for interest rates and foreign exchange converged toward expectations that government policies would bring inflation within the 8.5 percent IPCA target for 2004.

International financial markets clearly indicated improved perceptions of confidence in President Silva and the new government during second quarter 2003. While concern about reforms and regulatory changes remain, the worst scenarios among investors about political and economic policy disjuncture have clearly been abandoned. With Cbonds up from 48c last year to over 90c during second quarter 2003, the EMBI risk premium down from 2,400 points to below 780, all inflation indexes in sharp decline and the valuation of the real from 3.9 to 2.8 against the dollar suggest that Brazil has become somewhat of a darling among international investors. Indeed, perceptions are so positive that expectations about economic recovery and projections for growth in the years to come now may be overstated. Given the tendency of international investors to overshoot positions in emerging markets, analysts should beware of the structural constraints on economic growth in Brazil.

Theories of money and monetary economics suggest that changes in government debt are primarily caused by short-term phenomena money and finance rather than long-term trends in government accounts. This can also be seen as a shift away from use of government bonds indexed against inflation or foreign exchange to government bonds in domestic currencies without indexation. Once the market turned, economic indicators improved and levels of government debt declined. The valuation of the real from 4.0 to the dollar in 2002 to 2.8 in second quarter 2003 reduced both inflationary pressures and the level of government debt. Given that roughly 30 percent of government paper was indexed to foreign currencies, the 25 percent reduction in the value of foreign currencies translates into significant reductions in federal government debt.

Epistemic communities of monetary policy making

The politics of monetary policy making that ended inertial inflation and used emerging market currency crises as enabling constraints to implement reforms and Central Bank modernization also involved a new generation of monetary economists and policy makers. Independent research institutes, graduate schools of economics and the Central Bank research division have adapted new concepts and theories from monetary economics and frameworks for monetary policy making from abroad such as inflation targeting, credit and interest rate channels, pass-through estimates for foreign exchange rate fluctuations, the importance of market forecasts, futures markets for interest rates and foreign exchange and Central Bank policies of communication and transparency to ensure market confidence.

This section focuses on several contributions of research on monetary economics and policy that informed central banking and monetary policy making in Brazil.

The specification of monetary policy channels is critical for the management of down-market credit cycles and new strategies for financial inclusion. However, the importance of expectations as determinant of inflation also suggests that maintaining the confidence of economic agents is critical. This is at the centre of the theory of monetary statecraft because optimal monetary policy requires maintaining market confidence as a prerequisite for policy initiatives. Innovations in monetary theory and analysis have thereby specified the importance of monetary channels such as the interest rate channel, the credit channel and the channel for pass through of foreign exchange devaluation or valuation on domestic prices and economic growth. However, this new framework for monetary policy management also provides new parameters for policies of social inclusion.

Minela and Souza-Sobrinho (2011) improved estimates for the timing of adjustment by decomposing monetary policy transmission into interest rate channels for households, firms and foreign exchange fluctuations.[14] They find that households are the most important factor causing monetary shocks to decrease economic activity, but that both the household interest rate channel and foreign exchange rate are key mechanisms for transmission of Central Bank monetary policy, while expectations determine the impact of monetary policies on inflation (see Table 5.5). Minella and Souza-Sobrinho also emphasize the critical role of futures markets for SELIC benchmark interest rates as information source and reference for monetary policy committee interest rate decisions. Analyses of monetary shocks in Brazil also confirm steeper declines for household consumption, investments, exports, industrial capacity and steeper increases of unemployment and inflation.

Santos and Leon argue that liberalization of the Brazilian economy helped control inflation during 2008, confirming the globalization and inflation hypothesis whereby foreign competition places downward price pressures on domestic

Table 5.5 Monetary policy channels and expectations, 4–12 quarters

	Channel	4 quarters	8 quarters	12 quarters
GDP	Interest Rates on Households	41.1	37.2	32.9
	Interest Rates on Firms	15.9	15.1	13.1
	Foreign Exchange	4.4	24.9	40.6
	Expectations	38.4	22.7	13.5
	Total	100.0	100.0	100.0
Inflation	Interest Rates on Households	6.4	10.4	9.3
	Interest Rates on Firms	1.7	4	3.5
	Foreign Exchange	12.5	8.8	10
	Expectations	79.4	76.7	77.2
	Total	100.0	100.0	100.0

Source: Minella, André and Souza-Sobrinho, Nelson. 'Canais Monetários no Brasil sob a Ótica de um Modelo Semiestrutural,' in Central Bank of Brazil. 'Dez Anos de Metas para a Inflação no Brasil, 1999–2009', 2011, p. 81.

producers.[15] Figueiredo and Gouvea report further evidence of this downward pressure on prices in Brazil, but suggest that 15 *fold* variations in price rigidities across sector and products require that disaggregation is required to assess the impact.[16]

Another line of inquiry in monetary research in Brazil emphasizes the importance of market forecasts and futures markets for improved information that ensures that policies converge with market expectations. During the monetary chaos and repeated price and wage freezes of the 1980s and early 1990s, information about the state of the economy and markets remained poor. From 1994 to 1999, a fixed foreign exchange rate served as a nominal anchor for the convergence of expectations. Since floating the real amidst crisis and the adoption of inflation targeting, the Central Bank has adopted new strategies to improve the quality of information and ensure consonance between policies, expectations of economic agents and prices. Two innovations proved critical: the development and timely publication of Central Bank surveys designed to tap the forecasts of top banks and consulting firms and the organization of futures markets for interest rates and foreign exchange rates on the BMF commodity exchange in São Paulo. Monetary statecraft describes how new policies at the Central Bank promoted transition toward greater transparency and convergence between monetary policy targets and measures, the expectations of investor and market perceptions.

Carvalho and Minella find that market forecasts tapped by the *Focus* survey of top banks and consulting firms improved the credibility of inflation targeting and monetary policy making, while private sector forecasts more accurately predicted trends than standard (ARMA, VAR and BVAR) forecasting software *and have improved* over time since 2001.[17] The *Focus* survey has thereby helped align inflationary expectations, control inflation and sustain access to finance.

For Silva *et al.* (2011), Monetary Policy Committee communication strategies have evolved under inflation targeting to reduce information asymmetries and improve transparency by adapting best practices from abroad as promoted by the BIS and central banks in advanced economies.[18] Focusing investor perceptions on monetary policy decisions helped reduce uncertainty and improve access to capital markets. Silva *et al.* place the complexity of Central Bank communication under inflation targeting in Brazil on top of the scale of monetary regimes developed by Blinder *et al.*, requiring less complex management than multiple mandates retained by the US Federal Reserve (dollarization, currency board, managed foreign exchange, inflation targeting, multiple mandates). Compilation of Monetary Policy Committee decisions from 1996 to 2014 suggest the evolution of statements by monetary authorities from broad contextual justifications to more specific parameters for policy decisions.

Lima et al. (2011) review the economic models used to frame debate in the Monetary Policy Committee: inflation indicators, short-term VAR models, semi-structural models to estimate inflation scenarios; specification of inflation scenarios with intermediate macroeconomic models; DSGE model estimation of inflation scenarios.[19] However, the increasing importance of futures markets for interest rates and foreign exchange suggest that inferences from economic models are tempered by market perceptions and prices. This enables monetary authorities to align policy with markets and reinforces the importance of the quality and transparency of information supplied by the Central Bank and Treasury.

The modernization of Central Bank communication includes launch of new measures for government accounts, national accounts and credit risk. In 1998, the Central Bank and Treasury launched new measures for liquid government debt, monthly publication of sub-national government debt, and separated the results of state owned enterprises from government accounts. In 1999, the Central Bank and Treasury adopted daily reporting of international reserves, introduced a new measure for nucleus of inflation and required monthly reporting of credit portfolios held by banks in a new credit risk matrix composed of AA-H standards based on best practices from abroad. In 2000, quarterly reporting of national accounts and a new calendar for data publication schedules shortened intervals and increased the regulatory of information shared by the Central Bank and Treasury. In 2001, the Special Data Dissemination Standard of the International Monetary Fund was adopted, while gross central government debt and monthly reporting of M2, M3 and M4 monetary measures improved information about central economic indicators. In 2002, further position of international investments suggested by the IMF, and new quarterly indicators of long-term public debt and its determinants, measures of Brazilian foreign capital and separation of international reserve operations from current account and balance of payment market further improved the accuracy and relevance of information for market pricing. In 2003, a new payment-amortization index and foreign sustainability index were launched to improve information about government debt, while a new reporting system that integrated economic accounts with the IBGE was adopted in 2004. Finally, in 2005, national accounts were reported with seasonal adjustment, government debt stock was separated by instrument and the operations of credit cooperative and mercantile credit were also separated from other financial institutions.

In 2005, the International Institute for Finance (a Washington-based association of investment banks) ranked the Central Bank of Brazil at the top of all measures of transparency in monetary policy making.[20] In 2014, information management divisions of the Central Bank circulated publications (annual reports, quarterly financial stability reports and inflation reports, monthly bulletins, bi-weekly *Focus* forecasting surveys and investor relation presentations) to over 24,000 email addresses of investors, journalists, banks, financial institutions and Central Bank watchers and researchers. Annual Reports provide overviews of policy making. Financial Stability Reports provide quarterly overviews of global and domestic macroeconomic and monetary developments and in depth review of the performance and risk profile of banks, credit and capital markets. Annual Inflation Reports review monetary policy committee decisions and economic developments related to inflation targeting policies. Annual and Monthly Bulletins report data updates that provide grounds for monetary policy committee meeting decisions. Since 2000, 360 working papers have reported research on the theory and practice of central banking, monetary policy and economics (dozens republished in peer reviewed journals). Since 2001, the Central Bank conducts a fortnightly survey of forecasts by the top 120 bank and consulting firm in the country, publishing reports with average and standard deviation of over 15 monetary and economic variables for current and future two calendar years. Online provision of time series of forecasting data was recognized in 2010 by the World Bank as fundamental for monetary policy making that improved adjustment to the 2008 global financial crisis and permitted sustained social policy and antipoverty initiatives during the global economic downturn.

Monetary statecraft and the composition of money (1994–2014)

Before turning to new monetary channels of change in Brazil, discussion of trends in the composition of money after 1994 is in order. First, evidence from 1994–2014 suggests that the multiplication of money has occurred primarily because of the capitalization of corporate bonds and mutual funds. In comparison, traditional money categories such as cash and savings deposits have declined as a share of the total money supply. Second, a bias toward the private sector appears in this trend. The capitalization of private pension funds, mutual funds, and corporate bond issues is marked, while government bonds remain restricted to the federal treasury and a very select number of sub-national public entities; most state-owned enterprises transformed into mixed companies. In comparison to deep markets for local and state government bonds in advanced economies, prohibition of sub-national finance in in Brazil in 1997 (formalized in 2000 fiscal responsibility legislation) has hamstrung public finance and slowed the economy.[21]

Third, the changing composition of the money supply since 1994 suggests that past practices of monetary statecraft such as paper emissions pale in comparison to the multiplication of money by financial markets and banks (see Table 5.6). This suggests that post-Keynesian theories of money better describe the monetary phenomena explored in this section than neo-classical theories. The most traditional category of money is M1 and is composed of cash held by the public and sight deposits. This restricted measure of money increased nominally from 22.7 to 305.3 billion reals between 1994 and 2014 but declined as a percent of the broader money supply from 12.9 to 6.5 percent.

Traditional savings accounts also increased nominally from 45.7 to 628.9 billion reals between 1994 and 2014, but declined as a portion of the broader money supply from 25.9 to 13.4 percent. The second category of M2, that of corporate bonds, increased from 60.5 billion reals to over 1 trillion reals during this same period, representing over a twofold increase from 6.1 to 21.4 percent of the broader (M4) money supply. The total value of savings accounts and corporate bonds increased from R$132.5 billion to R$2.02 trillion, but declined by almost half as a percent of the broad money supply from 62.2 to 36.5 percent.

The bulk of increases in the broader money supply came from mutual funds and government bond operations, defined by the Central Bank as M3. From 1994 to 2014, mutual funds increased from 21.9 billion to over 1.8 trillion reals (from 12.4 to 39.4 percent of broad money supply), while secondary market operations

Table 5.6 Composition of money (1994–2014)

	M1	M1%	Savings Dep's	Corp Bonds	M2	M2%	Gov Mutual Funds	Bond Op's	M3	M3%	Gov Bonds Fed.	Gov Bonds S-M	M4%	Broad M4
1994	22.7	13%	45.7	60.5	132.5	60%	21.9		154.5	12%	18.2	3.6	12%	176.4
1995	28.4	11%	64.2	85.9	178.7	58%	46.2		225.0	18%	30.8	5.2	14%	261.1
1996	29.8	9%	72.6	86.2	188.7	47%	97.2		285.9	29%	45.7	4.4	15%	336.1
1997	47.3	12%	98.2	94.2	239.7	47%	100.4		340.2	25%	62.0	3.7	16%	405.9
1998	50.7	11%	108.4	95.8	254.9	44%	121.0		376.0	26%	80.9	2.3	18%	459.3
1999	62.7	11%	111.4	100.6	274.7	38%	184.3	9.5	468.7	35%	80.8	1.5	15%	551.0
2000	74.3	11%	111.9	97.4	283.7	32%	253.8	18.9	556.5	42%	93.6	1.8	15%	652.0
2001	83.7	11%	120.0	117.8	321.6	31%	285.3	18.1	625.0	40%	128.5	2.5	17%	756.1
2002	107.8	13%	140.8	148.7	397.5	36%	279.5	11.2	688.2	36%	117.3	1.9	15%	807.5
2003	109.6	11%	144.1	159.1	412.8	32%	408.0	17.3	838.3	44%	119.3	0.7	13%	958.4
2004	127.9	12%	159.5	205.5	493.4	33%	474.8	20.3	988.6	45%	120.0	0.8	11%	1,109.5
2005	144.7	11%	169.3	267.1	582.4	33%	559.1	24.8	1,166.5	45%	144.9	0.9	11%	1,312.3
2006	174.3	11%	187.8	295.5	661.5	31%	684.0	32.1	1,377.7	46%	180.8		12%	1,558.6
2007	231.4	12%	234.6	310.9	781.2	29%	793.8	42.5	1,617.6	44%	267.2		14%	1,884.8
2008	223.4	10%	271.1	575.0	1,072.9	38%	775.1	60.0	1,908.1	37%	333.9		15%	2,242.1
2009	250.2	10%	319.6	594.3	1,167.4	35%	930.4	108.4	2,206.3	40%	398.5		15%	2,604.9
2010	280.1	9%	379.6	697.6	1,360.6	35%	1,116.7	70.5	2,548.0	39%	490.7		16%	3,038.7
2011	285.3	8%	420.8	911.2	1,617.4	38%	1,326.3	86.4	3,030.2	40%	519.9		15%	3,550.2
2012	324.4	8%	497.1	942.4	1,764.0	35%	1,600.8	153.5	3,518.4	43%	584.6		14%	4,103.1
2013	344.8	8%	599.8	1,012.5	1,957.1	36%	1,736.9	130.0	3,824.2	42%	635.1		14%	4,459.3
2014	305.3	6%	628.9	1,088.1	2,022.3	37%	851.4	127.2	4,001.0	42%	697.3		15%	4,698.4

Source: Central Bank of Brazil, available at www.bcb.gov.br
S-M = State and municipal

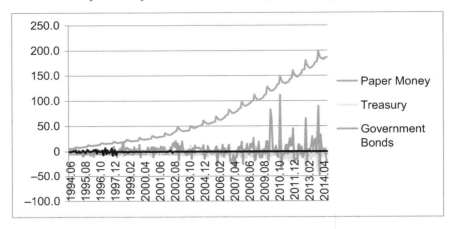

Figure 5.6 Means of money supply management (1994–2014, R$ billion)

Source: Ipeadata

involving government bonds increased nominally from 9.5 to 127.2 billion reals (but declined from 5.4 to 2.7 percent of the broad money supply) from 1999 to 2014.

Finally, the category of M4 (government bonds) increased nominally from R$176.4 billion to over R$4.6 trillion, representing a slight increased share of the total money supply, from 12.9 to 14.8 percent.

In sum, since the end of inertial inflation in 1994, the value of cash held by the public and traditional savings accounts increase nominally, but decline to a very small portion of the total money supply. Instead, corporate and government bond issues, mutual funds and secondary markets for government bonds are behind the increase in the broader money supply in Brazil.

This relative decline of paper money and bank deposits and increase in the capitalization of bond markets has led to changes in the means of monetary policy. Instead of past policies of Central Bank discount lending to banks, monetary authorities increasingly used Treasury operations on capital markets to issue or purchase treasury bonds by the Central Bank to manage the supply of money. Further data from the Central Bank on the factors that condition the money supply suggest this change in policy. Figure 5.6 reports the value of Central Bank discounting, Treasury operations and government bond issues and the total supply of paper money from 1994 to 2014.

Several observations are in order. First, the value of Central Bank discount loans to banks falls to zero after 1998 and, notably, does not recur as part of monetary policies after the global financial crisis hit Brazil during 2008. In comparison to the widespread use of Central Bank discount loans to sustain liquidity during the global financial crisis of 2007–2008, the Central Bank of Brazil did not use such policies. Second, Treasury operations and, especially, government bond issues increase in value during the period in question to become reach, briefly, near the total value of paper money circulating in Brazil, especially after 2010. Sales and purchases of government bonds by the Central Bank[22] increased substantially during 2010, not as emergency measures amidst crisis but as counter cyclical policies designed to increase the flow of credit from banks or, alternatively, to reduce the flow of credit and alleviate inflationary pressures. A proviso is needed here. Although sale and purchase of government bonds are widely seen to be a central monetary policy instrument, in Brazil and abroad, the large value of government bond sales after 2010 is such that it seems unlikely that this is the type of 'light touch' by a central bank through market operations that is usually referred to in this context. Instead, government bond operations appear to be caused by other cyclical phenomena in government accounts and the calendar of public finance obligations.

National financial accounts (2004–2009)

Another view of broader changes of money in Brazil is available from new national financial account data on the balance sheets of households, banks, firms, governments and the rest of the world produced by the Central Bank and Instituto Brasileiro de Geografia e Estatística (Brazilian Institute of Geography and Statistics, IBGE). Although currently limited to the 2004–2009 period, national financial account data nonetheless enable use of new methods and concepts from monetary economics to reconsider the politics of monetary policy in Brazil and draw comparative observations. Traditional national accounts measure the gross national product as a total of consumption and investment. The gross domestic product of Brazil sums to *far below* the value of financial accounts reported for the 2004–2009 period (see Table 5.7). From 2004 to 2009, the value of financial assets in Brazil increased from 9.1 to 18.2 *trillion* reals, far above the value and pace of GDP during the same period, which increased from 1.8 to 2.2 trillion reals.

The doubling of financial assets during five years in Brazil from 2005 to 2009 runs contrary to assumptions about the neutrality of money and financial flows. This section explores this anomaly for neo-classical theory through the following observations. First, from theories of financialization we attempt to trace how the

Table 5.7 Brazilian financial assets and GDP (2004–2009, R$ trillion)

	2004	*2005*	*2006*	*2007*	*2008*	*2009*
Banks	3.5	4.3	5.2	6.5	7.6	8.7
percent total financial assets	39%	41%	42%	45%	49%	48%
Firms	2.3	2.8	3.3	3.9	3.7	4.5
percent total financial assets	26%	27%	27%	27%	24%	25%
Government	1.8	1.9	2.1	2.2	2.3	2.6
percent total financial assets	20%	19%	17%	15%	15%	14%
Households*	1.3	1.5	1.6	1.9	1.9	2.3
percent total financial assets	15%	14%	13%	13%	12%	13%
Total Financial Assets	9.1	10.6	12.3	14.7	15.7	18.2
GDP	1.8	2.1	2.3	2.6	3.0	2.2

Source: Central Bank of Brasil, Contas de Patrimonio Financeiro, available at http://www.bcb.gov. br/?SERIECONTAPAF

capitalization of assets and increases in credit produce fundamental changes in political economy. Second, the fact that money and financial assets and liabilities are accumulate far differently across economic sectors suggests that stock-flow approaches in monetary economics provide opportunities for analysis of monetary statecraft. Third, the fact that financial assets and liabilities accumulate far differently across countries suggests that national financial accounts provide opportunities for comparative analysis of monetary statecraft.

These issues need to be discussed separately. First, the doubling of financial assets in Brazil from 2004 to 2009 suggests the importance of post-Keynesian theories of financial instability and recent debates about the causes and consequences of financialization. However, the doubling of financial assets in Brazil during the years of global financial crisis suggests that past vulnerabilities may have given way to different processes.

Second, the accumulation of financial assets in Brazil did not occur equally across sectors. Instead, banks increased financial assets from 3.5 to 8.7 trillion reals representing an increase in bank share of total financial assets in Brazil from 39 to 48 percent *in five years* (see Table 5.8). In a broader sense, this accumulation of assets (and liabilities) in bank balance sheets in Brazil from 2004 to 2009 is similar to processes of financialization reported in advanced and developing economies. Below we disaggregate these data from national financial accounts.

In comparative perspective, the valuation of financial assets in Brazil 2004–2009 stands out in several respects. First, banks in Brazil increased their share of

Table 5.8 Financial assets in Brazil by sector (2004–2009, R$billion)

	2004	2005	2006	2007	2008	2009
Non-financial Firms, total	2,377.7	2,824.6	3,347.1	3,915.1	3,760.4	4,549.0
Cash + Deposits	206.2	251.9	309.6	376.5	384.9	419.4
Bonds	100.4	119.6	134.8	126.3	237.0	225.8
Loans	110.4	131.7	150.8	60.4	52.8	52.5
Stocks	1,220.3	1,502.3	1,911.0	2,396.1	1,979.8	2,646.9
Reserves + Insurance	4.9	5.9	6.7	7.7	8.9	10.1
Other	735.3	812.9	833.9	947.8	1,096.8	1.194.0
Financial Institutions, total	3,583.7	4,311.8	5,206.4	6,575.0	7,693.6	8,758.8
Gold + Special Deposits at IMF	1.2	1.3	1.4	1.5	2.1	9.8
Cash + Deposits	304.0	372.5	465.9	694.5	668.7	773.4
Bonds	1,326.9	1.5	1,861.5	2,223.7	2,693.0	2,937.3
Loans	841.9	1,008.6	1,250.4	1,714.6	2,195.7	2,652.4
Stocks	814.4	1,058.4	1,300.6	1,611.4	1,625.1	1,924.8
Reserves + Insurance	1.4	1.6	2.1	2.3	2.8	2.9
Other	293.4	308.3	324.0	326.7	505.8	457.9
Government, total	1,828.9	1,981.0	2,113.0	2,285.4	2,345.9	2,644.6
Cash + Deposits	381.8	468.3	508.4	577.2	589.1	847.7
Bonds	40.9	46.8	49.0	55.7	77.2	72.1
Loans	461.6	461.9	475.3	479.0	565.5	652.9
Stocks	219.4	265.6	328.7	389.8	355.7	393.4

(Continued)

Table 5.8 (Continued)

	2004	2005	2006	2007	2008	2009
Reserves + Insurance	1	1	1	2	2	2
Other	724.9	738.0	751.3	783.3	758.0	677.9
Households,* total	1,367.0	1,509.0	1,658.5	1,967.1	1,974.8	2,310.6
Cash + Deposits	228.6	244.9	279.5	345.3	393.2	459.6
Bonds	46.9	63.5	77.2	86.1	186.5	192.5
Stocks	411.8	501.7	613.8	763.0	616.7	777.2
Reserves + Insurance	312.9	358.7	418.3	488.2	544.5	623.2
Other	368.5	340.0	269.5	284.3	233.8	257.9
Total	9,157.4	10,626.5	12,325.2	14,742.8	15,774.9	18,263.1
Gold + special deposits at IMF	1.2	1.3	1.4	1.5	2.1	9.8
Cash + Deposits	1,120.7	1,337.7	1,563.6	1,993.6	2,036.1	2,500.3
Bonds	1,515.3	1,790.8	2,122.6	2,492.0	3,193.9	3,427.9
Loans	1,423.5	1,612.3	1,887.1	2,264.6	2,827.8	3,370.9
Stocks	2,666.0	3,328.2	4,154.2	5,160.5	4,577.5	5,742.5
Reserves + Insurance	319.5	366.5	427.5	498.6	556.6	636.6
Other	2,110.9	2,189.4	2,168.4	2,331.6	2,580.7	2,574.9

Source: Central Bank of Brazil, Contas Patrimoniais available at http://www.bcb.gov.br/?SERIE CONTAPAF

Table 5.9 US financial assets and GDP (2004–2009, US$ trillion)

	2004	2005	2006	2007	2008	2009
Banks	53.0	57.4	63.3	69.5	68.9	69.9
percent total financial assets	37.7%	34.5%	31.4%	29.1%	30.6%	30.6%
Firms	34.8	38.7	41.8	45.5	42.8	39.2
percent total financial assets	24.80%	25.2%	24.8%	25.0%	24.8%	22.6%
Government	10.6	11.6	12.7	13.8	14.9	15.1
percent total financial assets	7.5%	7.6%	7.6%	7.6%	8.6%	8.7%
Households	41.9	45.5	50.3	53.0	46.0	48.6
percent total financial assets	29.8%	29.6%	29.9%	29.1%	26.6%	28.1%
Total Financial Assets	140.4	153.3	168.3	181.8	172.7	172.9
GDP	12.2	13.0	13.8	14.4	14.7	14.4

Source: Federal Reserve Bank, Z1 accounts

domestic financial assets from 39 to 48 percent between 2004 and 2009, a period of bubble and crisis during which banks in the United States lost share of total financial assets from 37.7 to 30.6 percent (see Table 5.9). The share of financial assets held by firms and governments remained largely stable during this period of crisis, both in the United States and Brazil, confirming that these sectors manage *liabilities* rather than assets.

However, households in the United States hold almost twice as large a share of national financial assets compared to Brazilian households. In the United States, the household share of financial assets declined in 2008 (from 29.1 to 26.6 percent of total) during the financial crisis, but recovered in 2009. In comparison, the share of Brazilian households of financial assets declined gradually from 2004 to 2009 to remain at 13 percent of the total.

National financial accounts also differ from traditional measures of gross national product because they measure *flows across sectors* in terms of financial products and services. Measures and models of national accounts define gross domestic product as the sum of total expenditure of final goods and services for private and government consumption and investment, plus the value of exports minus the value of imports. Private consumption and investment is traditionally separated into the respective consumption and investments of households, firms and banks, each with a different profile and place in the political economy. National *financial* accounts take a different approach that has few obvious relations to traditional measures of national accounts.

National financial accounts measure (1) the *flow of funds* between households, firms, banks and government *as a matrix of assets and liabilities* and (2) the *stock* of financial assets and liabilities *as capital or net worth* of households, banks and

Table 5.10 Financial liabilities in Brazil (2004–2009, R$billion)

Firms	2004	2005	2006	2007	2008	2009
Bonds	112.9	102.9	112.8	112.2	150.1	158.4
Loans	461.2	525.9	631.5	623.0	847.7	926.0
Stocks	1,765.7	2,135.8	2,646.4	3,458.0	2,717.8	3,682.7
Other	1,196.0	1,209.6	1,169.9	1,197.2	1,245.8	1,142.3
Total	3,536.0	3,974.3	4,560.8	5,390.5	4,961.6	5,909.5
Banks						
Cash & Deposits	1,043.9	1,276.8	1,507.5	1,949.4	1,984.6	2,454.2
Bonds	353.8	462.1	584.9	706.1	1,067.0	1,087.2
Loans	492.8	472.0	580.6	846.0	1,109.8	1,433.4
Stocks	1,336.1	1,711.5	2,129.6	2,627.7	2,480.2	3,056.9
Insurance	320.2	367.1	428.3	499.3	557.5	637.3
Other	348.4	378.9	347.0	354.5	441.9	381.0
Total	3,895.4	4,668.7	5,578.2	6,983.1	7,641.2	9,050.3
Government						
Bonds	1,228.0	1,354.4	1,473.7	1,610.5	1,811.4	2,083.4
Loans	518.5	509.6	524.7	511.4	575.7	561.4
Other	233.8	239.1	295.8	392.3	462.9	567.6
Total	1,980.4	2,103.2	2,294.3	2,514.4	2,850.1	3,212.5
Households						
Loans	193.6	249.6	304.5	394.8	505.3	596.3
Other	346.8	375.1	379.5	423.8	482.2	551.8
Total	540.5	624.7	684.1	818.7	987.5	1,148.1

Source: Central Bank of Brazil, Contas Patrimoniais available at http://www.bcb.gov.br/?SERIE CONTAPAF

government. Funds flow across sectors. Each sector retains different balances of assets and liabilities, but balance sheets offset one another such that the total value of national assets remains equal to the total value of national liabilities. The same applies to the balance sheets of countries with the rest of the world. The net worth of sectors and the total stock of national balance sheets may thereby increase or decrease.

The categories of assets and liabilities reported for Brazil from 2004 to 2009 are cash, deposits, loans, bonds and equities (see Table 5.10). This makes it possible to analyze money in a new way by tracing the financial assets and liabilities of households, firms, banks and governments and between these sectors and the rest of the world. This provides new perspectives on the politics of monetary policy. Although data from Brazil fail to report the entire repertoire of accounting categories used in broader monetary economics models, data do permit estimates of net flows of funds between households, firms, banks and government (and the rest of the world). Data from 2005–2009 capture a period of substantial growth culminating in credit crunch during 2008 as the global financial crisis abroad hit Brazil and caused a brief but steep retraction of GDP during second semester 2008. The net flows of financial assets from government to banks, firms and households suggest the importance of countercyclical policies through a variety of channels.

Table 5.11 summarizes a balance sheet matrix of money and financial flows and stocks in Brazil (leaving aside the question of relations with the rest of the world).

Table 5.11 Balance sheet matrix of national financial accounts

	Closed Economy	*R$*			*Total*
	Households	*Firms*	*Banks*	*Government*	
Cash	+Ch			−Cg	0
Deposits	+Dh		−Db		0
Loans	−Lh	−Lf	+Lb		0
Bonds	+Bh		+Bb	−Bg	0
Equities	+Eh	−Ef			0
Financial Net Worth	*NWh*	*NWf*	*NWb*	*NWg*	*K*

Source: Godley, Wynne and Lavoie, Marc. *Monetary Economics: An Integrated Approach to Credit, Money, Income, Production and Wealth* (London: Palgrave, 2007).

National Financial Accounts Categories, Closed Economy
+Ch = Household cash assets   −Cg = Government cash liabilities
+Dh = Household deposit assets   −Db = Bank deposit liabilities
−Lh = Household loan liabilities   −Lf = Firm loan liabilities
+Lb = Bank loan assets   +Bh = Household bond assets
+Bb = Bank bond assets   +Eh = Household equity assets
−Ef = Firm equity liabilities   NWh = Household net worth
NWf = Firm net worth   NWg = Net worth government
K = Total capital

Table 5.12 Net financial flows (2005–2009, R$billion)

	2005	2006	2007	2008	2009
Households	10.0	10.8	6.7	8.1	3.1
Firms	20.8	28.4	−22.9	−69.8	2.5
Banks	56.7	92.1	139.4	92.0	83.3
Government	−61.4	−109.9	−128.2	−86.5	−149.3
Brazil/World	26.1	21.4	−5.0	−56.1	−60.3

The four columns of the matrix for a closed economy (households, firms, banks and government) and five categories of money and financial assets (cash, deposits, loans, bonds and equities) sum to describe the net worth of each sector and totals for financial capital in Brazil.

To this matrix of a closed economy, one can add relations with the rest of the world that capture monetary phenomena of an open economy (see Table 5.12). Because flows between Brazil and the rest of the world also sum to the total financial capital, this implies that international financial flows into and out of Brazil must be absorbed as assets or liabilities by households, firms, banks and government.

Comparing national financial account data from Brazil with data from the United States and Germany suggests promising means to reassess politics and monetary policy. First, competing theories and approaches in political economy differ about how economic sectors and different types of financial assets and liabilities interact to determine development, growth, welfare and business cycles. Households tend to hold positive balance sheets consisting of cash, bank deposits and personal investments. However, by taking on loans for homes or consumption, debt may increase liabilities over assets. Firms tend to hold negative balance sheets because investments produce growth, with liabilities created through sale of equities or loans from banks. Banks traditionally balanced assets and liabilities, while market-based banking emphasizes how banks increasingly manufacture assets on capital markets. Governments traditionally hold large liabilities in the form of cash, as provider of the domestic currency. Governments also issue bonds that anticipate tax receipts to finance public works or to provide liquidity to reverse economic downturns and financial crises. Negative or positive financial balances thereby differ fundamentally across and within households, firms and banks and between national economies and the rest of the world.

One of the central arguments of this book is that large marginal gains, and risks, incur during the recovery of markets for money, credit and finance. Because of the extremely shallow point of departure in the early 1990s, money and financial balance sheets in Brazil still pale in comparison to advanced economies. Tables 5.13–5.15 on the following pages present the value of liabilities and assets held by banks, firms, households, governments and their domestic economies with the rest of the world for Brazil, the United States and Germany from 2005 to 2009, both in US dollars and as percent of GDP.

Based on data from 2005 to 2009, the balance sheets of Brazilian banks remain, in US dollars, less than 1 percent of US banks and 4.2 percent of German banks. Even if measured more favorably as a percent of GDP, the balance sheets of Brazilian banks hold *8 percent* of US banks and *8.7 percent* of German banks. Brazilian banks remain profoundly underdeveloped, a legacy from the disorganization of money, banking and finance during military and transition governments in the 1980s and early 1990s.

Table 5.13 Brazilian sectoral financial balance sheets (2005–2009, US$billion)

		2005	*2006*	*2007*	*2008*	*2009*
Banks	Liabilities US$ billion	302.8	333.9	617.5	364.3	631.3
	Liabilities %GDP	34.3%	30.6%	45.1%	22.0%	38.9%
	Assets	328.8	376.8	696.3	404.3	679.7
	Assets %GDP	37.2%	34.6%	50.9%	24.4%	41.9%
	Net Fin.Worth US$ billion	26.0	42.8	78.8	40.0	48.4
Firms	Liabilities US$ billion	123.9	88.1	109.8	191.2	122.7
	Liabilities %GDP	14.0%	8.0%	8.0%	11.5%	7.5%
	Assets	133.4	101.3	96.8	160.9	124.2
	Assets %GDP	15.1%	9.3%	7.0%	9.7%	7.6%
	Net Fin.Worth	9.5	13.2	−12.9	−30.3	1.5
Households	Liabilities US$ billion	38.7	27.6	76.1	73.2	93.7
	Liabilities %GDP	4.3%	2.5%	5.5%	4.4%	5.7%
	Assets	43.3	32.7	79.9	76.8	95.5
	Assets %GDP	4.9%	3.0%	5.8%	4.6%	5.8%
	Net Fin.Worth	4.6	5.0	3.8	3.5	1.8
Government	Liabilities US$ billion	78.1	83.8	125.5	110.3	215.9
	Liabilities %GDP	8.9%	7.7%	9.2%	6.7%	13.3%
	Assets	49.9	32.7	53.1	72.7	129.1
	Assets %GDP	5.6%	3.0%	3.8%	4.4%	7.9%
	Net Fin.Worth	−28.2	−51.1	−72.4	−37.6	−86.8
	Net Fin.Worth %GDP	−3.2%	−4.7%	−5.3%	−2.3%	−5.4%
Rest of World	Liabilities US$ billion	11.4	62.7	119.7	10.5	54.6
	Liabilities %GDP	1.2%	5.7%	8.7%	0.6%	3.3%
	Assets	−0.6	52.7	122.5	34.9	89.7
	Assets %GDP	−0.1%	4.8%	8.9%	2.1%	5.5%
	Net Fin.Worth	−12.0	−10.0	2.8	24.4	35.1
	Net Fin.Worth %GDP	−1.4%	−0.9%	0.2%	1.5%	2.2%
GDP		882.1	1088.9	1366.8	1653.5	1620.1

Source: Central Bank of Brazil. Contas Patrimoniais.

Table 5.14 US sectoral financial balance sheets (US$ trillion)

		2005	2006	2007	2008	2009
Banks	Liabilities US$ trillion	56.1	61.9	68	67.3	68.4
	Liabilities %GDP	428.2%	448.5%	472.2%	457.8%	475.0%
	Assets US$ trillion	58.6	64.8	69.8	67.6	68.9
	Assets %GDP	447.3%	469.5%	484.7%	459.8%	478.4%
	Net Fin. Worth	2.4	2.9	1.8	0.2	0.5
Firms	Liabilities US$ trillion	11.9	12.6	13.7	12.9	13.3
	Liabilities %GDP	90.8%	91.3%	95.1%	87.7%	92.3%
	Assets US$ trillion	23.8	26.4	28.6	23.2	25.4
	Assets %GDP	181.6%	191.3%	198.6%	157.8%	176.3%
	Net Fin. Worth	11.9	13.7	14.8	10.3	12.0
Households	Liabilities US$ trillion	12.1	13.4	14.3	14.2	14.0
	Liabilities %GDP	92.3%	97.1%	99.3%	96.6%	97.2%
	Assets US$ trillion	45.5	50.3	53.0	46.0	48.6
	Assets %GDP	347.3%	364.4%	368.0%	312.9%	337.5%
	Net Fin. Worth	−33.3	−36.8	−38.6	−31.7	−34.5
Government	Liabilities US$ trillion	10.7	11.0	11.6	14.1	15.7
	Liabilities %GDP	81.7%	79.7%	80.6%	95.9%	109.0%
	Assets US$ trillion	2.9	3.2	3.4	3.9	4.0
	Assets %GDP	22.1%	23.2%	23.6%	26.5%	27.8%
	Net Fin. Worth	−7.8	−7.8	8.2	−10.2	−11.7
	Net Fin. Worth %GDP	−59.5%	−56.5%	56.9%	−69.4%	−81.3%
Rest of World	Liabilities US$ trillion	10.6	12.8	14.5	13.6	14.3
	Liabilities %GDP	80.9%	92.7%	100.6%	92.5%	99.3%
	Assets US$ trillion	9.0	11.0	13.4	10.6	12.1
	Assets %GDP	68.7%	79.7%	93.0%	72.1%	84.0%
	Net Fin. Worth	−1.6	−1.7	−1.1	−3.0	−2.2
	Net Fin. Worth %GDP	−12.2%	−12.3%	−7.6%	−20.4%	−15.3%
GDP		13.1	13.8	14.4	14.7	14.4

Source: Federal Reserve Board. 'Z.1 Financial Accounts of the United States Flow of Funds, Balance Sheets, and Integrated Macroeconomic Accounts. Historical Annual Tables 2005–2014' (New York: Federal Reserve Board, 2015). Available at http://www.federalreserve.gov/releases/z1/Current/annuals/a2005-2014.pdf

The financial balance sheets of Brazilian firms also present much shallower profile than firms in the United States and Germany. In studies of corporate finance and monetary economics, firms are seen to manage financial balance sheets with negative net worth; because the real assets, types of capital and investments for the realization of future earning means that the liabilities, usually in the form of equity ownership or loans from banks Liabilities therefore remain far above financial assets held by firms. In this respect, one of the central indicators of financial and monetary development is the ability of firms to take on liabilities to accelerate innovation and production. In the high interest rate

Table 5.15 German sectoral financial balance sheets (US$ trillion)

		2005	2006	2007	2008	2009
Banks	Liabilities US$ trillion	15.40	11.70	14.20	12.10	14.70
	Liabilities %GDP	570.4%	403.4%	430.3%	336.1%	445.5%
	Assets US$ trillion	15.30	11.50	13.80	12.10	14.50
	Assets %GDP	566.7%	396.6%	418.2%	336.1%	439.4%
	Net Fin. Worth	−0.10	−0.20	−0.30	0.00	−0.20
Firms	Liabilities US$ trillion	6.00	4.70	6.10	4.50	5.50
	Liabilities %GDP	222.2%	162.1%	184.8%	125.0%	166.7%
	Assets US$ trillion	3.90	2.90	3.70	3.00	3.60
	Assets %GDP	144.4%	100.0%	112.1%	83.3%	109.1%
	Net Fin. Worth	−2.10	−1.80	2.30	−1.50	−1.80
Households	Liabilities US$ trillion	2.70	2.00	2.20	1.90	2.20
	Liabilities %GDP	100.0%	69.0%	66.7%	52.8%	66.7%
	Assets US$ trillion	7.40	5.40	6.60	5.40	6.60
	Assets %GDP	274.1%	186.2%	200.0%	150.0%	200.0%
	Net Fin. Worth	4.60	3.40	4.30	3.40	4.30
Government	Liabilities US$ trillion	2.80	2.00	2.30	2.10	2.70
	Liabilities %GDP	103.7%	69.0%	69.7%	58.3%	81.8%
	Assets US$ trillion	0.80	0.60	0.80	0.70	1.00
	Assets %GDP	29.6%	20.7%	24.2%	19.4%	30.3%
	Net Fin. Worth	−1.90	−1.40	−1.50	−1.30	−1.70
	Net Fin. Worth %GDP	−70.4%	−48.3%	−45.5%	−36.1%	−51.5%
Rest of World	Liabilities US$ trillion	7.20	5.90	7.50	6.30	7.70
	Liabilities %GDP	266.7%	203.4%	227.3%	175.0%	233.3%
	Assets US$ trillion	6.80	5.90	7.40	5.80	7.10
	Assets %GDP	251.9%	203.4%	224.2%	161.1%	215.2%
	Net Fin. Worth	−0.40	0.00	−0.10	−0.50	−0.60
	Net Fin. Worth %GDP	−14.8%	0.0%	−3.0%	−13.9%	−18.2%
GDP		2.70	2.90	3.30	3.60	3.30

Source: OECD national financial accounts available at https://stats.oecd.org/Index.aspx?DataSetCode=
SNA_TABLE610

environment of Brazil, the total value of liabilities held by firms also remains below 1 percent of US firms and below 2 percent of German firms. And, once again, even as a percent of GDP, the value of liabilities held by firms in Brazil remains *below 10 percent* of the value of liabilities taken on by firms in the United States and Germany.

A similar shallow profile obtains from data on households in Brazil in comparison to the United States and Germany. The high indebtedness of US households is universally seen as one of the major structural problems of the country and reason behind both the severity of the 2007 crisis and problems since. In terms of US dollars, the total liabilities of Brazilian households remains 0.66 percent of the value of households in the United States (93.7 US$billion vs 14 trillion) and

5.8 percent in terms of domestic GDPs (5.7 vs 97.2 percent of GDP). Brazilian households have emerged from monetary chaos amidst a still unprecedently high regime of interest rates to hold balance sheets largely matching liabilities with assets; both sides of household balance sheets increased gradually from 2005 to 2009. The liabilities of Brazilian households increased from 38.7 to 93.7 US$billion (4.3 to 5.7 percent of GDP), while their assets increased from 43.3 to 95.5 US$billion (4.9 to 5.8 percent of GDP). Households in Brazil thereby retain a total positive net financial worth of 4.6 US$billion in 2005, declining to 1.8 US$billion in 2009.

In comparison, US households increased liabilities from 12.1 to 14.0 trillion dollars 2005 to 2009, while assets reached from 45.5 to 53.0 trillion in the period 2005–2007 before declining to 46.0 trillion in 2008, leaving the total net financial worth reaching 38.6 trillion dollars in 2007. German households hold liabilities at far lower levels: 2.7 trillion dollars or 100.0 percent of GDP in 2005, declining to 2.2 trillion dollars or 66.7 percent of GDP. Meanwhile, the value of assets held by German households also declined from 7.4 to 6.6 trillion dollars or 274.1 to 200.0 percent GDP in the period 2004–2009, such that the net financial worth of households in Germany remained positive, albeit declining from 4.6 trillion to 4.3 trillion.

In sum, monetary statecraft in Brazil implied shaping monetary policy toward overcoming underdevelopment amidst still shallow markets for money and finance such that the conservatism of household financial management has just begun to emerge from past lifetime financial management strategies of saving to purchase homes and consumer durables in cash rather than obtain credit or finance. The cautious monetary policies of the Central Bank and monetary policy committee reinforce this extremely shallow level of financial portfolios and development in Brazil, made clearer by the comparative data that place Brazil far below levels of assets held by German households and liabilities enjoyed, in excess, by households in the United States.

The financial balance sheet of the Brazilian government also suggests how shallow markets for money and finance remain as context for monetary statecraft in the country. Theories of public finance and monetary economics emphasize the importance of government management of liabilities. We have traced the politics of monetary statecraft in Brazil since launching the first national bank in 1808 – 24 years before independence from Portuguese colonial rule. However, in comparative perspective, government liabilities remain dramatically lower than levels in advanced economies.

In comparative perspective based on the financial balance sheets of sectors, the Brazilian government increased dramatically access to domestic money by increasing liabilities from 78.1 to 215.9 billion dollars between 2005 and 2009, representing an increasing from 33.6 to 93.7 percent of GDP (government assets during this period increased from 49.9 to 129.1 billion dollars or 5.6 to 7.9 percent of GDP). This increased the negative net financial worth of the Brazilian government from −12 to 135.1 billion dollars or −3.2 to −5.5 percent of GDP.

In comparison, the US government increased liabilities from 10.7 to 15.7 trillion dollars in the period 2005–2009, representing an increase from 81.7 to

109.0 percent of GDP, while US government assets increased from 2.9 to 4.0 trillion, representing an increase from 22.1 to 27.8 percent of GDP. The negative net financial worth of the US government thereby increased from −7.8 to −11.7 trillion dollars (−59.5 to −81.3 percent of GDP). The different profile of the German government also obtains in decreasing liabilities from 2.8 to 2.0 trillion in 2005–2006 before crisis, but retaining liabilities at 2.7 trillion in 2009. This represents a decline of liabilities from 103.7 to 69.0 percent of GDP 2005–2006 and a return to 81.8 percent of GDP by 2009. The negative net worth of the German government thereby declined as a percent of GDP from 70.4 to 36.1 percent in 2005–2008 before returning to 51.5 percent GDP in 2009.

Comparing the financial accounts of the Brazilian government with data from the United States and Germany suggests the fundamentally different contexts for monetary statecraft. The value of government liabilities[23] in Brazil remain 1.3 percent of the value of liabilities assumed by governments in the United States in nominal terms and 12.2 percent in terms of respective gross domestic products. Brazilian government liabilities also remain 7.9 percent of the value of German government liabilities and 16.0 percent in terms of their respective gross domestic products. The negative net worth of governments provides further evidence of how shallow financial portfolios remain in Brazil. In 2009, the negative net worth of governments in Brazil (−5.4 percent of GDP) also remained far below the figures of −81.3 percent for the United States and −51.5 percent for Germany.

Finally, financial balance sheets between Brazil and the rest of the world provides further evidence of the different context for monetary statecraft in Brazil compared to advanced economies. Although total liabilities between Brazil and the rest of the world increased from 11.4 to 119.7 US dollars from 2005 to 2007, liabilities declined thereafter to 10.5 billion US dollars in 2009 to remain at 54.6 billion in 2009. These levels pale in comparison to data from the United States and Germany. The total liabilities of the United States with the rest of the world increased from 10.6 to 14.3 trillion dollars or from 80.9 to 99.3 percent of GDP. And Germany increased liabilities with the rest of the world nominally from 7.2 to 7.7 trillion US dollars, representing 266.7 and 233.3 percent of German GDP. It is of note that German assets overseas remain more balanced than the United States, also increasing from 6.8 to 7.1 trillion dollars (an increase from 2.7 to 3.3 trillion dollars at average annual euro–dollar exchange rate).

The negative net financial worth of the US domestic economy with the rest of the world therefore remains far greater than Germany or Brazil, increasing from −1.6 trillion in 2006, to 3.0 trillion in 2008, to decline to 2.2 trillion in 2009. This represents an increase from 12.2 to 20.4 percent of US GDP 2005–2008 before declining to 15.3 percent in 2009. This suggests the significant comparative advantage of the US for monetary policy making. Despite originating the global financial crisis in 2007–2008, the domestic economy of the United States, largely through issue of government securities, retained access to inexpensive money to fund emergency measures and counter-cyclical policy.

In comparison, the financial balance sheet of Brazil with the rest of the world suggests a much shallower relation, with liabilities and assets more balanced or matched than the United States. First, in comparison to the United States and, to a lesser degree, Germany, the different context for monetary statecraft in Brazil can be seen in the shallow financial relation between Brazil and the rest of the world. Brazilian liabilities with the rest of the world remain *0.38 percent* the value of US liabilities with the rest of the world if measured in US dollars, and 12.2 percent the value if measured in terms of respective GDPs (Brazil with 3.3 percent of GDP; the United States with liabilities of 99.3 percent of GDP in 2009). This represents a significant difference for monetary statecraft and indicates how the US dollar serving as reserve currency and US capital markets serving as global money markets provide the United States to massive amounts of cheap money for emergency policies and counter-cyclical monetary policies.

Second, both the assets and liabilities of Brazil with the rest of the world increased from 2005 to 2009 to produce a more matched balance sheet and positive net financial worth. While liabilities with the rest of the world increased from 11.4 to 54.6 billion dollars, assets also increased from −0.6 to 89.7 billion dollars or −0.1 to 5.5 percent of GDP. The net financial worth of the Brazilian economy with the rest of the world thereby increased from −12.0 billion (−1.4 percent GDP) to 35.1 billion (2.2 percent GDP from 2005 to 2009).

Further inferences from these comparisons of financial balance sheets are limited because no data from the United States and Germany are available to consider how real or fixed assets relate to the accumulation of financial assets and liabilities in and across these sectors. Moreover, the limited time span, from 2005 to 2009, and the aggregation of data on the specific types of financial assets and liabilities within each sector counsel caution regarding inferences from comparisons between Brazilian sectoral balance sheets and the United States and Germany. The global financial crisis in 2007–2008 surely is an outlier in terms of historical trends, one that inspires considerable debate across a variety of disciplines and fora in public policy. The balance sheets of banks, firms, households, government and domestic economies with the rest of the world also will need to be disaggregated to separate short-term accumulation of liabilities and assets from longer-term trends.

However, this exercise of reporting the balance sheets of sectors in Brazil and comparison of data with two advanced economies is limited in scope but nonetheless important; it clearly illustrates the wide gap between Brazilian markets for money and finance, the persistence of underdevelopment and the incipient levels of assets and liabilities held by banks, firms, households, governments and with the rest of the world.

Before turning to how monetary channels have served to accelerate financial inclusion and manage consumer-led growth, two observations about finance and inequality are in order.

Finance and inequality

Two broader concerns about finance and inequality suggest the importance of reconsidering theories of politics and monetary policy. First, in contexts of high financial returns and inequality such as Brazil, finance is transformed from a means to smooth consumption and investment across generations and social

Table 5.16 Simulation of lifetime personal asset accumulation by income quintiles for São Paulo City (1991–2040, R$)

Year	1/5	2/5	3/5	4/5	5/5	> 10%
1991	956.8	2,143.2	3,496.1	5,993.8	19,587.2	28,623.8
2000	735.7	1,965.4	3,424.0	6,353.4	24,124.2	36,022.0
2010	1,908.3	5,097.6	8,880.9	16,479.1	62,572.0	93,431.7
2020	4,949.6	13,222.0	23,034.7	42,742.5	162,295.6	242,337.7
2030	12,837.9	34,294.4	59,746.1	110,863.0	420,952.9	628,561.7
2040	33,298.1	88,950.7	154,965.9	287,550.2	1,091,843.3	1,630,327.1

Source: Prefeitura de São Paulo (2000).

Note: Calculations based on quintiles and top 10 percent income in Municipal Atlas. The 1991 and 2000 baselines are average monthly income for each income quintile. Figures from 2020 to 2040 simulate annual financial returns of 10 percent.

groups into *a mechanism that increases inequalities*. Second, we estimate the time needed for Brazil to reach levels of financial inclusion typical of advanced economies under four different policy frameworks. Frameworks based on private banking fare the worst.

First, regarding finance as a mechanism that increases inequality, Table 5.16 projects financial returns of 10 percent from 2000 to 2040 based on average incomes of population quintiles in 2000 estimated by the São Paulo Municipal Atlas (Prefeitura de São Paulo, 2000). Figures for 1991 and 2000 are average monthly incomes compiled from census data. Declines for lower income quintiles 1991–2000 suggest reverses typical of periods of economic reform and, presumably, the result of migration to metropolitan São Paulo. After 2000, hypothetical figures are calculated by simply adding 10 percent per year to income quintiles (and the top 10% income cohort) across decades. The result from these scenarios is clear: financial returns on personal assets dramatically increase inequalities.

This exercise suggests that finance increases inequality in settings of inequality and high financial returns, one typical of many developing countries. Indeed, given that most Brazilians have little or no income to save and that 55 percent still had no bank account in 2010, this exercise *underestimates* the extent to which finance increases inequality. In sum, from the notorious starting point of Gini coefficients for Brazil in 1990 (0.60), the reality of geometric financial returns over time can be said to multiply inequality significantly.

A second theoretical exercise suggests that private banking in Brazil is insufficient to promote financial inclusion. If we extrapolate the pace of bank inclusion in Brazil recorded during the period 2000–2010 for the decades 2010–2030, a simple linear projection suggests that reaching levels of bank inclusion typical of advanced economies (say 80 percent) will take another *two decades*.

To consider alternatives, compare four alternative hypothetical supply curve scenarios for the banking market in Brazil in 2030. The first scenario, that of upmarket banking with an expensive supply curve, can be estimated to serve approximately 50 million Brazilians (of 300 million in 2030). The second scenario, according to standard private bank supply curve, the number of bank accounts would remain at 33 percent of the population (100 of 300 million Brazilians). A third scenario representing the coverage of a cheaper supply curve of savings banks that specialize in simplified (no-cost, 'no-questions-asked') bank accounts would reach roughly 66 percent or 200 of 300 million Brazilians.

A fourth hypothetical scenario is based on recent experiments with issue of identity cards as no-charge bank cards. This supply curve at zero cost (to users) is horizontal. Accordingly, full bank inclusion of all Brazilians could be completed well before 2030. Although hypothetical, these scenarios for bank accounts in Brazil suggest that exclusive reliance on private banks is sub-optimal for financial inclusion.

These general concerns about finance and inequality leverage the importance of our findings about monetary statecraft and new monetary channels for change.

Monetary channels of change

Monetary statecraft in Brazil during the 2000s also involves different strategies of social inclusion. Monetary theory and policy usually assume zero sum relations between social inclusion and central banking. To the contrary, positive-sum relations may obtain in contexts of inequality and financial exclusion such as Brazil; this reverses standard views of politics, money, banking and central banking. Since 2000, a federal government savings bank, basic income policies (albeit conditional, see Soares *et al.*, 2010) and other social policies have reached vast numbers of bankless Brazilians (Mettenheim *et al.*, 2013). Conceptions of citizenship and social justice (Leão Rego and Pinzani, 2013; Brandtstädter *et al.*, 2011), new social policies, Central Bank modernization and reform of government banks have helped reverse social exclusion, improve monetary authority and maintain price stability amidst democratization in Brazil.

These monetary channels of change differ from past experiences. Since the 'end of the electoral road to socialism', exemplified by military coup against President Salvador Allende in Chile in 1973, social scientists and policy communities have focused on fiscal constraints to social policies. For Gold, Lo and Wright (1975), new structural theories of the state improved on instrumental and functional theories by describing how individual investors price markets, limit social policy spending and veto change; because government policies require either tax increases or budget cuts, social policies may become counterproductive by reducing the profits of firms and, in turn, tax revenue and public funds. This vicious cycle, in the worst cases, contributed to political-economic crisis and the breakdown of democracy in developing countries (O'Donnell, 1973). Similar forces in advanced economies, from this perspective of fiscal constraints, produced stagflation in the 1970s and electoral turns to neo-conservative politics to dismantle Welfare States (Pierson, 1996).

These explanations are now incomplete. Old views of fiscal dominance and structural constraints to change fail to account for advances both in monetary economics during the 1990s and monetary policy making during the 2000s

(Bernanke and Gertler, 1995). Central Bank modernization, new regulatory frameworks and better supervision of banks and markets (despite opting for deregulation in the United States and select tax havens and financial centres) provide a new setting for monetary channels of change and financial roads to more social economies. Structural theories of the state and conceptions of hard fiscal constraints predate modern studies of credit channels and interest rate channels. Since the 1990s, new concepts from monetary economics have improved central banking and monetary policy making; they also require rethinking constraints to change and social policy.

Monetary channels provide new opportunities, and risks, for social policy, public banking and financial inclusion. Many developing countries have accumulated large stocks of foreign reserves through sustained trade surpluses to overcome past vulnerabilities. Moreover, in Brazil, transparent policy frameworks such as inflation targeting, tough fiscal targets, and a flexible foreign exchange regime have remained in place since 1999 (Fraga *et al.,* 2004). The current situation of Brazil and many developing countries is thus different from the 1970s. In Brazil, the modernization of state banks (after mismanagement under military rule and capture by oligarchs during prolonged transition), and a sequence of economic reforms have approximated government policies and markets to provide new channels for financial inclusion.

In the new context created by liberalization and Central Bank modernization the Caixa Econômica Federal (Caixa) functioned both as agent of federal government social policy and savings bank to promote financial inclusion. The Caixa developed new channels such as simplified accounts, electronic card technology, and correspondent banking to deliver income grants and modernize social policy provision, thereby providing citizens with access to banking and public services in vast numbers. Since transition from military rule and price stability (1994), financial liberalization (1995) and incorporation of new banking technologies during the 2000s, public banking, social policies and conceptions of citizenship and social justice have proved more much effective to reach bankless Brazilians than private banks or microfinance firms, funds or organizations.

This is an anomaly for neo-liberal policies, contemporary banking theory, and the international microfinance movement that abhors state banks in favour of private initiative, philanthropy and non-governmental organizations. However, the record in Brazil and other developing countries is clear. Since liberalization of banking systems during the 1990s and 2000s, government banks (where they were not privatized) have remained dominant players in many developing economies, especially the largest ones.[24] Instead of transitions to private, market-based banking,[25] state banks have instead realized competitive advantages over private and foreign banks to remain central agents of credit, finance and public policy. Indeed, the modernization of government banks during the 2000s occurred just in time to counter crisis in 2008. The capitalization, reform and reorientation of large public banks provided policy makers in many developing countries with counter-cyclical policy alternatives once global crisis hit (Schclarek Curutchet, 2014). State banks have also proved critical agents for financial inclusion. This article reports evidence of how a federal government savings bank provided new channels for social policies based on conceptions of citizenship and social justice in Brazil.

From Keynesian demand management to reaching the bankless

Monetary channels, basic income and public bank agency also differ from aggregate demand management traditionally pursued by working-class parties. New policies of social and state banking aim to improve provision of social services and increase access to banking services. Supply-side policies are usually associated with neo-liberalism and neo-conservatism. However, recent strategies suggest different political correlates. Since liberalization of banking in many developing countries, state banks have outperformed private and foreign banks by mixing provision of banking services and social services to reach large numbers of unbanked citizens to help reverse inequality and social exclusion. These policies involve microeconomics of social inclusion and differ fundamentally from the macroeconomics of populism, and fiscal constraints, in the past (Dornbusch and Edwards, 1991).

Monetary channels of change also differ from concerns in studies of central banking and monetary policy in advanced economies that assume banked populations, zero-sum games, and profit-maximizing actors amidst stable prices and economies. Stark inequalities in developing countries provide large marginal gains from financial inclusion that improves monetary authority. For example, compare Brazil in the 1990s and the 2000s. To regain market confidence during financial crises in the 1990s, the Central Bank of Brazil increased SELIC benchmark overnight interbank interest rates to 42 percent (Mexico, 1994–1995, Asia 1997, Russia, 1998, Brazil 1999). Progress can be seen by recourse to 23 percent interest rate hikes during crises in the early 2000s (Argentina, 2001, Brazil 2003) and 12 percent (7 percent real) rates adopted in 2008–2009 to counter crisis abroad. Worse begets better. The relation between politics, social inclusion and monetary policy here is not a zero-sum game optimized by legislating Central Bank independence. Instead, the construction of monetary authority (after decades of inertial inflation and monetary chaos in Brazil) reaps large marginal returns from reforms and declining, albeit still high, costs of adjustment.

Monetary policies and social inclusion are also positive sum because the large number of Brazilians brought within credit and interest rate channels improves the effectiveness of policy. During the first year of inflation targeting in Brazil (2000), an estimated 20 percent of Brazilians had bank accounts. Central Bank interest rate policies and government credit policies therefore failed (directly) to reach 80 percent of citizens that remained outside channels of credit and interest rates. By 2010, the number of Brazilians with bank accounts had increased to an estimated 45 percent (still roughly half levels found in most advanced economies). Notwithstanding the remaining challenges for financial inclusion, doubling the number of Brazilians with bank accounts 2000–2010 has been fundamental both for social inclusion and improving monetary policy.

Monetary policy frameworks (such as inflation targeting, the Taylor rule and models of dynamic general equilibrium) and Central Bank monitoring and supervision of credit flows and the portfolios of banks and credit institutions provide new means to monitor market signals and inflation that set limits to basic income payments, social policies and downmarket credit programs such as popular home mortgage finance. This differs from both theories of hard fiscal constraints and the primary concern of economists about monetary policy shocks. Research on central banking, monetary theory and channels of credit and interest rates assume the contexts of advanced economies with banked populations and mature markets for loans and bonds. These assumptions do not hold in developing countries if 80 percent of citizens remain bankless and shallow bond markets restrict issues to a select number of corporate issuers and the central government.

Broader concerns about finance and inequality suggest the large marginal returns to monetary statecraft in Brazil. In a context of high financial returns and inequality such as Brazil, finance is transformed from phenomena that, in other contexts, may smooth consumption and investment across generations and social groups into a mechanism that increases inequalities. Indeed, given that most Brazilians have little or no income to save and that 55 percent still had no bank account in 2010, this exercise underestimates the extent to which finance increases inequality. In sum, from the notorious starting point of Gini coefficients for Brazil in 1990 (0.60), the reality of geometric financial returns over time can be said to multiply inequality significantly.

Another broader concern about bank modernization informs our findings about monetary statecraft in Brazil. Case studies (Mettenheim, 2006) and comparative studies (Ayadi *et al.,* 2010) suggest that many public savings banks have realized competitive advantages over private and foreign banks (even, and especially, after liberalization of national banking systems). This counters expectations that opening banking and credit markets would lead to the dominance of private and foreign banks and provides new concepts, theories, and policy alternatives that avert biases in microfinance toward private banks, non-governmental organizations and market funding.

In Brazil, since transition to democracy, the end of inertial inflation (1994), liberalization of banking (1995) and capitalization of federal government banks to meet Basel Accord I requirements (2001), the Caixa has consistently outperformed private and foreign banks in terms of profits, returns, non-performing loans and a variety of standard indicators. The Caixa used large-scale institutional foundations of competitive advantage to reform and modernize during transition to international regulations and new Central Bank policies of supervision and control. Critics of government banking emphasize political capture. The Caixa (and other Brazilian government banks) did indeed suffer mismanagement under military rule (1964–1985) and were captured by traditional elites during the prolonged transition to democracy (1974–1994). However, since 1994, Caixa management has used institutional foundations of competitive advantage to outperform private and foreign banks amidst more open, transparent and better regulated markets for banking, credit and finance.

In this sense, modernization of Caixa savings bank operations and concessions for government policy implementation proved complementary. Family grants, other social services (unemployment insurance, social security and payroll savings funds) and microfinance programs have been widely credited with reducing notorious levels of inequality in Brazil. The Caixa retains most government concessions to manage these policies. This helps bring citizens and prospective clients into Caixa points of sale and expand branch offices and bank correspondent networks cheaper than private and foreign banks.

Simplified bank accounts and correspondent banking are further innovations that have mixed social policy agency and public banking to promote financial inclusion in Brazil. The Central Bank of Brazil introduced rules for simplified bank accounts in 1999 to reduce barriers that kept roughly 80 percent of citizens bankless. Banks were initially required to accept applications for simplified accounts upon presentation of Brazilian identity cards (neither proof of income nor residence necessary). If clients of simplified accounts retained a positive balance for 90 days, then they became eligible for loans up to R$200 (with no further information from clients nor credit analysis). Moreover, positive balances for two further 90-day periods increased credit lines to R$600 – still without any information about clients except for identity card numbers. Simplified accounts at the Caixa reached 8.75 million by 2010. Caixa market share of simplified accounts increased from 58 to 87 percent from 2004 to 2010.[26] Most private banks no longer offer simplified accounts.

In comparison, the Caixa offered simplified accounts to family grant recipients enabling direct deposit of basic income grants, providing bank accounts, for the first time, to most (women) recipients of family grants. Direct debit of family grants into simplified bank accounts (no charges, no questions asked) eliminates the need to appear in person at the branch office, reduces risk of theft, facilitates payments for goods and services by card instead of cash and provides proof of address, often for the first time, so that women may apply for further services.

In 2010, the Caixa began to automatically extend overdraft privileges if simplified account balances remained positive. This effectively transforms a simplified bank account into a payroll credit – on per-monthly basic income grants of R$36–306 (US$18–153 in February 2013). Further research into family grants and simplified accounts as gender-based social policy for financial inclusion will be required. However, this combination of basic income, social policy and government savings bank operations are fundamentally different phenomena than expected by mainstream and critical theories, that is the predominance of private banking after financial liberalization.

Use of bank correspondents by the Caixa also differs from these expectations. In Brazil, economic reforms, financial liberalization, democratization after military rule and socioeconomic heterogeneity provide a quasi-experimental setting for testing the effectiveness of policies for financial inclusion. Change has differed from the expectations of both mainstream and critical observers. Opening Brazilian banking to foreign competition and privatization of most state government banks sought to dismantle the state-centred banking system built under national-populists (1930–1945), developmentalists (1945–1964) and military rule

(1964–1985). However, transition to private, foreign and market-based banking has not ensued. Instead, a back to the future modernization of social and state banking has occurred. The Caixa, a traditional government savings bank, has realized competitive advantages over private and foreign banks by combining social policies and a focus on popular savings and credit to remain the third largest financial institution in the country. These new monetary channels provide financial roads to more social economies. However, caution about institutional change is also in order. The Caixa has yet to be rid of two legacies: corporate centralization and capture under military rule and prolonged transition, typical of the still significant challenges for reform and democratization in Brazil.[27]

Monetary statecraft and consumption-led growth

Management of consumer-led growth is the second different characteristic of monetary statecraft in Brazil during the 2000s. In comparison to other emerging and developing countries, especially China, Brazil appears on the opposite end of a spectrum that runs from excessive savings at the expense of consumption, to excessive consumption at the expense of savings and investment. The broader political economy of development paths in BRIC countries is beyond the scope of this chapter. Instead, we focus on the implications of new monetary channels for management of consumer-led growth as an additional fact behind the strategies of social inclusion in Brazil amidst democracy.

Consumer-led growth has helped reverse legacies of inequality and countered shocks from abroad but encountered bottlenecks because of weak investment in infrastructure. From 2004 to 2012, Brazil experienced its first sustained period of growth since the 1980s. From 2002 to 2012, the monthly minimum wage that indexes all formal salaries increased from 240 to 622, that is, 66 percent discounting inflation. Substantial improvement from very high levels of inequality in Brazil under military rule can be seen in standard indicators such as the Gini coefficient and Thiel T (see Figure 5.7) and measures of poverty and extreme poverty (see Figure 5.8).The number of family grant recipients increased from 4.4 to 13.4 million during 2003–2011, providing 17.4 billion reals in family grant payments that serve as the exclusive source of income to an estimated 48 million Brazilians (of 292 million) (Figure 5.7).

Growth through real income increases and social inclusion also defines the upswings in the Brazilian business cycles during the 1990s and 2000s. Sustained growth from 2004 until the global crisis hit the country in 2008 served to consolidate support for the policy tripod that had been adopted during the late 1990s, namely, fiscal control, inflation targeting and a flexible foreign exchange regime. Adjustment was required in 2008 and once again in 2011 when the crisis in Europe deepened. However, policy makers in Brazil have managed growth since 2004 by balancing, on the one hand, the entry of 30–40 million new consumers (thereby improving the notorious levels of inequality in Brazil), and on the other, the strong pressures placed on domestic producers due to the valuation of the real during the upswings and capital inflows that cheapened imports.

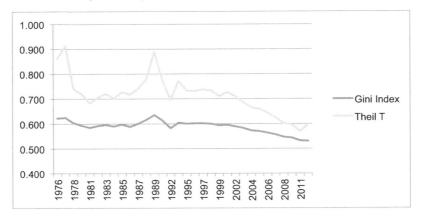

Figure 5.7 Indicators of reduction in inequalities (1976–2012)
Source: Ipeadata

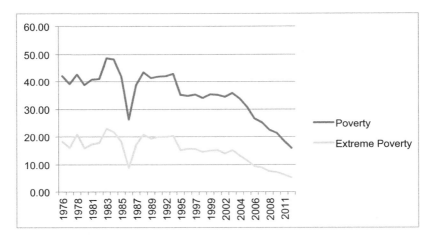

Figure 5.8 Poverty and extreme poverty (1976–2012)
Source: Ipeadata

Downmarket consumer-led growth suggest that monetary policy may manage
social inclusion in terms fundamentally different than past strategies of social
policy that encountered structural fiscal constraints. The recent terms of debates
about slow growth in Brazil suggest the fundamentally different channels of
change and removal of past constraints. Despite the continued impact of crisis and
slow recovery abroad, macroeconomic vulnerabilities have been reduced, more
transparent policies remain in place and fundamentals of finance and banking
remain solid. Liquidity buffers guarantee counter-cyclical funds. Foreign currency
reserves held by the Central Bank of Brazil increased from a precarious US$34
billion in the late 1990s (half as credit from the IMF) to over US$376 billion in

June 2012. A full 45 percent of private deposits at banks are held at the Central Bank to ensure liquidity and provide policy levers to counter credit crunches from abroad. Brazilian banks also continue to avert leverage and to retain prudent levels of capital reserves. The average Basel Index of banks in Brazil has remained at 16.8 in 2012. Public debt also declined from 60 percent of GDP in 2003 to 35.1 percent of GDP (June 2012). And, for the first time since the Latin American debt crisis of the 1980s, foreign debt constraints have largely disappeared. Brazilian sovereign issues acquired investment grade status and further upgrades by Fitch, Moody's and S&P during 2011. Sovereign issues reached record levels of 2.4 percent for Global 2021 bonds and 3.9 percent for Global 2041 bonds.

Solid macroeconomic fundamentals, financial expansion and banking solidity provide room for further credit and consumer-led growth. Indeed, the series of reductions in interest rates initiated by monetary authorities in August 2011 were widely criticized as being risky, given the apprehensions about inflationary pressures. In retrospect, Pessoa (2012) argues that the Central Bank of Brazil had correctly anticipated the depth of the crisis abroad in August 2011 and therefore correctly perceived the room for interest rate reductions, unlike markets and observers who erred on the side of caution and criticized what they perceived as the politicization of policy at the Central Bank of Brazil. SELIC benchmark overnight interest rates have since declined from 12.5 percent in August 2011 to 7.5 percent (4.3 after discounting inflation) by July 2012. This helped avert the escalation of household debt and bad credit that had threatened to complicate the adjustment to the downturn in the business cycle.

In sum, consumer-led growth has reinforced the popularity of two PT presidents and helped reverse high inequality in Brazil. Record low levels of unemployment and persistent real income increases have also provided powerful political support for credit and consumer-led growth. Credit expansion and social inclusion have not run their course as growth factors because prudent bank lending, Central Bank supervision and the response of domestic industry have averted the formation of asset bubbles and/or bad debts. Moreover, a principal driver of growth has been home construction, especially low-cost public housing programs. Viable interest rates, the absence of bad credit problems and the securitization of mortgages provide solid grounds for further growth, despite this sector being the cause of asset bubbles, crises and problems for banks, homeowners and policy makers abroad. Household debt as a percentage of GDP also remained at 20.9 percent in 2012, far below levels in advanced economies. And the consequences of the crisis abroad (lower interest rates) permitted the stabilization of accumulated debt during 2011–2012. Finally, non-paying loans in Brazil remain at 3.8 percent of total loans, far below levels in the past and currently below levels reported in advanced economies amidst the crisis and its fallout.

Currency wars and capital tsunamis

The primary threats to this growth model from abroad are strong trade surpluses and capital inflows that tend to increase the value of the real against hard currencies. Booming demand and increased commodity prices for Brazilian exports during the late 2000s produced record trade surpluses and alleviated investor concerns about Brazilian sovereign debt and government deficits. However, since the 2008 crisis, expansive monetary policies designed to reverse the crisis in the advanced economies have further increased capital inflows to Brazil and the valuation of the real. In 2010, Brazilian Finance Minister Guido Mantega described this as a new situation of 'currency war'. For Mantega, the devaluation of currencies by advanced economies is also designed to reduce or has the unintended 'protectionist' consequence of reducing the competitiveness of exports from emerging economies to advanced economies. According to Mantega, US$8.8 trillion of emergency measures and quantitative easing undertaken by central banks in advanced economies led to the need to adopt capital controls and other measures to reverse the excessive valuation of the real.

While a flexible foreign exchange rate regime has been fundamental for the adjustment and modernization of the Brazilian economy since its adoption amidst crisis in 1999, domestic monetary authorities have nonetheless developed several policy instruments to intervene in regard to the specific characteristics of markets for foreign exchange in Brazil. For example, Central Bank of Brazil circular 3458 of 8 July 2011 increased compulsory deposits for bank operations with foreign exchange to 60 percent of the value of transactions in order to discourage arbitrage in currency markets. Foreign currency operations not directly related to trade are estimated to have amounted to over US$15 billion at Brazilian banks, while foreign banks purchased an additional US$15 billion in foreign exchange notes (cupom cambial) on BMF-BOVESPA futures markets. This indicates the importance of financial flows over traditional forces of trade in currency exchange markets. Financial operations taxes were also levied on export finance and loans in bonds under 180 days, policies also designed to counter the use of export finance facilities to hedge against foreign currency risks in other operations.

These policies effectively reversed the valuation of the real from 1.5 against the US dollar in July 2011 to 1.8 by October. They allayed fears of further declines in exports and the trade balance and concerns over the impact of quantitative easing in advanced economies on capital inflows and further valuation of the real. Equally important is the fact that reversing the valuation of the real assuaged fears of industry associations that cheap imports would be used to sustain consumer-driven growth at the expense of local industry. From the perspective of political economy, it is important to note that capital controls were thus used to exercise macroeconomic policy change. This averted piecemeal protection of industrial sectors sought by lobbies or escalation of diplomatic discord and lengthy issues of unfair trade pursued through international institutions such as the World Trade Organization.

Brazilian policy makers thereby averted further deindustrialization, already responsible for the virtual elimination of textile production and other sectors suffering from imports that had secured competitive advantage through the revaluation of the real. However, what to do with Brazilian industry is a structural problem that is far from being resolved. The boom in export of minerals, basic commodities and agricultural goods during the 2000s reaffirmed the traditional competitive advantage of Brazil in these areas. Primary exports remain a fundamental comparative advantage of Brazil as a large country with a wealthy base of natural resources. However, booming primary exports have placed industrial groups on the defensive as large export surpluses have sustained imports and growth. This is a new swing of the pendulum that requires policy makers to adopt a balancing act in Brazil. Primary exports sustain consumption-led growth, but in excess (and coupled with excessive capital inflows) this may threaten domestic industry. Inflation targeting and prudent monitoring of asset bubbles and credit risk could avert problems that may arise from growth. Moreover, domestic manufactured goods may compensate for declining exports as the real rises in value against foreign currencies (and productivity of Brazilian industry lags). For another, excessive valuation of the real leads to the substitution of domestic goods for imports much as several industrial sectors in the country have also suffered widespread bankruptcies. Policy makers must therefore balance sustaining consumption without increasing inflation and control the excessive valuation of the real that may facilitate imports and break domestic industry.

The weight of consumption in the Brazilian economy favours this cycle. Data from 2006 indicate that household consumption (59.7 percent GPD) far outweighs government consumption (20.3 percent GDP) and investment (17.0 percent GDP). Moreover, services comprised 65.7 percent GDP in 2006, compared to industry (28.8 percent) and agriculture (5.4 percent). Government policies in the new political economy of growth in Brazil thus closely monitor consumer-led growth and real income expansion within a regime of inflation targeting and a flexible foreign exchange regime. Recent capital controls and interventions in the foreign exchange markets were mentioned earlier. Before the mid-2000s, the problem was the reverse. Upon adoption of the flexible foreign exchange regime in 1999, the real lost value from 1.6 to reach nearly 4 against the US dollar in 2003 amidst a lack of confidence among foreign investors about the new PT government of President Lula. This magnitude of change (valuation of the real against the dollar from 4–1 to 1.5–1 in 2003–2010) permitted shifting to imports to meet the rising consumer demand. However, as domestic Brazilian industries suffered during the late 2000s under competition from imports, concerns about deindustrialization emerged.

This has often set consumers and producers against one another as policy makers seek to sustain growth without bankrupting traditional industries. In a structural sense, recent growth is buffered from international pressures because of the relatively closed character of the Brazilian economy and dispersion of export destinations. Total exports remain at 12 percent of GDP, with destinations spreading risk across Latin America (2.4 percent GDP), Europe (2.4 percent), China (2.1 percent), the United States (1.3 percent) and the rest of the world (3.8 percent). This ameliorates shocks coming from specific regions and permits reorientation and adjustment.

Conclusion

Monetary statecraft shaped Brazilian development since transition from military rule first as muddling through implementation of heterodox theory to reverse inertial inflation; then through use of financial crises as enabling constraints whereby policy makers pushed further reforms of liberalization, privatization and modernization of central banking; then, after 2003, as acceptance of a more liberal monetary policy regime by Worker's Party opposition permitted reaping returns of reforms by accelerating social inclusion through new methods of managing monetary channels.

This trajectory of politics and monetary policy differs from theories of central bank independence in economics and corporate capture in sociology. In October 2005, legislation designed to formalize Central Bank independence was taken off the agenda of the PT coalition government under President Lula. The construction of more effective central banking and improved monetary authority occurred in Brazil without definition of operational independence or constitutional Central Bank autonomy. Instead, a new, somewhat reluctant, but nonetheless solid consensus emerged in Brazilian politics that monetary policies may best be entrusted to technical authorities. This sober conclusion is based on recognition of past mistakes that contributed to the breakdown of democracy in 1964 and witness of further financial abuses under military rule and the political vacuum of prolonged transition. The severity of financial crisis in neighboring Argentina reinforced this reluctant consensus among Brazilian politicians. Surveys of political elites suggest a sober realization that government policies must respect market constraints. For perhaps the first time in Brazilian history, policy involving the domestic money supply, foreign currency exchange markets, interest rate policies, hard currency reserves, credit risk and prudent banking principles have been delegated to specialist subsecretaries in the Central Bank of Brazil, Treasury and Ministry of Finance.

In this respect, recent developments suggest a gradual separation and specialization of institutions responsible for monetary policies in the federal government. Since the late 1980s and early 1990s, a fundamental shift has occurred away from the need for a small group of economists responsible for quickly adapting policies to volatile change under high inflation and repeated attempts to de-index financial instruments. Since price stability in 1994, the trend toward specialization and differentiation is unmistakable. Instead of centralizing a variety of decisions and reacting to circumstances by attempting to coordinate a wide variety of monetary, fiscal, tax, finance and bank lending policies, Central Bank officials increasingly delegate decisions to specialized departments in the attempt to monitor markets, regulate banks, and anticipate crises rather than react to events. This specialization and differentiation of central banking in Brazil suggests both the opportunities for statecraft during the first decade of price stability in the country and the importance of the separation of powers in Brazilian political institutions. Indeed, scholars of Brazilian politics have emphasized the simultaneous empowerment of legislative, judiciary, and executive since the 1988 Constitution. Review of monetary policy and central banking suggests that congressional oversight, judicial review, and executive capacity appear to involve an increasingly complex, positive-sum policy process involving all branches of government.

Central banking in new democracies requires statecraft – the gradual construction of institutions through politics – rather than the simple imposition of orthodoxies or reforms from abroad. Scholars, policy makers and markets now appear to agree that considerable progress has been made in Brazil during the last decade in terms of liberalization, privatization, macroeconomic adjustment and a variety of fiscal, administrative and monetary reforms. However, far from confirming the correct adoption of policies from abroad, or now providing models for emulation by other developing nations, advances in central banking occurred in Brazil through a tempered realism about the need to reconcile democratization and monetary authority. Since price stability in 1994, the costs of adjustment to economic shocks from abroad and at home have been high, and the legacies of underdevelopment are still cruel. The cumulative impact of reforms has made the Brazilian economy more resistant to the crises and dramatic reversals that have marked emerging economies and new democracies. This chapter suggests that federal government banks and new monetary policies of social inclusion may further transform what has traditionally been seen as a zero-sum relation into a more positive-sum cycle capable of reinforcing property rights, prudent banking, economic development and citizenship, deepening both financial markets and democracy.

Notes

1 On the Phillips curve in Brazil, see: Machado, Vicente G. and Portugal, Marcelo S. 'Phillips curve in Brazil: an unobserved components approach' (Central Bank of Brazil Working Paper no. 354, 2014). Sachsida, A., Ribeiro, M. and Santos, C. H. 'A curva de Phillips e a experiência brasileira' (Textos para Discussão IPEA, no. 1429, 2009).

2 Carvalho, Fabia A., and Minella, André. 'Survey forecasts in Brazil: A prismatic assessment of epidemiology, performance, and determinants', *Journal of International Money and Finance*, 31(6) (2013), 1371–1391. Silva Filho, Tito N. T. 'Banks, Asset Management or Consultancies' Inflation Forecasts: is there a better forecaster out there?' (Brasilia: Central Bank of Brazil Working Paper 310, July 2013). Ornelas, José R. H. and Silva Jr, Antonio F. A. 'Testing the Liquidity Preference Hypothesis using Survey Forecasts' (Brasilia: Central Bank of Brazil Working Paper 353, 2014). Araujo, C. H. and Gaglianone, W. P. 'Survey-based inflation expectations in Brazil'. In Bank for International Settlements, Monetary and Economics Department 'Monetary policy and the measurement of inflation: prices, wages and expectations' (Bank for International Settlements, BIS papers, no. 49, 2010).

3 Nóbrega, Mailson and Loyola, Gustavo. 'The Long and Simultaneous Construction of Monetary and Fiscal Institutions', in Sola, Lourdes and Whitehead, Laurence (eds.), *Statecrafting Monetary Authority: Democracy and Financial Order in Brazil* (Oxford: Centre for Brazilian Studies, 2006), note 12, p. 83

4 See Mettenheim, Kurt. *Federal Banking in Brazil: Policies and Competitive Advantages* (London: Pickering and Chatto, 2010).

5 The Asset Management Firm (Empresa Gestora de Ativos, EMGEA) was created in 2001 to liquidate, recover, or sell problematic assets from federal government banks. Caixa liabilities to the FGTS, FDS and FAHRE were also transferred to the EMGEA. Subsequent injections of Itaupu receivables (R$5.8 billion) and Caixa mortgage contracts (R$4.3 billion) increased EMGEA capital in 2002 and 2003. The 2006 EMGEA financial statements report R$26.8 billion assets and R$11.0 billion losses accumulated since formation of the asset management company in 2001. Further costs reported by federal government since the 2001 capitalization of federal government banks include transfer of a further R$551.0 million mortgage contracts from the Caixa to EMGEA and R$20.5 million reported in 2006 budget for cost of acquiring credits under the PROEF program.

6 On reserve requirements in Brazil, see: Areosa, Waldyr D. and Coelho, Christiano A. 'Using a DSGE Model to Assess the Macroeconomic Effects of Reserve Requirements in Brazil' (Central Bank of Brazil Working Paper 303, 2013).

7 Inflation targeting requires that monetary authorities adopt a forward-looking attitude and take preemptive action, given the lags between policy decisions and their effect on output and prices. Bogdanski, Joel, Tombini, Alexandre and Werlang, Sergio. 'Implementing Inflation Targeting in Brazil' (Brasilia: Central Bank of Brazil Working Paper, No. 1, 2000), p. 5.

8 'In Brazil, the monetary authorities chose the full disclosure strategy, in the same line as the Bank of England. The publication of Inflation Reports is an integral part of the communication efforts, allowing the general public to understand and assess the quality of the monetary policy decisions, in a continuous process that ultimately leads to earning credibility and permits achieving the inflation targets with lesser costs' (p. 28). Bogdanski, Tombini and Werlang cite: Batini, N. and Haldane, A. G. 'Forward-Looking Rules for Monetary Policy' (Bank of England Working Paper no. 91, 1999); Britton, E., Fischer, P. and Whitley, J. 1998. 'The Inflation Report Projections: Understanding the Fan Chart'. *Bank of England Quarterly Bulletin*, no. 38; and Haldane, A. G. 'Some Issues in Inflation Targeting' (Bank of England Working Paper no. 74, 1997).

9 Bogdanski, Tombini and Werlang (pp. 9–10) cite the following readings in preparation for the implementation of inflation targeting: 'Two key books were very useful: Bernanke *et al., Inflation Targeting: Lessons from the International Experience* (Princeton, NJ: Princeton University Press, 1998); and Taylor, John B. (ed.), *Monetary Policy Rules* (Chicago: University of Chicago Press, 1999). Some other articles and books entered a 'minimum kit', a mandatory reading for anyone in the group. (1) General readings and cases: King, Mervyn (1997), *The Inflation Target Five Years On*; Massad, Carlos (1998), *La Politica Monetaria en Chile*; Masson, P. R. *et al.* (1997), *The Scope for Inflation Targeting in Developing Countries*; Taylor, John (1999), *A Historical Analysis of Monetary Policy Rules*. (2) Optimization models: Backus, David *et al.* (1986) *The Consistency of Optimal Policy in Stochastic Rational Expectations Models*; Currie, David *et al.* (1993), *Rules, Reputation and Macroeconomic Policy Coordination*; Svensson, Lars (1998), *Open-Economy Inflation Targeting*. (3) Applied work: Taylor, John (1993) *Discretion versus Policy Rules in Practice*; Taylor, John (1994), *The Inflation/Output Variability Trade-off Revisited*'.

10 Experts from Australia, Canada, Chile, Israel, Mexico, New Zealand, Sweden, United Kingdom and United States made presentations on their country's experiences. Researchers from the Central Bank of Brazil presented their initial work on inflation targeting, titled 'Issues in the Adoption of an IT Framework in Brazil', May 1999.

11 Santiso, Javier. 'Wall Street and Emerging Democracies: Financial Markets and the Brazilian Presidential Elections', in Sola and Whitehead, *Financial Order in Brazil* (Oxford: University of Oxford Centre for Brazilian Studies, 2006), pp. 269–324.

12 Whitehead, Laurence, 'The Political Dynamics of Financial Crises in 'Emerging Market' Democracies', in Sola and Whitehead, *Financial Order in Brazil*, p. 29.

13 Subnational debt was two-thirds from São Paulo city, arising from mismanagement during Maluf and Pitta mayorships. See Olenscki, Antonio R. B. 'Modelo Brasileiro de Crédito Municipal (2000–2006): Uma Análise de Controles Governamentais e Características da Oferta' (FGV-EAESP doctoral dissertation, 2008).

14 Minella, André and Souza-Sobrinho, Nelson. 'Canais Monetários no Brasil sob a Ótica de um Modelo Semiestrutural', in Central Bank of Brazil, 'Dez Anos de Metas para a Inflação no Brasil, 1999–2009', 2011, pp. 35–94.

15 Santos, Rafael and Leon, Márcia. 'Globalização – Implicações para a política monetária no Brasil' in Central Bank of Brazil, 'Dez Anos de Metas para a Inflação no Brasil, 1999–2009', 2011, pp. 95–126.

16 Figueiredo, Francisco M. R. and Gouvea, Solange. 'Repasse Cambial para a Inflação: o papel da rigidez de preços', in Central Bank of Brazil, 'Dez Anos de Metas para a Inflação no Brasil, 1999–2009', 2011, pp. 127–168.

17 Carvalho, Fabia A. and Minella, André. 'Previsões de Mercado no Brasil: desempenho e determinantes', in Central Bank of Brazil, 'Dez Anos de Metas para a Inflação no Brasil, 1999–2009', 2011, pp. 169–226.

18 Silva, Alzira R. M., Hennings, Katherine and Gutierrez M. C. 'A Comunicação de Política Monetária no Regime de Metas para a Inflação: a experiência brasileira entre 1999 e 2009', in Central Bank of Brazil, 'Dez Anos de Metas para a Inflação no Brasil, 1999–2009', 2011, pp. 227–350.

19 Lima, Eduardo J. A., Araujo, Fabio and Costa e Silva, José R. 'Previsão e Modelos Macroeconômicos no Banco Central do Brasil', in Central Bank of Brazil, 'Dez Anos de Metas para a Inflação no Brasil, 1999–2009', 2011, pp. 351–400.

20 Brazil was scored according to investor relations office; investor relations staff identifiable and reachable via website; websites in English; links to other government agencies; subscription for information; SDDS compliance; transparent market relevant data; friendly macroeconomic data format; historical policy information; forecasting information; legal and regulatory information availability; investor contact list; online communication, presentations, roadshows with investors, and investor confidence calls (archived online); investor feedback inputs policy; policy makers accessible to investors; assessment of investor relations.

21 Mettenheim, Kurt. 'Municipal Bond Market in Brazil. Theory, Repression and Prospects'. *Revista de Administração de Empresas,* 52/6 (2012): 692–703.

22 Because fiscal responsibility legislation prohibits Central Bank issue of debt, the Central Bank acts as counterparty for Treasury. Carvalho Junior, Simonsen and Cysne.

23 This value seems incongruent with gross debt and government bond data.

24 Mettenheim, Kurt. 'BRIC Statecraft and Government Banks', in Olivier Butzbach and Kurt Mettenheim (eds.), *Alternative Banking and Financial Crisis* (London: Pickering and Chatto, 2014), pp. 179–210.

25 Hardie, Iain and Howarth, David (eds.). *Market Based Banking and the International Financial Crisis* (Oxford: Oxford University Press, 2013).

26 In comparison to simplified current accounts, the number of simplified *savings* accounts *decreased* to just 6,031 in June 2010, after reaching over 230,000 in 2006. This suggests the difficulty of expanding financial inclusion. Interviews with Caixa staff and clients – and the aggregate data on income declines among lower income quintiles – confirm the difficulty of accumulating savings. This reinforces the importance of basic income policies and confirms the difficulty of market-centred policies for financial inclusion.

27 For example, the *Revista das Caixas Econômicas* was a bi-monthly publication of independent savings banks ended by military rulers in 1964. Published since 1949, articles on themes such as popular savings and home finance, urban sanitation and development, municipal bond metrics, risk analysis and management, legal frameworks for savings bank operations and monetary policy provide evidence of vibrant epistemic communities and policy debates before military coup in 1964. Consolidation of 26 independent savings banks into a single corporation run by administrative troika under military rule shifted Caixa policies toward middle-class housing and repressed alternative views.

Conclusion

This book has elaborated the theory of monetary statecraft to capture the autonomy of politics, the complexities of policy making, and political development in the sense of social inclusion – all of which shape supply and demand to determine monetary phenomena. This book drew theories and concepts from political science and studies of public policy to demonstrate that politics cannot be eliminated as economic calculations of optimal monetary policy would have it. Nor do the politics of monetary policy always involve capture by banks and special interests, as sociological theories suggest. The empirical chapters of this book used concepts and theories from studies of public policy to explain how ideas, agenda setting, and recursive phases such as problem identification, formulation, and implementation shape monetary policy and money. Policy tracing confirmed the importance of muddling through, unexpected consequences, limited rationality and satisficing, and recursive, open-ended processes in government. The theory of political development sharpened the focus of monetary statecraft on the sequence of challenges to include social classes within political institutions – first oligarchy, then middle classes, then popular classes. Political underdevelopment matters in Brazil because – especially important because it is still underway in Brazil; such that political reversals under military rule were not been regained during transition from military rule, monetary chaos, and record levels of inertial inflation in the 1980s and early 1990s.

The qualitative methods used in this book such as historical institutional analysis, process tracing, case study, and focused comparisons produced causal observations and inferences better than statistical analyses of aggregate cross-national data. Since J. S. Mill described the comparative method as most adequate for study of phenomena not amenable to experimental or statistical analysis, the social sciences have improved techniques to generate causal inferences. Given the need to reconsider core ideas about politics and monetary policy in the wake of the global financial crisis of 2007–2008, qualitative methods provide more agile and more effective proving grounds for new theories and concepts than statistical analysis of cross-national aggregate data that, to date, have succumbed to fallacies of aggregation, proved unable to control for alternative explanations, and tend to conceal rather than reveal causal processes. Qualitative methods provided effective tests for theories and concepts about monetary statecraft while controlling for competing explanations from economics and sociology.

In Brazil, the construction of central bank capacity and modernization of monetary policy since transition from military rule occurred in precisely the reverse causal order expected by economic theories of central bank independence: only *after* price stability was restored through the (gradualist) implementation of heterodox policies in 1993–1994. Moreover, removal of legislation to formalize central bank independence from the agenda of PT coalition governments under presidents Lula and Dilma (2003–2014) confirms the reality that the central bank and monetary policy committee (COPOM) lack full independence from the executive and political pressures set by law. Two further anomalies appeared for theories of politics and monetary policy in economics and sociology. In Brazil, monetary reforms gained political legitimacy because of the (positive) redistributive effects of price stability and because policy makers used financial crises as enabling constraints to usher in new reforms. Instead of zero-sum relations, the evidence from Brazil suggests positive-sum relations between political development and monetary policy. Democratization in Brazil since 2000 also reinforced monetary policy modernization because financial inclusion policies (based on conceptions of citizenship and basic income rather than market-based microfinance or other ideas from economics) accelerated social inclusion through new monetary channels of change. None of these important developments that have shaped Brazilian development and democracy over the last decades can be explained by theories of politics and monetary policy from economics or sociology.

Indeed, insistence on central bank independence shares biases with other claims about reforming government such as the virtues of parliamentarism, party discipline, district electoral systems or a long list of economic reforms deemed essential for growth. These prescriptions for reform underestimate the *out-of-place* character of institutions from advanced economies in developing economies. Aggregate cross-national correlations between independent central banking and economic indicators such as lower inflation and higher growth presuppose the existence of mature markets, effective regulatory agencies and a multiplicity of factors enjoyed by advanced economies and old democracies. Because parameters for monetary policy fluctuate much more dramatically in developing countries, transplanting central bank independence consistently disappoints.

Somewhat paradoxically, this greater instability produces further analytic advantages of analyzing underdevelopment and increases the value of qualitative methods used herein. The primary constraint for analysis of politics and monetary policy is that the number of relevant events such as public policy reforms and crises are too few, while the number of possible causes are too many for statistical analysis. Because underdevelopment produces more volatile phenomena and more frequent crises, this provides analytic advantages for study of politics and monetary policy. We therefore broadened the scope of study to include the long history

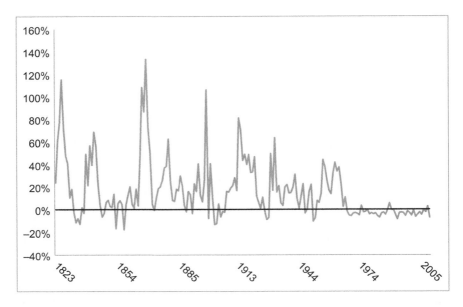

Figure 6.1 Federal government spending as percent government receipts (1823–2009)
Source: Ipeadata

of monetary policy in Brazil since 1808. Another analytic advantage ensued. The larger number of monetary problems in Brazilian history also generated a large number of debates and studies that provided a largely untapped record of primary and secondary sources. Policy process tracing and historical institutional analysis thereby helped skirt the constraints of randomization that have impeded inferences from statistical analyses of politics and monetary policy.

We also conclude by reminding readers that monetary statecraft in Brazil is about coming out of underdevelopment (see Figure 6.1). A core idea about money shared by virtually every classic and contemporary observer is that monetary phenomena take on greatest importance when things get 'out of order'. As a proxy for things getting out of order, consider Brazilian government spending as a percent of central government receipts from independence in 1823 through 2009. This long view indicates the 'out of order' context for monetary policy and, at the same time reveals a long record of policy makers, politicians, and independent observers searching for solutions adequate for developing countries (remember Ardant's suggestion at the outset of this book?). For the first time in Brazilian history, government accounts (perhaps the most fundamental indicator capable of recovering, building and sustaining market confidence) have remained in surplus. The fact that fiscal targets in Brazil remain *surpluses* (3.5 percent reduced to 1.2 percent since 2013), while similar targets in European Community accords remain *deficits* (3.0 percent repeatedly waved amidst crisis) suggests the continued importance of differences between political economies at the global centre and periphery. Moreover, such targets appear not apply to the United States as primary global currency provider or Japan where firms and government entities emit mostly yen-denominated debt (i.e., money, according to broader measures of money).

A wide variety of evidence has been presented in this book to suggest that monetary policies have been central to democratisation and political development in Brazil. However, in comparative perspective, the value of credit and financial balance sheets (assets and liabilities that, in a broad sense, are money) in Brazil still stand out as shallow. The volume of credit in developed economies generally exceeds 100 percent of the gross domestic product (GDP). Credit in Brazil has indeed grown (from 23 to 58 percent of GDP in 1990–2014) to remain less than two-thirds levels common in advanced economies. In terms of financial balance sheets, chapter five estimated the assets and liabilities of Brazilian households, firms, governments, and between Brazil and the rest of the world to remain *below one-tenth* levels in the United States and Germany during the 2005–2009 period.

The construction of monetary authority in Brazil is also a story of the organizational modernization of the central bank and the separation and differentiation of powers amidst democratization. Monetary policy makers in Brazil after the end of inertial inflation in 1994 increasingly delegated decisions to specialized departments able to monitor markets, regulate banks and anticipate crises rather than react to events. Worse begot better here in two senses. This specialization and differentiation of central banking in Brazil suggests both the extent of opportunities for statecraft from newly won price stability and the importance of the separation of powers in Brazilian political institutions. Studies of Brazilian politics emphasize the empowerment of all three (legislative, judiciary and executive) branches since the 1988 Constitution. The findings reported in this book about congressional oversight, judicial review and executive capacity in the sphere of monetary policy are also positive sum. Increasingly complex relations between branches of government (and the media, press, lobbies, and think tanks) are required in areas that are as technical as monetary policy and central banking.

Transition from military rule, the end of inertial inflation and change of government from reformism under Cardoso (1995–2002) to two coalition governments under PT presidents Lula and Dilma (2003–2014), have placed central banking and democracy on a new footing in Brazil. The reconstruction of central banking and monetary authority after 1994 opened new monetary channels for social inclusion. In this respect, the challenges of democratization and central banking in Brazil today can be said to differ fundamentally from past paradigms such as welfare states in Europe, market-driven (often asset bubble) growth in the United States and past experiences in Brazil and Latin America with national populism and state-led developmentalism or state capitalism. Since reversing inertial inflation in 1994, the costs of adjustment to shocks from abroad and at home have been high and the legacies of underdevelopment are still cruel. Nonetheless, new monetary channels of social inclusion have transformed politics and monetary policy from what is usually seen as zero-sum relations into more positive-sum cycles of sound banking, basic income policies, social inclusion, more effective counter-cyclical policies and the deepening of citizenship, credit, and money and its markets.

This is a fundamentally different combination of politics and monetary policies: that of accelerating social inclusion and development by basing policies on core concepts of social justice and citizenship as much as market equilibrium and property rights. Recent political theories suggest that basic income policies may respect economic constraints but provide monetary channels of change able to accelerate social inclusion and political development. For Pateman and Barry, we have failed to tap new possibilities for citizenship and democratization through basic incomes policies.[1] Evidence from this study of Brazil concurs: debates about politics and monetary policy need a broader theoretical and programmatic horizon.

This casts doubts on longstanding ideas about economic constraints to change. By integrating advances in monetary economics (such as concepts about credit and interest rate channels that improve adjustment policies) with broader concerns in political theory and public policy (about social justice, relief of poverty, equality of opportunity, the flexibility of labour markets, and individual freedom), a variety of new research agendas on politics and monetary policy come into view. Reforms in Brazil involving liberalization, privatizations and greater transparency have enabled new monetary policies of social inclusion far more than expected. Given the large numbers reached by new social policies in Brazil (such as the basic income policy of basic grants for mothers and children in school that sum to over 48 million, or a quarter of all Brazilians). Basic income policies have proved compelling in terms of social justice, viable in terms of monetary economics and essential for political socialization and citizenship.

Monetary statecraft and the classics

Our findings may be further leveraged by a look at classic works in political economy. The work of classic authors supports the theory of monetary statecraft because many share the following analytic shift. Broader accounts of political economy by classic authors tend to strongly assert that money and monetary policies are *not* relevant to broader economic processes. However, this supposition gives way precisely *when and to the extent that they examine money and monetary policy*. Once classic authors shift away from general causal schemes to focus on money and monetary policy, they arrive at a common conclusion – that money, monetary phenomena and monetary policy evidence causal processes that, now upon closer inspection, are seen to be independent from broader causes in the real economy and produce substantial consequences for the real economy.

A second message we draw from the classics has to do with a bias that appears to be widely, shared by classic and contemporary analysts of money and monetary policy – an almost exclusive focus on commercial monetary transactions. This underestimates the importance of households, government, and non-profit organizations. By focusing on private commercial transactions to the detriment of money saved, exchanged, lent, invested or otherwise transacted outside the circuits shaped by private firms, private banks, the new opportunities for monetary policies, social inclusion and political development remain out of view. Research in political economy focuses, almost exclusively, on commercial monetary transactions conducted by private firms in banking and finance. This ignores broader questions about money, credit, finance, debt and monetary phenomena related to cooperative banks, public savings banks, government-owned special purpose banks and other non-joint stock banking institutions that often retain important market shares to multiply money and shape monetary phenomena. Brief considerations follows of these issues in Marx, Schumpeter and Keynes, and other observations about monetary statecraft and the classics.

Marx

Marx's works on monetary phenomena share this analytic shift away from his broader studies that assume phenomena of money, credit, banking and finance to be secondary. Fortunately, his empirical analyses of historical problems of money, credit, banking, and finance find independent causal phenomena. This is not a flaw. Instead, this difference arises because the empirical, problem-oriented studies of Marx identify and problematize important anomalies about money and monetary policy, anomalies not only for Marx but also for broader theories of political economy. By turning away from general theory toward a better account of money and monetary policy, Marx produces several observations that remain relevant to studies of money, banking, credit, financial markets and crises today. Our reading of Marx's empirical texts on money and monetary policy suggest that they are consistent with core ideas in the theory of monetary statecraft: about muddling through, reacting to circumstances and the importance of timing, and recursive causal loops in public policy. Marx also serves as inspiration for Minsky's financial instability hypothesis, while Keynes sees Marx's concept of hoarding as a forerunner to his concept of liquidity preference; both of which remain central references for study of the politics of monetary policy.

Recent studies of money in Marx confirm the importance of this difference between his broader theories and his discussion the independent causal forces of monetary phenomena.[2] Foley argues that, in terms of definitions and concepts that are part of his broader theory, Marx insists that the value of money retains a strict relation to value in terms of labour time such that once exchange values and prices enter into focus, *unequal exchange* ensues because of the 'law of the conservation of values'. This concept of unequal exchange in Marx provides new opportunities for study of national financial accounts in ways that may build on in the contributions of stock-flow and balance sheet approaches in recent monetary economics (used in this book to compare Brazil, the United States and Germany in chapter five). A core idea in studies of national financial accounts is that data on the balance sheets of households, banks, firms, governments and the rest of the world can reveal negative and positive flows across sectors.[3] This runs counter to the assertion in recent balance sheet models of monetary economics that assume stable values across sectors. Estimation of wealth effects and other measures of gains and losses on the balance sheets of domestic sectors and, for those interested in international relations, between countries and the rest of the world, provide promising research agendas that are explored in chapter five.

Marx's empirical, problem-oriented analyses provide further opportunities for reassessment of politics and monetary policy. For Foley, Marx's empirical studies of money and credit abandon the idea that money matters less than broader trends in the real economy. Once again, money and credit become independent causal factors rather than consequences of other economic factors. For Foley, two views of monetary policy drawn from Marx provide promising theories relevant today. Recent 'post crisis' debates about the state as lender of last resort[4] and gold as a commodity for ultimate mediation during crises[5] resonate with core ideas about money in Marx. This promises to help rethink relations between politics and monetary policy. The importance of Marx for Minsky's theory of financial instability has also been widely noted; providing further promising agendas for reassessing politics and monetary policy.

Schumpeter

Schumpeter also insists on the neutrality of money when concerned about economic theory in general. However, upon consideration of specific problems of credit, banking and monetary policy, he indicates otherwise. Schumpeter first appears adamant:

> Money enters the picture only in the modest role of a technical device that has been adopted in order to facilitate transactions. This device can no doubt get out of order, and if it does it will indeed produce phenomena that are specifically attributable to its *modus operandi*.
>
> (Schumpeter, *History of Economic Analysis,* p. 265)

The bulk of Schumpeter's opus is indeed dedicated to themes of the real economy such as questions of income, production, innovation and the supply, demand and circulation of goods and services.

However, in his history of economic theory, Schumpeter clearly demarcates monetary economics in ways contrary to his general assertion that money matters only if, and indeed has a modus operandi, if and only if it gets out of order:

> Monetary Analysis, in the first place, spells denial of the proposition that, with the exception of what may be called monetary disorders, the element of money is of secondary importance in the explanation of the economic process of reality . . . We are thus led, step by step, to admit monetary elements into Real Analysis and to doubt that money can *ever* be 'neutral' in any meaningful sense.
>
> (Schumpeter, *History of Economic Analysis,* p. 265)

This is a compelling example of the shift in classic political economy that occurs when authors turn from broader questions about political economy to focus on problems of money and monetary policy.

Schumpeter also supports our assertion that monetary data provide a privileged source for qualitative methods to analyze politics and public policy. This study used monetary aggregates to unravel the causes and consequences of politics and monetary policies over time in a variety of settings. In this respect, the evidence acquired implies a back-to-basics approach to analysis of data based on historical institutional and process tracing methods. This way of working is supported by the following warning of Schumpeter:

> [M]onetary aggregates are homogeneous, whereas most nonmonetary ones are but meaningless heaps of hopelessly disparate things; and if we wish to work with a small number of variables, we can hardly help resorting to monetary ones.
>
> (Schumpeter, *History of Economic Analysis,* p. 266)

Monetary aggregates provide a rich source of evidence for problem-oriented, open-ended qualitative multivariate analysis if handled with care.

For example, Schumpeter signals the importance of considering broader categories of money. We have indeed used standard monetary measures as compiled and aggregated by the Central Bank of Brazil such as M0, M1, M2, M3 and M4, and new financial balance sheet categories of assets and liabilities that have been compiled in accord with recent advances in monetary economics.[6] For Schumpeter, when items such as credit instruments, bank notes and checking deposits perform functions of money (not necessarily all functions of money), then these instruments 'intrude into the monetary system'.[7] We have followed these 'intrusions' as they have occurred both in Brazilian history and, especially, amidst the recent period of price stability and democratization to understand the politics of monetary policy.

Schumpeter also traces the emergence of core ideas about money in terms of *minimal and descriptive definitions of money* which bring conceptual order to different monetary aggregates. First, a minimal definition of money as coin and currency is proposed by Schumpeter. Then, broader definitions of money are proposed to include credit, bank deposits, government bonds, and other securities and derivatives to consider their effect on money and monetary phenomena. For Schumpeter, two core positions emerge in the history of economic theory: one a strict metallist view of money that insisted on a minimal definition of money (and, by extension, other instruments that imply legal or other claims to money or market operations in money). For Schumpeter, a second, broader, 'descriptive' definition of money began with John Law, such that he begins with the following exclamations: 'Manufacture of money! Credit as a creator of money! Manifestly, this opens up other theoretical vistas'.[8] Minimal and descriptive (or limited and broader) definitions of money pervade differences in monetary economics until today. This turn in Schumpeter suggests the need to focus on credit, bank deposits, bonds and other instruments as money that take causal precedence far more than may be suggested by focusing on his general position.

Schumpeter also leverages our findings about method. Most of the advances reported by Schumpeter in the history of economic theory toward understanding money arise from empirical, problem-oriented studies of monetary policy. Chapter seven of Schumpeter's history of economic theory opens with discussion of 'England's problems' and, the work of Henry Thornton. Indeed, Schumpeter suggests that monetary economics first emerged as a sub-discipline during debates about whether inflation was caused by the Bank of England or not (leading up to the Bank Charter Act of 1844 that sought to separate banking from management of the money supply by imposing 100 percent metal reserves against bank notes). Here arise the advantages of Thornton's broader view of money

> that included full-value and token coins, bank notes, deposits subject to check or, alternatively, the checks themselves, and, under certain conditions, bills of exchange. This was all right: obviously, the total of All We Pay With is a meaningful notion; its chief analytic value consists in the recognition it implies of the fact that there is no *essential* difference between bank notes and deposits.

> (Schumpeter, *History of Economic Analysis,* p. 668)

This begins a long debate about categories of money. Several ideas reviewed by Schumpeter support core ideas about monetary statecraft presented in this book.

First, Schumpeter's discussion of chartalist theories of money help describe how governments shape money. Take, for example, Schumpeter's citation of Ricardo's position on seigniorage: 'Ricardo, not inelegantly, construed paper money as money, the whole cost of which "may be considered as seigniorage"' (Schumpeter, *History of Economic Analysis,* p. 669).

Seniorage is one of many ways whereby governments shape money, both in the sense of a minimal definition of money as currency and broader categories of money such as bank deposits, bonds and other securities.

As Schumpeter proceeds through his history of economic theory, he shifts away from disregard for monetary phenomena to recognition of their independent causal importance. This culminates in his endorsement of *a credit theory of money*: 'practically and analytically, a credit theory of money is possibly preferable to a monetary theory of credit'.[9] From this perspective, Schumpeter reviews debates about money between advocates of the 'banking principle' and advocates of the 'currency principle' that problematized Bank of England policy. He then reviews subsequent monetary policy debates about the gold standard, bimetallism, international monetary cooperation, and problems of stabilization and money management.

Given the importance of monetary channels for social inclusion, and the conceptions of social justice and citizenship behind new basic income policies in Brazil, it is also of note that Schumpeter raises questions about justice when discussing money and prices.[10] In reference to Took and Newmarch's *History of Prices*,[11] Schumpeter notes that 'the variations in the purchasing power of money brought up the question of "justice" as between creditors and debtors (or else, so far as the public debt was concerned, taxpayers)'.[12] For Schumpeter, earlier analyses about tradeoffs (such as between higher prices and widespread bankruptcy, or debtors as an active part of the economy whose relief may benefit all), became lost in the shift to broader treatments of general prices, especially after numerical methods of indexation in the work of Fisher became widely adopted.[13]

These observations from Schumpeter help broaden the study of politics, money, and monetary policy. The redistributive effects of inflation and price stability, the importance of new theories of basic income, and the problem of wealth effects in new approaches to stock-flow balance sheets of financial accounts sum to suggest that much work remains to be done on normative and empirical theories of money and justice. In this sense, conclusions from this study of Brazil differ. Across advanced economies, a reluctant consensus now prevails that globalization, financialization, and crises confirm the insights of *critical approaches* to money and monetary phenomena. We report a different experience in Brazil: the reality that monetary channels have been used to accelerate financial and social inclusion. Monetary policy may be at the centre of democratization.

Keynes and monetary statecraft

Evidence from Brazil has also provided new perspectives on problems at the centre of the Keynesian tradition. Keynes' landmark considerations on money also evidence a shift away from general views of political economy as determined by real factors of production and consumption (that supposes monetary phenomena to be secondary), to recognition of stronger causal roles for money and monetary phenomena. Keynes introduces this shift with his famous metaphor: 'If, however, we are tempted to assert that money is the drink which stimulates the system to activity, we must remind ourselves that there may be several slips between the cup and the lip' (Keynes, *General Theory*, Ch. 13, III).

Keynes builds on this observation in several ways. Take, for example, the following passage of the *General Theory:*

> For whilst an increase in the quantity of money may be expected, *cet. par.,* to reduce the rate of interest, this will not happen if the liquidity-preferences of the public are increasing more than the quantity of money; and whilst a decline in the rate of interest may be expected, *cet. par.,* to increase the volume of investment, this will not happen if the schedule of the marginal efficiency of capital is falling more rapidly than the rate of interest; and whilst an increase in the volume of investment may be expected, *cet. par.,* to increase employment, this may not happen if the propensity to consume is falling off. Finally, if employment increases, prices will rise in a degree partly governed by the shapes of the physical supply functions, and partly by the liability of the wage-unit to rise in terms of money. And when output has increased and prices have risen, the effect of this on liquidity-preference will be to increase the quantity of money necessary to maintain a given rate of interest.
>
> (Keynes, *General Theory,* Ch. 13, Part III)

This passage is critical for understanding money and monetary policy. It differs from Keynes' previous treatment of 'bearishness' and refines Marx's conception of hoarding. Liquidity preference 'corresponds' to, but is more than bearishness as Keynes describes in his *Treatise on Money.*[14] Hoarding, a concept at the centre of Marx's analysis of money as noted above, also, from this perspective, anticipates Keynes' concept of liquidity preference. However, for Keynes, liquidity preference is[15] a more accurate scale that expands on Marx's observations.

Keynes provides further support for our problem-oriented approach and the use of minimal and descriptive definitions as the best ways of working with essentially contested concepts of money. The historical chapter of this book focused on paper money, bank notes, credit and deposits, government bonds, discounting from the central bank and national bank and other sources that shape the supply of money *depending on the question about politics and monetary policy at hand*. In the *General Theory* (p. 111), Keynes suggests this research strategy:

> Without disturbance to this definition,[16] we can draw the line between 'money' and 'debts' at whatever point is most convenient for handling a particular problem. For example, we can treat as money any command over general purchasing power which the owner has not parted with for a period in excess of three months, and as *debt* what cannot be recovered for a longer period than this; or we can substitute for 'three months' one month or three days or three

hours or any other period; or we can exclude from *money* whatever is not legal tender on the spot. It is often convenient in practice to include in *money* time-deposits with banks and, occasionally, even such instruments as (*e.g.*) treasury bills. As a rule, I shall, as in my *Treatise on Money,* assume that money is coextensive with bank deposits.

Recent advances in the use of minimal and descriptive definitions for research designs sustain this view of Keynes. This implies that problem-oriented, qualitative methods such as case studies, focused comparisons and historical institutionalism using process tracing may best identify causal relations.

A final, more critical comment about the classics is in order. In their discussions of monetary policy, Marx, Schumpeter and Keynes unfortunately share a bias toward commercial transactions and private banking to the detriment of money and monetary transactions not only from the point of view of households and alternative banking institutions, but also politics. The theory of monetary statecraft seeks to avert this bias by placing citizens at the forefront of the politics of monetary policy, such that monetary policy is not amenable to calculations of economic efficiency but, instead, is constructed through political support and the vagaries of policy making. Schumpeter does mention justice as a criteria (that, for him, remained too limited by discussions of wealth effects due to differential price change). However, none of the other classic authors considered in this conclusion (and indeed few if any contemporary studies of money and monetary policy), treat politics as relevant to shaping markets for money and monetary policy. This observation is not a slight of hand to insert normative questions into empirical and causal analysis. This is a warning; without taking the autonomy of politics and policy making into account, theories of money and monetary policy will remain limited, misconceived, and wrong.

Stock-flow approaches in monetary economics

Recent advances in monetary economics promise to bridge this gap between politics and money avert the biases toward commercial transactions and private banking that weaken so many studies of money. The inability of standard approaches in economics to predict or explain the asset bubbles that produced global financial crisis in 2007–2008 has led to reassessment of theory and method. Monetary economists have returned to stock-flow approaches and other theoretical traditions that use concepts from accounting and finance to study the balance sheets of households, banks, firms, government and relations between domestic economies and the rest of the world. These models were used in this book to compare the context for monetary statecraft in Brazil with different realities in the United States and Germany in the period 2005–2009.

Stock-flow approaches to money and monetary policy emerged in the 1970s as innovations within Keynesian economics. Tobin, Davidson and Minsky returned to Keynes' *Treatise on Money* and chapter 17 of his *General Theory* to rethink monetary phenomena. Because stock-flow approaches have disaggregated broader monetary measures into financial assets and liabilities held, respectively, by households, firms, banks, governments and between countries and the rest of the world, the data and methods developed by researchers in this tradition promise to explain further aspects of politics and monetary policy. However, one presupposition seems wrong: that a steady state obtains wherein the stocks and flows of each economic sector *grow at the same rate*, such that the composition of balance sheets across sectors remain constant. We found the contrary. In chapter five, comparison of the financial balance sheets of banks, households, firms, governments and between Brazil and the rest of the world from 2005–2009 (and similar data from the United States and Germany) suggest a fundamentally different situation. The balance sheets of sectors do not remain constant. Instead, banks increase their share of financial assets substantially in all three cases. And monetary relations between countries and the rest of the world differ dramatically according to where countries sit in the global system.

Monetary channels of change

Classics and stock-flow approaches in monetary economics help leverage the findings of this study. However, the central conclusions of this book are drawn from historical institutional analysis and policy tracing. A wide variety of primary and secondary sources sum to suggest that theories of politics and monetary policy in economics and sociology fall short. This opens a variety of research agendas. Theories of political development and public policy seem especially useful to reassess central banking and monetary policy. They bring politics to the fore as an independent causal factor; clarify how political imperatives arise from the expanding scope of social conflicts that require resolution and inclusion in political institutions. We thereby hope to have demonstrated that monetary policy making is an open-ended, recursive process that remains subject to political and social forces through agenda setting, problem identification, epistemic communities and other causes emphasized by the accumulated knowledge about how public policy works.

   We hope that the theories and concepts about monetary statecraft, and the methods for its study presented in this book may also contribute to reassessment of central banking in academia, international institutions, and public policy fora. After all, the independence of central banking so dear to economic approaches to politics has, in fact, disappeared since the global financial crisis of 2007–2008. Massive lending of last resort, costly recapitalization of banks, capture of government policy by banks and financial institutions, manipulation of global money markets and staggering bailouts of 'too large to fail' banks and financial institutions require new approaches. However, to the contrary, international financial institutions, government agencies, and public policy debates appear, as this book goes too press, still to be reeling not only from the crisis and its consequences, but also from the unprecedent large scale of novel monetary policies used by central banks and government entities across the advanced economies such as zero interest rates and massive infusions of money into banks and other agents described as quantitative easing.

The variety, complexity, and large scale of monetary policies since the global financial crisis of 2007–2008 stand in stark contrast to the poverty of our theories about politics and monetary policy. Neo-classical derivations of optimal non-politics no longer hold. Statistical comparison of aggregate data has also failed to produce convincing theories about politics and monetary policy. It follows that the best way to elaborate theories and concepts about the politics of monetary policy is to turn to qualitative methods such as case studies, policy tracing, and historical institutionalism. These methods are better able to design research capable of producing causal inferences amidst multiple causes, the non-linearities of politics and public policy, and the complexities of path dependence experiences. Qualitative methods may more effectively advance understanding of the large number of new monetary policy tools adopted since crisis in 2007–2008.

In this respect, Brazil and other developing countries retain another analytic advantage. Because so-called unconventional monetary policy tools (such as policy interest rates and reserve requirements), prudential policy tools (such as capital requirements), balance sheet tools such as intervention into domestic financial markets (interbank lending markets, sovereign bond markets, credit markets, mortgage markets) and foreign exchange markets (foreign exchange intervention, foreign currency reserve management) have, in fact, been used as part of broader repertories of monetary policies, both amidst crisis and more positive periods when great expectations prevailed about reaching currency convertibility and price stability. The experience of Brazil has provided more effective natural experiments to understand the politics of monetary policy while observers in advanced economies remain shell shocked by crisis and their loss of parsimonious theories of central bank independence.

Brazil presents a different story, one of coming out of underdevelopment and monetary chaos caused by military rule and delayed transition to democracy. Large political returns ensued from putting money into order. And notwithstanding terribly high interest rates, shallow credit markets, volatile parameters, elevated risk premia and declining marginal gains to consumer-led growth, this novelty is notable. Monetary channels of change in Brazil have produced positive-sum relations between social inclusion, democratization and the modernization of central bank capacity and monetary authority. This is an anomaly for both economic theories of politics and monetary policy *and* sociological theories of policy capture. This book has explored these anomalies and indeed the long history of monetary policy making in Brazil from the perspective of statecrafting in comparative political economy. We hope thereby to have contributed to the suggests that reassessment of monetary policy by broadening the scope of monetary economics analysis to include theories of political development and public policy, while reaping the analytic advantages of exploring the largely uncharted trajectories of emerging economies such as Brazil.

Notes

1 Pateman, Carole. 'Democratizing Citizenship: Some Advantages of a Basic Income'. *Politics & Society*, 32/1 (2004): 89–105; Barry, Barry. 'Real Freedom and Basic Income'. *Journal of Political Philosophy*, 4/3 (1996): 242–276.

2 Foley, Duncan. 'On Marx's Theory of Money', *Social Concept*, 1/1 (1983): 5–19; Foley, Duncan. *Understanding Capital: Marx's Economic Theory* (Cambridge, MA: Harvard University Press, 1986).

3 Foley, ibid., p. 7. 'For any particular capital or group of capitals (a firm, sector, industry, or nation) the value flows measured in money terms may deviate from true value flows because of unequal exchanges in which value is either transferred to or drained out of the sector in question. Thus the notion of value is an operational and measurable concept if we specify the degree to which we believe unequal exchange is an important factor in the situation and the concrete circumstances that permit the inequality of exchange'.

4 Foley, ibid., p.12: '[T]he State might stand at the apex of the chain of promises of higher and higher social validity. State credit, rather than gold, then would be the ultimate means of payment for private transactors. This second theoretical path inverts Marx's order of credit are only substitutes (or supplements, as Jacques Derrida would say [1976, pp. 141ff]), which stand in for gold and must vanish in the ultimate moment of payment'.

5 Foley, ibid., p. 12: 'Following the second theoretical path, we would view credit as analytically the first form of money, and gold only as an ultimate mediation brought forcibly into play when exchange reaches a point of crisis, either in the relations of two agents or in the system as a whole. The question of what role, if any, gold plays in a monetary system would remain open to examination in concrete instances'.

6 Godley, Wynne and Lavoie, Marc. *Monetary Economics: An Integrated Approach to Credit, Money, Income, Production and Wealth* (London: Palgrave, 2007). On the importance of balance sheet approaches for reassessment of monetary policy and theory since the global financial crisis of 2007–2008, see Bezemer, Dirk J. 'Understanding Financial Crisis Through Accounting Models' (University of Groningen, memo, 2009) and the papers presented to the International Monetary Fund seminar, 'Balance Sheet Approaches and Macroeconomics'.

7 Schumpeter, *History of Economic Analysis*, p. 305.

8 Ibid.

9 Ibid., p. 686.

10 Ibid., p. 682.

11 Tooke, Thomas and Newmarch, William. *History of Prices and of the State of the Circulation from 1792 to 1856* (London: Longman, 6 volumes, 1838–1857).

12 Schumpeter, *History of Economic Analysis*, p. 682.

13 Fisher, indexation.

14 'For "bearishness" is there defined as the functional-relationship, not between the rate of interest (or price of debts) and the quantity of money, but between the price of assets and debts, taken together, and the quantity of money. This treatment, however, involved a confusion between results due to a change in the rate of interest and those due to a change in the schedule of the marginal efficiency of capital, which I hope I have here avoided' (*General Theory*, Ch. 13, Part IV).

15 'Indeed if we were to substitute "propensity to hoard" for "hoarding", it would come to substantially the same thing. But if we mean by "hoarding" an actual increase in cash-holding, it is an incomplete idea – and seriously misleading if it causes us to think of "hoarding" and "not-hoarding" as simple alternatives. For the decision to hoard is not taken absolutely or without regard to the advantages offered for parting with liquidity – it results from a balancing of advantages, and we have, therefore, to know what lies in the other scale. Moreover it is impossible for the actual amount of hoarding to change as a result of decisions on the part of the public, so long as we mean by "hoarding" the actual

holding of cash. For the amount of hoarding must be equal to the quantity of money (or – on some definitions – to the quantity of money minus what is required to satisfy the transactions-motive); and the quantity of money is not determined by the public. All that the propensity of the public towards hoarding can achieve is to determine the rate of interest at which the aggregate desire to hoard becomes equal to the available cash. The habit of overlooking the relation of the rate of interest to hoarding may be a part of the explanation why interest has been usually regarded as the reward of not spending, whereas in fact it is, the reward of not-hoarding' (Keynes, *General Theory,* Ch.13, V).

16 Keynes refers to the definition of the rate of interest in the *General Theory,* Ch. 13, Part II: 'For the rate of interest is, in itself, nothing more than the inverse proportion between a sum of money and what can be obtained for parting with control over the money in exchange for a debt for a stated period of time'.

Bibliography

Official and historical documents

Albuquerque, Laurenço de C. *A crise financeira e sua solução*. (Rio de Janeiro: Imprensa Americana – Fabio Reis and c., 1897).

Almanak Laerte. (Rio de Janeiro: 1888–1895, 1900, 1905).

Amaral, Angelo. *O Accôrdo financeiro*. (Rio de Janeiro: Livraria Brazileira, 1898).

Andrada, Antonio C. R. de. *Bancos de Emissão no Brasil*. (Rio de Janeiro: Leite Ribeiro, 1923).

Annuario estatístico de São Paulo, 1901–1920. (São Paulo: Typographia do Diario Official, 1904–1923). 29 volumes.

Annuario estatistico do Brasil, 1908–2006. (Rio de Janeiro: Typographia da Estatistica, 1916–2006). 67 volumes.

Aranha, Oswaldo. *Relatório apresentado a Getúlio Vargas por Oswaldo Aranha. Exposição relativa ao período de 3 de novembro de 1931 à 15 de novembro de 1933*. (Rio de Janeiro: Ministério da Fazenda, 1933).

Azevedo, J. Lúcio. Novas epanáforas: *estudos de história e literatura*. (Lisbon: A. M. Teixeira, 1932).

Azevedo, Manoel A. D. *Considerações sobre o crédito real*. (Rio de Janeiro: Typ. Leuzniger, 1892).

Balanço da receita e despeza da Republica no exercicio de 1889–1914. (Rio de Janeiro: Imprensa Nacional, 1892–1928). 26 volumes.

Balanço da receita e despeza do Imperio no exercicio de 1856–1888. (Rio de Janeiro: Typographia Nacional, 1859–1891). 19 volumes.

Banco do Brasil, *Relatório anual*. (Rio de Janeiro, 1889–1894, 1905–1930).

Barbosa, Rio. *O Papel e a Baixa no Câmbio*. (Rio de Janeiro: Reler, 2005).

Barbosa, Rui. *Finanças e Política da Republica*. (Rio de Janeiro: Companhia Impressora, 1892).

Barbosa, Rui. *Obras Completas de Rui Barbosa*. (Rio de Janeiro: Casa da Rui Barbosa, 1949–75). 53 volumes.

Boucas, Valentim. *Finanças do Brasil*. (Rio de Janeiro: Ministério da Fazenda, 1955).

Brant, R. *As Illusões financeiras*. (Rio de Janeiro: Imprensa Nacional, 1921).

Breve noticia do estado financeiro das províncias. (Rio de Janeiro: Imprensa Nacional, 1887).

Bulhões Jardim, José Leopoldo de. *Ministros da Fazenda do Brasil, 1856–28*. (Rio de Janeiro: Edições Financeiros, n.d.).

Bulhões Jardim, José Leopoldo de. *Os financistas do Brasil*. (Rio de Janeiro: Jornal do Comércio, 1914).

Bulhões, Octávio G. *Depoimento. Programa de História Oral*. (Rio de Janeiro: CPDOC, 1990).

Bulhões, Octavio G. *À margem de um relatório; texto das conclusões da Comissão Mista Brasileiro-Americana de Estudos Econômicos (Missão Abbink)*. (Rio de Janeiro: Edições Financeiras, 1950).

Caixa de Conversão, Documentos Parlamentare. (Paris: Typ. Aillard, Alves and Cia. 1914). 2 volumes.

Calogeras, J. G. *La Politique Monétaire du Brésil*. (Rio de Janeiro: Editora Nacional, 1910).

Calogeras, João P. *Problemas de Governo*. (São Paulo: Empresa Gráfica Rossetti, 1928).

Carlos, Antonio and Brant, Mario. *Economia e finanças do Brasil (1914–1924)*. (Rio de Janeiro: Imprensa Nacional, 1924).

Castro Carreria, Liberato. *Historia financeira e orçamentaria do Imperio do Brazil desde sua fundação*. (Rio de Janeiro: Imprensa Nacional, 1889).

Cavalcanti, A. *Resenha financeira do Império*. (Rio de Janeiro: Imprensa Nacional, 1893).

Cifras e notas: (Economia e finanças do Brasil). (Rio de Janeiro: Typ. da 'Revista do Supremo Tribunal', 1925).

Collecção de mappas estatisticos do commercio e navegação do Imperio do Brasil no anno financeiro de 1841–1850. (Rio de Janeiro: Typographia Nacional, 1848–1855). 6 volumes.

A Conferência Nacional de Economia e Administração. (Rio de Janeiro: Imprensa Nacional, 1940).

Contas apresentadas á Assembléa Geral Legislativa pelo Marques de Itanhaem, tutor de S. M. I. e Altezas, precedidas de hum relatorio explicativo do anno financeiro da casa imperial de 1838–1839. (Rio de Janeiro: Typographia Nacional, 1839).

Correspondencia entre o Ministerio da Fazenda e a Legação de Londres Concernente ao Emprestimo Contrahido em 1865. (Rio de Janeiro: Typographia Nacional, 1866).

A crise commercial do (Rio de Janeiro em 1864). (Rio de Janeiro: B. L. Garnier, Livreiro Editor, 1864).

A crise financeira: As emissões e o Ministro da Fazenda do Governo Provisório. (Bahia: Typographia e Encadernação do 'Diario da Bahia', 1892).

Curso forçado. (Rio de Janeiro: Typographia Laemmert, 1888). 2nd edition.

Departamento Nacional de Estatística, *Movimento Bancário*. (Rio de Janeiro: Editora Nacional, 1927–1928, 1929–1930, 1930–1933).

Departamento Nacional de Indústria e Comércio, *Sociedades mercantis autorizadas a funcionar no Brasil, 1806–45*. (Rio de Janeiro: Imprensa Nacional, 1947).

Dívida interna fundada da União. (Rio de Janeiro: Contadoria Central da Republica, 1914).

Documentação para o historico das Tarifas Aduaneiras no Brasil 1808–1889. (Rio de Janeiro: Livraria J. Leite, n.d.).

Du Pin e Almeida, Miguel C. *Factos econômicos*. (Rio de Janeiro: Livraria Francisco Alves, 1913).

Economical data about Brazil 1808–1929. (Rio de Janeiro: Impensa Nacional, 1924–1929). 3 volumes.

Elementos de estatistica: comprehendendo a theoria da sciencia e a sua aplicação á estatistica commercial do Brasil. (Rio de Janeiro: Typographia Nacional, 1865). 2 volumes.

Elementos de finanças (estudo theorico-pratico. (Rio de Janeiro: Imprensa Nacional, 1896).

Estatistica das Finanças do Brasil: receita, despesas e dividas publicas da União, dos Estados e dos Municipios. (Rio de Janeiro: Typ. da Estatistica, 1926).

Estudo economico e financeiro sobre o Estado de S. Paulo. (São Paulo: Typographia do Diario Official, 1896).

Estudo para a solução das questões do cambio e o papel-moeda no Brazil. (Rio de Janeiro: Typographia Laemmert, 1888).

Estudo sobre a situação econômica e financeira do Brasil. (Rio de Janeiro: Typ. do Jornal do Commercio, de Rodrigues and C., 1915).

Exposição de motivos sobre a situação financeira e idéas de reforma apresentadas pelo Exm. Sr. Barão de Lucena – Ministro da Fazenda ao Generalissimo Presidente da Republica: Enviada em mensagem ao Congresso a 19 de setembro de 1891. (Rio de Janeiro: Imprensa Nacional, 1891).

Exposição do Estado da Fazenda Publica. (Rio de Janeiro: Typographia Nacional, 1823).

Falcão, Waldemar. *O Empirismo Monetário no Brasil.* (Rio de Janeiro: Companhia Editoria Nacional).

Finanças. (Rio de Janeiro: Comp. Typ. do Brasil, 1899). 2nd edition.

As finanças brasileiras. (Rio de Janeiro: Officinas Grafficas do 'Jornal do Brasil', 1927).

As finanças da regeneração estudo politico: offerecido aos mineiros. (Rio de Janeiro: Typographia da Reforma, 1876).

Os financistas do Brasil: conferencia realisada na Bibliotheca Nacional no dia 22 de Dezembro de 1913. (Rio de Janeiro: Rodrigues and C, 1914).

Finanças do Brasil (1824–1942). Finanças dos Estados do Brasil. (Rio de Janeiro: Typ. do Jornal do Commercio; Rodrigues and C., 1932–1942). 11 volumes.

As Finanças do Manifesto: Refutação – Collecção de artigos publicados em 'O Debate'. (Rio de Janeiro: Imprensa Nacional, 1898).

Finanças e politica da Republica: Discursos e Escriptos. (Rio de Janeiro: Companhia Impressora, 1892).

Finanças: quadros synopticos da receita e despeza do Brazil, periodo de 1822 a 1913. (Rio de Janeiro: Typographia do Ministerio da Agricultura, 1914).

Freire, Felisbelo. *História do Banco do Brasil.* (Rio de Janeiro: Typ. O Economista Brasileiro, 1907).

A grande política: balanço do Imperio no reinado actual: liberaes e conservadores: Estudo politico-financeiro. (Rio de Janeiro: Imperial Instituto Artistico, 1877).

Guanabara, Alcindo. *A presidência Campos Sales.* (Rio de Janeiro: Laemert, 1902).

Historico da dívida externa federal. (Rio de Janeiro: Imprensa Nacional, 1923).

Leis de Orçamento da Republica. (Rio de Janeiro: Imprensa Nacional, 1892–1922).

Leis de Orçamento do Imperio. (Rio de Janeiro: Imprensa Nacional, 1879–1889).

Meili, Julius. *Brasilianische Geldwesen.* (Zurich: Typographia de Jean Frey, 1905). 2 volumes.

Niemeyer, Otto E. *The Niemeyer Report to the Brazilian Government.* (London: W. Neeley, 1931).

Nogueira, Dênio. *Depoimento.* (Rio de Janeiro: Programa de História Oral do CPDOC/ FGV, Editora FGV, 1993).

O balanço da dynastia: Despezas da casa e Familia Imperial desde o anno de 1808 até o dia 15 de Novembro de 1889. (Rio de Janeiro: Imprensa Nacional, 1890).

Observações sobre o melhoramento do meio circulante no Imperio do Brazil. (Rio de Janeiro: Ministério da Fazenda, 1835).

O orçamento do Imperio desde sua fundação. (Rio de Janeiro: Typographia Nacional, 1883).

Orçamento da Republica do Brazil. (Rio de Janeiro: Imprensa Nacional, 1892–1911).

Orçamento do Imperio do Brazil. Orçamento da despeza e receita do Imperio. (Rio de Janeiro: Typographia Nacional, 1833–1889).

Orçamento dos Ministerios. (Rio de Janeiro: Imprensa Nacional, 1886–1920).

Organisações e Programmas Ministeriaes desde 1822 a 1889. (Rio de Janeiro: Imprensa Nacional, 1889).

Ortigão, Ramalho. *O anno commercial economico e financeiro de 1918.* (Rio de Janeiro: Typ. Besnard Frères, 1919).

Pereira de Barros, José M. F. *Apontamentos de direito financeiro brasileiro.* (Rio de Janeiro: Eduardo and Henrique Laemmert, 1855).

Politica economica, valorisação do café (Documentos Parlamentares, 1895–1915. (Rio de Janeiro: Typ. do Jornal do Commercio, de Rodrigues and C, 1915).

Problemas de administração: relatorio confidencial apresentado em 1918 ao Conselheiro Rodrigues Alves sobre a situação orçamentaria e administrativa do Brasil. (São Paulo: Companhia Editora Nacional, 1933).

Quadro dos municípios brasileiros vigorante no quinquênio de 1 de Janeiro de 1939 a 31 de dezembro de 1943. (Rio de Janeiro: Imprensa Nacional, 1943).

Reflexões sobre as finanças do Brasil operações de credito do Thesouro e o emprestimo contrahido em Londres em cinco milhões de libras esterlinas no corrente anno. (Rio de Janeiro: Typographia Universal de Laemmert, 1865).

Reforma monetária: O ouro. (Rio de Janeiro: Imprensa da Casa da Moeda, 1893). 2nd edition.

Reforma monetaria: parecer e discurso sobre o projecto que concretiza o plano financeiro do Presidente Washington Luis. (Rio de Janeiro: Imprensa Nacional, 1926).

Relatório da Commissão de Inquerito nomeada por aviso do Ministro da Fazenda de 10 de outubro de 1859. (Rio de Janeiro: Ministério da Fazenda, no date).

Relatório da commissão nomeada para examinar o Estado da escripturação dos Bancos Rural e Agrícola. (no date or publisher).

Relatório do Ministro da Fazenda em 1908. (Rio de Janeiro: Imprensa Nacional, 1908).

Relatorio dos trabalhos apresentados pela Comissão Tecnica á Comissão de Estudos Financeiros e Economicos dos Estados e Municipios. (no date or publisher).

Reorganização das finanças brasileiras: Relatorio apresentado ao Governo Brasileiro. (Rio de Janeiro: Imprensa Nacional, 1931).

Resenha financeira do ex-imperio do Brasil em 1889. (Rio de Janeiro: Imprensa Nacional, 1890).

Resumo de varias estatisticas economico-financeiras. (Rio de Janeiro: Typographia da Estatistica, 1924).

Retrospecto commercial de 1876–1939. (Rio de Janeiro: Typographia Imperial e Constitucional de J. Villeneuve and C.; Typographia do Jornal do Commercio de Rodrigues and C. [1877–1933]).

Ribeiro, João. *Bancos, memória apresentado ao congresso industrial de Minas Gerais.* (Juiz de Fora, MG: Typographia Central, 1903).

Rodriquez, J. C. *Alguns artigos sobre finanças: publicados no Jornal do Commercio.* (Rio de Janeiro: Typografia do Jornal do Commercio de Rodrigues and C., 1899).

Souto, L. R. Vieira. *O Papel Moeda e o Cambio.* (Paris: Imprimerie Vaugirard, 1925).

Souza, Carlos. *Anarquia Monetária e suas Conseqüências.* (São Paulo: Monteiro Lobato, 1924).

Sturz, J. J. *A review, financial, statistical, and commercial, of the Empire of Brazil and its resources: together with a suggestion of the expediency and mode of admitting, Brazilian and other foreign sugars into Great Britain for refining and exportation.* (London: Effingham Wilson, 1837).

Tesouro Nacional, 1808–1908: resumo historico. (Rio da Janeiro: Imprensa Nacional, 1908).

A unificação do padrão monetario. (Rio de Janeiro: Imprensa Nacional, 1923).

Vianna, Victor. *O Banco do Brasil: sua formação, seu engrandecimento, sua missão nacional.* (Rio de Janeiro: Jornal do Comércio, 1926).

A vida econômica e financeira do Brasil. (Rio de Janeiro: Imprensa Nacional, 1915).

Whitaker, José M. *A administração financeira do Governo Provisório de 4 de novembro de 1930 a 16 de novembro de 1931.* (São Paulo: Revista dos Tribunais, 1933).

Whitaker, José M. *Seis Meses, de novo, no Ministério da Fazenda.* (Rio de Janeiro: E.G.O.C.S.A., 1956).

Wileman, J. P. *Brazilian Exchange: the study of an inconvertible currency.* (Buenos Aires: Galli Bros., Calli San Martin, 1896).

Wileman's Brazilian Review; a weekly journal of trade, finance, economics, and shipping. (Rio de Janiero: 1898–1940). 2,184 issues.

Secondary sources

Abreu, Marcelo P. 'On the Memory of Bankers: Brazilian Foreign Debt, 1824–1946', *Political Economy, Studies in the Surplus Approach*, 4/1 (1988): 45–82.

Abreu, Marcelo P. 'A missão Niemeyer', *Revista de Administração de Empresas*, 14/4 (1974): 7–28.

Abreu, Marcelo P. (ed). *Ordem do Progresso: Cem Anos de Política Econômica Republicana, 1889–89.* (Rio de Janeiro: Campus, 1990).

Abrucio, Fernando. *Os Barões da Federação.* (São Paulo: Edusp, 1999).

Admati, Anat R., DeMarzo, Peter M., Hellwig, Martin F. and Pfleiderer, Paul. 'Fallacies, irrelevant facts and myths in the discussion of capital regulation: why bank equity is *not* expensive,' (Stanford University, working paper, 2011).

Aguiar, Pinto de. *Rui e a Economia Brasileira.* (Rio de Janeiro: Fundação da Casa Rui Barbosa, 1971).

Alesina, Alberto. 'Macroeconomics and Politics', in Fischer, Stanley (ed). *NBER Macroeconomics Annual.* (Chicago: University of Chicago Press, 1988), pp. 13–62.

Alesina, Alberto and Drazen, Allen. 'Why Are Stabilizations Delayed?' *American Economic Review*, 81/5 (1991): 1170–1188.

Alesina, Alberto and Summers, Lawrence. 'Central Bank Independence and Macroeconomic Performance: Some Comparative Evidence', *Journal of Money, Credit and Banking*, 25/2 (1993): 151–162.

Alesina, Alberto, Roubini, Nouriel, and Cohen, Gerald. *Political Cycles and the Macroeconomy.* (Cambridge, MA: MIT Press, 1997).

Alesina, Alberto F. and Andrea, Stella. 'The Politics of Monetary Policy' (May 2010). Harvard Institute of Economic Research Discussion Paper No. 2183.

Allen, Franklin and Gale, Douglas. *Comparing Financial Systems.* (Cambridge, MA: MIT Press, 2000).

Alves, José de Brito. *O Mercado Aberto no Brasil.* (Rio de Janeiro: Sindicato dos Bancos do Estado da Guanabara, 1973).

Amann, Edmund and Baer, Werner. 'The Illusion of Stability: The Brazilian Economy Under Cardoso', *World Development*, 28/10 (2000): 1805–1819.

Ames, Barry. *The Deadlock of Democracy in Brazil.* (Ann Arbor, MI: University of Michigan Press, 2001).

Ames, Barry. *Political Survival: Politicians and Public Policy in Latin America.* (Berkeley: University of California Press, 1987).

Andrews, David. 'Capital Mobility and State Autonomy: Toward a Structural Theory of International Monetary Relations', *International Studies Quarterly*, 38/2 (1994): 193–218.

Andrews, David. (ed). *International Monetary Power*. (Ithaca, NY: Cornell University Press, 2006).

Ardant, Gabriel. 'Financial Policy and Economic Infrastructure of Modern States and Nations' in Charles Tilly (ed). *The Formation of National States in Western Europe*. (Princeton, NJ: Princeton University Press, 1975), pp. 164–242.

Areosa, Waldyr D. and Coelho. Christiano A. 'Using a DSGE Model to Assess the Macroeconomic Effects of Reserve Requirements in Brazil' (Central Bank of Brazil Working Paper 303, 2013).

Arida, Persio and Lara-Resende, André. 'Inflação Inercial e Reforma Monetária,' in Persio Arida (ed). *Inflação Zero*. (Rio de Janeiro: Paz e Terra, 1986), pp. 11–35.

Armijo, Leslie and Katada, Saori (eds). *The Financial Statecraft of Emerging Powers*. (New York: Palgrave Macmillan, 2014).

Armijo, Leslie E. 'Inflation and Insouciance: The Peculiar Brazilian Game', *Latin American Research Review*, 31/3 (1996): 7–46.

Ayadi, Rym, Schmidt, Reinhard H. and Valverde, Santiago Carbo (eds). *Investigating Diversity in the Banking Sector in Europe: The Performance and Role of Savings Banks*. (Brussels: Centre for European Policy Studies, 2009).

Baer, Mônica. *A Internacionalização Financeira no Brasil*. (Petrópolis, RJ: Vozes, 1986).

Baer, Werner. *The Brazilian Economy: Growth and Development*. (New York: Praeger, 1995). 4th edition.

Baer, Werner. 'Social Aspects of Latin American Inflation,' *Quarterly Review of Economics and Finance*, 31/3 (1991): 45–57.

Baleeiro, Aliomar. *Rui, um Estadista no Ministério da Fazenda*. (Rio de Janeiro: Fundação da Casa Rui Barbosa, 1949).

Baldwin, David A. *Economic Statecraft*. (Princeton, NJ: Princeton University Press, 1985).

Barker, W. J. *Banks and Industry in Contemporary Brazil: Their Organization, Relationship and Leaders*. (New Haven, CT: Yale University Press, 1990).

Barro, Robert and Gordon, David. 'Rules, Discretion and Reputation in a Model of Monetary Policy', *Journal of Monetary Economics*, 12/1 (1983): 123–125.

Bates, Robert. *Open-economy Politics: The Political Economy of the World Coffee Trade*. (Princeton, NJ: Princeton University Press, 1998).

Bates, Robert and Krueger, Anne O. *Political and Economic Interactions in Economic Policy Reform*. (Cambridge, MA: Blackwell, 1993).

Batista Jr., Paulo. N. and Belluzzo, Luiz G. (eds). *A Luta pela Sobrevivência da Moeda Nacional*. (São Paulo: Paz e Terra, 1992).

Bell, Stephanie. 'The role of the state and the hierarchy of money', *Cambridge Journal of Economics*, (2001) 25: 149–163.

Belluzzo, Luiz G. and Almeida, Júlio G. *Depois da Queda: A Economia brasileira da crise da dívida aos impasses do Real*. (Rio de Janeiro: Civilização Brasileira, 2002).

Berger, Allen, Molyneux, Phillip, and Wilson, John (eds.). *The Oxford Handbook of Banking*. (Oxford: Oxford University Press, 2010).

Berger, Suzanne and Dore, Ronald (eds). *National Diversity and Global Capitalism*. (Ithaca, NY: Cornell University Press, 1996).

Bernanke, Ben and Gertler, Mark. 'Inside the black box: the credit channel of monetary policy transmission', *Journal of Economic Perspectives*, 9/4 (1995): 27–48.

Bernhard, William (1998). 'A Political Explanation of Variations in Central Bank Independence', *American Political Science Review*, 92/2 (1998).

Bernstein, E. M. 'A inflação em relação ao Desenvolvimento Econômico', *Revista Brasileira de Economia*, 6/3 (1952): 107–169.

Besouochet, Lídia. *Mauá e seu Tempo*. (São Paulo: Editora Anchieta, 1942).

Bethell, Leslie (ed.). *Cambridge History of Latin America*. (Cambridge: Cambridge University Press, 1984–2008). 11 volumes.

Bett, Virgil M. *Central Banking in México: Monetary Policies and Financial Crisis, 1864–1940)*. (Ann Arbor, MI: University of Michigan Press, 1957).

Bevilaqua, Afonso S., Loyo, Eduardo, and Minella, André. 'Brazil: Taming Inflation Expectations'. (Brasilia: Central Bank of Brazil Working Paper 129, 2007).

Bhattacharya, Sudipto and Thakor, Anjan. 'Contemporary Banking Theory', *Journal of Financial Intermediation*, 3 (1993): 2–50.

Blinder, Alan S. *Central Banking in Theory and Practice*. (Cambridge: MIT Press, 1998).

Bogdanski, Joel, Tombini, Alexandre, and Werlang, Sergio. 'Implementing Inflation Targeting in Brazil'. (Brasilia: Central Bank of Brazil Working Paper 1, 2000).

Bonomo, Marco A. and Brito, Ricardo B. 'Regras monetárias e dinâmica macroeconômica no Brasil: uma abordagem de expectativas racionais', *Revista Brasileira de Economia*, 56/4 (2002): 551–589.

Bordo, Michael D. and Schwartz, Anna J. *A Retrospective on the Classical Gold Standard, 1821–1931*. (Chicago: University of Chicago Press, 1984).

Borges, Maria A. *Eugênio Gudin: Capitalismo e Neoliberalismo*. (São Paulo: Educ, 1996).

Boylan, Delia. *Defusing Democracy: Central Bank Autonomy and the Transition from Authoritarian Rule*. (Ann Arbor, MI: University of Michigan Press, 2001).

Brandstädter, Suzanne, Wade, Peter, and Woodward, Kathrine. 'Introduction: rights, cultures, subjects and citizens', *Economy and Society*, 40/2 (2011) 167–183.

Bresser-Pereira, Luiz C. *Development and Crisis in Brazil, 1930–8*. (Boulder, CO: Westview Press, 1984)

Bresser-Pereira, Luiz C. 'Estabilização em um ambiente adverso: a experiência brasileira de 1987', *Brazilian Review of Political Economy*, 13/4 (1993), 16–36.

Bresser-Pereira, Luiz C., José L. Oreiro, and Nelson Marconi. *Development Macroeconomics: New Developmentalism as a Growth Strategy*. (London: Routledge, 2014).

Bresser-Pereira, Luiz C. and Nakano, Yoshiaki. *The Theory of Inertial Inflation*. (Boulder, CO: Lynne Rienner, 1987).

Brito, Ney O. (1979). 'Inflação e o mercado de Letras do Tesouro Nacional', *Revista Brasileira de Economia*, 33/2 (1979): 189–210.

Brunner, Karl and Meltzer, Allan H. *Money and the Economy*. (Cambridge: Cambridge University Press, 1993).

Bulhões, Octavio G. De and Kingston, Jorge. 'A política monetária para 1947', *Revista Brasileira de Economia*, 1/1 (1947): 9–50.

Canuto, Octaviano and Ghosh, Swati (eds.). *Dealing with the Challenges of Macro Financial Linkages in Emerging Markets*. (Washington, DC: World Bank, 2013).

Cardoso, Eliana A. 'Indexação e acomodação monetária: um teste em processo inflacionário brasileiro', *Revista Brasileira de Economia*, 37/1 (1983): 3–11.

Cardoso, Fernando H. and Falleto, Enzo. Dependency and Development in Latin America. (Berkeley, CA: University of California Press, 1979).

Carneiro Netto, Dioníso D. and Fraga Neto, Armínio. 'Variáveis de Credito e Endoginidade da Oferta de Moeda no Brasil', *Pesquisa e Planejamento Econômico,* 14/1 (1984): 175–196.

Carvalho, Carlos E. 'Bloqueio da Liquidez e Estabilização: o fracasso do Plano Collor'. (Doctoral Dissertation, Instituto de Economia, Unicamp, Campinas, 1996).

Carvalho, Fabia A., and Minella, André. 'Survey forecasts in Brazil: A prismatic assessment of epidemiology, performance, and determinants', *Journal of International Money and Finance*, 31/6 (2013): 1371–1391.

Castro, Ana C. *As empresas estrangeiras no Brasil, 1860–13*. (Rio de Janeiro: Zahar, 1979).

Castro, Antonio B. and Souza, Francisco E. P. *A Economia Brasileira em Marcha Forçada*. (Rio de Janeiro: Paz e Terra, 1985).

Chang, Kelly H. *Appointing Central Bankers: The Politics of Monetary Policy in the United States and the European Monetary Union*. (Cambridge: Cambridge University Press, 2003).

Clark, William R. *Capitalism, not Globalism: Capital Mobility, Central Bank Independence and the Political Control of the Economy*. (Ann Arbor, MI: University of Michigan Press, 2003).

Cohen, Benjamin J. 'The Macrofoundation of Monetary Power', (Florence: European University Institute, Robert Schuman Centre for Advanced Studies, Working Paper, 2005, no. 8).

Collier, David. 'Understanding Process Tracing', *PS: Political Science and Politic, 44/4* (2011): 823–830.

Conaghan, Catherine and Malloy, James. *Unsettling Statecraft: Democracy and Neoliberalism in the Andes*. (Pittsburgh, PA: University of Pittsburgh Press, 1994).

Corazza, Gentil. 'O Banco Central do Brasil: Evolução Histórica e Institucional', *Perspectiva Econômica, 2/1* (2006): 1–23.

Cuckierman, Alex. *Central Bank Strategy, Credibility and Independence*. (Cambridge, MA: MIT Press, 1992).

Cysne, Rubens P. and Lisboa, Paulo C. C. *Imposto inflacionário e transferências inflacionárias no Brasil: 1947–2003*. (Rio de Janeiro: EPGE-FGV Ensaios Econômicos, No. 539, 2004).

Dantas, San Tiago. *Dois Momentos de Rui Barbosa*. (Rio de Janeiro: Casa da Rui Barbosa, 1949).

Da Silva, Peri A. 'O controle monetário e a contribuição do open market', *Revista Brasileira de Economia*, 35/2 (1981): 105–155.

Deutsch, Karl. 'Social Mobilization and Political Development', *American Political Science Review*, 55/3 (1961): 493–514.

Dickson, Peter. *The Financial Revolution in England* (New York: St Martin's, 1967).

Dornbusch, Rudiger. 'Brazil's Incomplete Stabilization and Reform', *Brookings Papers on Economic Activity*, (No. 1, 1997): 367–404.

Dornbusch, Rudiger and Edwards, Sebastian (eds). *The Macroeconomics of Populism in Latin America*. (Chicago: University of Chicago Press, 1991).

Douglas, William O. *Democracy and finance: the addresses and public statements of William O. Douglas as member and chairman of the Securities and Exchange Commission*. (New Haven, CT: Yale University Press, 1941).

Drake, Paul. *The Money Doctor in the Andes: U.S. Advisors, Investors, and Economic Reform in Latin America from World War I to the Great Depression*. (Durhan, NC: Duke University Press, 1989).

Dymski, Gary A. 'Banking on Transformation: Financing Development, Overcoming Poverty'. (Paper presented to UFRJ Economics Institute, 2003).

Eckstein, Harry. 'Case study and theory in political science', in Nelson Polsby and Fred Greenstein (eds). *Handbook of Political Science*. (Greenwich. CT: Addison-Wesley), pp. 79–137.

Eichengreen, Barry, Hausmann, Ricardo, and Panizza, Ugo. (2007). 'Currency Mismatches, Debt Intolerance and Original Sin: Why They Are Not the Same and Why it Matters'. *Capital Controls and Capital Flows in Emerging Economies: Policies, Practices and Consequences.* (Chicago: University of Chicago Press, 2007), pp. 121–170.

Ekerman, Raul. 'A comunidade de economistas do Brasil: dos anos 50 aos dias de hoje', *Revista Brasileira de Economia*, 43/2 (1989): 113–138.

Elgie, Robert. 'Democratic Acountability and Central Bank Independence: Historical and Contemporary, National and European Perspectives', *Western European Politics*, 21 (1998): 53–76.

Federal Reserve Board. 'Z.1 Financial Accounts of the United States Flow of Funds, Balance Sheets, and Integrated Macroeconomic Accounts. Historical Annual Tables 2005–2014'. (New York: Federal Reserve Board, 2015).

Feinstein, Charles. (ed.). *Banking, Currency and Finance in Europe Between the Wars.* (Oxford: Oxford University Press, 1995).

Féis, Herbert. *Europe: The World's Banker, 1870–14.* (Oxford: Oxford University Press, 1931).

Ferrer, James and Langoni, Carlos G. (eds.). *The Quest for Monetary Stability.* (Washington, DC: DA Publishing and Fundação Getulio Vargas, 1996).

The Financial Crisis Inquiry Commission. 'The Financial Crisis Inquiry Commission Report', (Washington, DC: US Government Printing Office, 2011).

Fischer, Stanley. *Indexing, Inflation and Economic Policy.* (Cambridge, MA: MIT Press, 1986).

Fishlow, Albert. 'Brazilian Development in Long Term Perspective', *American Economic Review,* 70/2 (1980): 102–108.

Fishlow, Albert. 'Origins and consequences of import substitution in Brazil', in Luis E. DeMarco (ed.), *International Economics and Development Essays in Honor of Raul Prebish.* (New York, Academic Press, 1972).

Fishlow, Albert. 'Thirty Years of Combating Inflation in Brazil: From the PAEG (1964) to the Plan Real (1994)'. (University of Oxford Centre for Brazilian Studies, Working Paper).

Foley, Duncan. 'On Marx's Theory of Money', *Social Concept,* 1/1 (1983): 5–19.

Foley, Duncan. *Understanding Capital: Marx's Economic Theory.* (Cambridge, MA: Harvard University Press, 1986).

Fraga, Arminio, Goldfajn, Ilan, and Minella, André. 'Inflation Targeting in Emerging Market Economies', in Mark Gertler and Kenneth Rogoff (eds). *NBER Macroeconomics Annual 2003.* (Cambridge, MA: MIT Press, 2004), pp. 365–416.

Fraga, Armínio and Werlang, Sérgio. 'Uma visão da inflação como conflito distributivo', *Revista Brasileira de Economia,* 37/3 (1983): 361–367.

França, Paulo. 'A 'Conta-Movimento' entre o Banco Central e o Banco do Brasil', *Conjuntura Econômica.* 40/3 (1986).

Franco, Gustavo H. B. *Reforma monetária e estabilidade durante a transição republicana.* (Rio de e Janeiro: BNDES, 1983).

Franco, Gustavo H. B. 'Taxa de Câmbio e Oferta de Moeda 1880–1897: Uma Análise Econométrica', *Revista Brasileira de Economia,* 40/1 (1986): 63–88.

Frankel, Jeffrey. 'No Single Currency Regime is Right for All Countries or At All Times,' (NBER Working Paper no. 7228, 1999).

Frieden, Jeffry A. *Currency Politics: The Political Economy of Exchange Rate Policy.* (Princeton, NJ: Princeton University Press, 2014).

Friedman, Milton (ed.). *Studies in the Quantity Theory of Money.* (Chicago: University of Chicago Press, 1956).

Friedman, Milton and Schwartz, Anna J. *A Monetary History of the United States, 1867–1960.* (Princeton, NJ: Princeton University Press, 1963).

Fritsch, Winston. *External Constraints on Economic Policy in Brazil.* (London: Macmillan, 1988).

Fry, Maxwell J. *Money, Interest and Banking in Economic Development.* (Baltimore, MD: Johns Hopkins University Press, 1998).

Furtado, Celso. *The Economic Growth of Brazil: A Survey from Colonial to Modern Times.* (Berkeley, CA: University of California Press, 1959).

Furth, J. Herbert. 'A ação dos Bancos Centrais e o equilíbrio econômico', *Revista Brasileira de Economia,* 4/4 (1950): 43–70.

Furth, J. Herbert. 'Conversão da Moeda e inflação reprimida', *Revista Brasileira de Economia,* 3/2 (1949): 35–51.

Gabor, Daniela, *A step too far? The European Financial Transactions Tax on Shadow Banking.* (Brussels: Progressive Economy Forum, 2014).

Gallie, W. B. 'Essentially Contested Concepts', *Proceedings of the Aristotelian Society,* 56 (1956): 67–198.

Garrett, Goeffrey. *Partisan Politics in the Global Economy.* (Cambridge: Cambridge University Press, 1998).

George, Alexander and Bennet, Andrew. *Case Studies and Theory Development in the Social Sciences,* (Cambridge, MA: MIT Press, 2005).

Gerschenkron, Alexander. *Economic Backwardness in Historical Perspective.* (Cambridge, MA, Harvard University Press, 1962).

Godley, Wynne and Lavoie, Marc. *Monetary Economics: An Integrated Approach to Credit, Money, Income, Production and Wealth.* (London: Palgrave, 2007).

Goertz, Gary and Mahoney, James. 'Case Selection and Hypothesis Testing', in Gary Goertz and James Mahoney (eds.). *A Tale of Two Cultures: Contrasting the Qualitative and Quantitative Research Paradigms* (Princeton: Princeton University Press, 2012), pp. 177–191.

Gold, David A., Lo, Clarence, and Wright, Erik O. 'Recent developments in Marxist theories of the capitalist state'. *Monthly Review,* 27/5 (1975): 29–43.

Goldsmith, Raymond. *Financial Structure and Development.* (New Haven, CT: Yale University Press, 1996).

Goodhart, Charles. *The Evolution of Central Banks.* (Cambridge: Cambridge University Press, 1990).

Goodhart, Charles. 'Two Theories of Money', *European Journal of Political Economy,* 14 (1998): 407–432.

Gorton, Gary and Metrick, Andrew. 'Securitized Banking and the Run on Repo,' (NBER Working Paper no. 15223, 2009).

Gourevitch, Peter. 'Democracy and Economic Policy: Elective Affinities and Circumstantial Conjunctures', *World Development,* 21/8 (1993): 1271–1281.

Gudin, Eugênio. *Inflação, Crédito e Desenvolvimento.* (Rio de Janeiro: Agir, 1956).

Gudin, Eugênio. *Princípios de economia monetária.* (Rio de Janeiro: Civilização Brasileira, 1962).

Guttmann, Robert. *How Credit-Money Shapes the Economy: The United States in a Global System.* (New York: M. E. Sharpe, 1994).

Haddad, Claudio. *Crescimento do Produto Real no Brasil, 1900–47).* (Rio de Janeiro: Editora Fundação Getulio Vargas, 1978).

Haddad, Claudio. *As Operações com Títulos Públicos Federais e a Execução da Política Monetária.* (São Paulo: Adeval, 1982).

Haggard, Stephan, Lee, Chung H., and Maxfield, Sylvia (eds). *The Politics of Finance in Developing Countries.* (Ithaca, NY: Cornell University Press, 1993).

Hagopian, Frances. *Traditional Politics and Regime Change in Brazil.* (Cambridge: Cambridge University Press, 1996).

Hahner, June. *Civil-Military Relations in Brasil, 1889–98.* (Columbia, SC: University of South Carolina Press, 1969).

Halloway, Thomas H. *The Brazilian Coffee Valorization, 1906.* (Madison, WI: University of Wisconsin Press, 1966).

Hammond, Bray. *Banks and Politics in America, from the Revolution to the Civil War.* (Princeton, NJ: Princeton University Press, 1957).

Hardie, Iain David Howarth, David (eds.). *Market Based Banking and the International Financial Crisis*, (Oxford: Oxford University Press, 2013).

Hartz, Luis. *The Liberal Tradition in America.* (New York: Harcourt Brace, 1955).

Henning, C. Randall. 'The Exchange Rate Weapon and Macroeconomic Conflict', in David Andrews (ed.). *International Monetary Power.* (Ithaca, NY: Cornell University Press, 2006), pp. 117–138.

Henning, C. Randall, 'Systemic Conflict and Regional Monetary Integration: The Case of Europe', *International Organization.* 52 (1998): 537–573.

Hermann, Jennifer. 'Financial system structure and financing models: the Brazilian experience and its perspective (1964/1997).' *Journal of Latin American Studies*, (2002), 34: 71–114.

Hilton, Stanley. *Oswaldo Aranha: uma biografia.* (Rio de Janeiro: Objetivo, 1994).

Hirschman, Albert O. *Essays in Trespassing: Economics to Politics and Beyond.* (Cambridge: Cambridge University Press, 1981).

Hirschman, Albert O. 'Ideologies of Development in Latin America', in *Latin American Issues: Essays and Comments.* (New York: The Twentieth Century Fund, 1961).

Hirschman, Albert O. 'The Social and Political Matrix of Inflation: Elaborations on the Latin American Experience', in A. O. Hirschman, *Essays in Trespassing: Economics to Politics and Beyond.* (Cambridge: Cambridge University Press, 1981).

Jensen, Henrik. 'The Credibility of Optimal Monetary Delegation', *American Economic Review*, 87 (1997): 911–920.

Kafka, Alexandre. 'Experiências de estabilização monetária', *Revista Brasileira de Economia*, 17/4 (1963): 5–26.

Katzenstein, Peter. *Small States in World Markets: Industrial Policy in Europe.* (Ithaca, NY: Cornell University Press, 1985).

Keynes, John M. *Economic Consequences of the Peace.* (New York: Harcourt, Brace and Howe, 1920).

Kindlberger, Charles P. *A Financial History of Western Europe.* (London: George Allen, 1984).

Kindleberger, Charles P. *Power and Money.* (New York: Basic Books, 1970).

Kingston, Jorge. 'A expansão de crédito no sistema bancário brasileiro', *Revista Brasileira de Economia*, 2/3 (1948): 7–29.

Kirshner, Jonathan. *Currency and Coercion: The Political Economy of International Monetary Power.* (Princeton: Princeton University Press, 2003).

Knapp, Georg. *Staatliche Theorie des Geldes.* (Munich: Duncker & Humblot, 1905).

Krugman, Paul. *Currencies and Crises.* (Cambridge, MA: MIT Press, 1992).

Lall, Ranjit. 'From failure to failure: The politics of international banking regulation,' *Review of International Political Economy*, (2012), 19(4): 609–638

Leão Rego, Walquiria and Pinzani, Allesandro. *Vozes do Bolsa Família. Autonomia, dinheiro e cidadania.* (São Paulo: Unesp, 2013).

Lees, Francis A., Botts, James M., Cysne, Rubens Penha. Banking and Financial Deepening in Brazil. (London: Palgrave Macmillan, 1990).

Leff, Nathaniel H. *Economic Policy Making and Development in Brazil, 1947–64.* (New York: Wiley, 1968).

Lemgruber, Antonio C. 'A inflação brasileira e a controvérsia sobre aceleração inflacionária', *Revista Brasileira de Economia*, 27/4 (1973): 31–50.

Lijphart, Arendt. 'Comparative Politics and Comparative Method.' *American Political Science Review*, 65 (1971): 682–693.

Lindblom, Charles E. 'The Science of Muddling Through'. *Public Administration Review*, 19/2 (1958): 79–88

Lowi, Theodore. 'American Business, Public Policy, Case Studies and Political Theory', *World Politics*, 16/4 (1964): 677–715.

Loureiro, Maria R. *50 Anos de Ciência Econômica no Brasil: Pensamento, Instituições, Depoimentos.* (São Paulo: Fipe/Vozes, 1997).

Loureiro, Maria R. *Os Economistas no Governo.* (Rio de Janeiro: Editora FGV, 1997).

Lundberg, Eduardo. *Saneamento do Sistema Financeiro – A Experiência Brasileira dos Últimos 25 Anos.* (Brasilia: Central Bank of Brazil, Memo, 2005).

Lynch, Edward S. and Parker, Newton B. 'Alterações no suprimento monetário brasileiro desde 1939', *Revista Brasileira de Economia*, 2/2 (1948): 93–121.

Machado, Vicente G. and Portugal, Marcelo S. 'Phillips curve in Brazil: an unobserved components approach'. (Central Bank of Brazil Working Paper no. 354, 2014).

Magalhães, Augusto F. R. *Os Bancos Centrais e Sua Função Reguladora da Moeda e Crédito.* (Rio de Janeiro: A Casa do Livro, 1971).

Mainwaring, Scott. *Rethinking Political Systems in the Third Wave of Democratization: The Case of Brazil.* (Stanford, CA: Stanford University Press, 1999).

Marques, Maria S. B. 'Moeda e inflação: a questão da causalidade'. *Revista Brasileira de Economia*, 37/1 (1983): 13–38.

Marques, Maria S. B. 'A aceleração inflacionária no Brasil 1973–1983', *Revista Brasileira de Economia*, 39/4 (1985): 343–384.

Maxfield, Sylvia. *Gatekeepers of Growth: The International Political Economy of Central Banking in Developing Countries.* (Princeton, NJ: Princeton University Press, 1998).

McKinnon, R. *Money and Capital in Economic Development.* (Washington, D.C.: Brookings Institution, 1973).

Mettenheim, Kurt. 'Back to Basics in Banking Theory and Varieties of Finance Capitalism', *Accounting, Economics and Law,* 3/3 (2013): 357–405.

Mettenheim, Kurt. 'BRIC Statecraft and Government Banks', in Olivier Butzbach and Kurt Mettenheim (eds.). *Alternative Banking and Financial Crisis.* London: Pickering and Chatto, 2014), pp. 179–210.

Mettenheim, Kurt. 'From the Economics of Politics to the Politics of Monetary Policy', in Lourdes Sola and Laurence Whitehead (eds.). *Statecrafting Monetary Authority: Democracy and Financial Order in Brazil.* (Oxford: University of Oxford Centre for Brazilian Studies, 2006), pp. 325–358.

Mettenheim, Kurt. *Federal Banking in Brazil: Policies and Competitive Advantages.* (London: Pickering and Chatto, 2010).

Mettenheim, Kurt. 'Municipal Bond Market in Brazil. Theory, Repression and Prospects', *Revista de Administração de Empresas,* 52/6 (2012): 692–703.

Mettenheim, Kurt. 'Observations on the Brazilian presidency, democracy and governance', *Revista de Administração de Empresas*, 39/3 (1999): 53–72.

Mettenheim, Kurt (ed.). *Presidential Institutions and Democratic Governance: Comparing Regional and National Contexts.* (Baltimore, MD: Johns Hopkins University Press, 1997).

Minella, André and Souza-Sobrinho, Nelson. 'Canais Monetários no Brasil sob a Ótica de um Modelo Semiestrutural', in Central Bank of Brazil. 'Dez Anos de Metas para a Inflação no Brasil, 1999–2009', 2011.

Minsky, Hyman P. *Stabilizing an Unstable Economy*. (New Haven: Yale University Press, 1986).

Mishkin, Frederic. *Monetary Policy Strategy*. (Cambridge, MA: MIT Press, 2007).

Moraes, Pedro B. 'Política monetária e oferta de crédito durante o Plano Cruzado', *Revista Brasileira de Economia*, 44/2 (1990): 21–33.

Mundell, Robert. 'A Theory of Optimum Currency Areas', *The American Economic Review*, 51/4 (1961): 657–665.

Neuhaus, Paulo. *História Monetária do Brasil, 1900–45*. (Rio de Janeiro: Editora FGV, 1975).

Nóbrega, Mailson and Loyola, Gustavo. 'The Long and Simultaneous Construction of Monetary and Fiscal Institutions', in Lourdes Sola and Laurence Whitehead (eds.). *State-crafting Monetary Authority: Democracy and Financial Order in Brazil*. (Oxford: Centre for Brazilian Studies, 2006), pp. 57–68.

Nun, José. 'The Middle Class Military Coup', in Claudio Veliz (ed). *The Politics of Conformity in Latin America*. (Oxford: Oxford University Press, 1967), pp. 66–118.

O'Donnell, Guillermo. *Modernization and Bureaucratic-Authoritarianism: Studies in South American Politics* (Berkeley, CA: Institute of International Studies, University of California, 1973).

Olenscki, Antonio R. B. 'Modelo Brasileiro de Crédito Municipal (2000–2006): Uma Análise de Controles Governamentais e Características da Oferta', (FGV-EAESP doctoral dissertation, 2008).

Paes, Julieda P. P. 'Bancos Estaduais, 'Criação' de Moeda e Ciclo Político'. (Masters Dissertation, EAESP-FGV, São Paulo, 1986).

Pastore, Affonso C. 'Inflação e expectativas com a política monetária numa regra de taxa de juros', *Revista Brasileira de Economia*, 44/4 (1990): 499–528.

Pastore, Affonso C. 'Inflação e política monetária no Brasil', *Revista Brasileira de Economia*, 23/1 (1969): 92–123.

Pastore, Affonso C. 'A Reforma Monetária do Plano Collor', *Revista Brasileira de Economia*, 45 (1991): 157–174.

Paulo, Mauro, Sussman, Nathan, and Yishay, Yafeh. *Emerging Markets and Financial Globalization Sovereign Bond Spreads in 1870–1913 and Today*. (Oxford: Oxford University Press, 2006).

Pelaez, Carlos M. 'As conseqûencias econômicas da ortodoxia cambial e fiscal no Brasil entre 1889–1945', *Revista Brasileira de Economia*, 25/3 (1971): 5–82.

Pelaez, Carlos M. 'A política econômica do Presidente Vargas: Wirth e the Politics of Brazilian Development, 1930–1954', *Revista Brasileira de Economia*, 24/3 (1970): 183–187.

Pelaez, Carlos M. and Suzigan, Wilson. *História Monetária do Brasil: Análise da Política, Comportamento e Instituições Monetárias*. (Rio de Janeiro: IPEA/INPES, 1976).

Pierson, Paul. *Dismantling the Welfare State? Reagan, Thatcher and the Politics of Retrenchment*. (Cambridge: Cambridge University Press, 1995).

Pierson, Paul. 'When Effect Becomes Cause: Policy Feedback and Political Change,' *World Politics*, 45/4 (1993): 595–628.

Polanyi, Karl. *The Great Transformation: The Political and Economic Origins of Our Time*. (New York: Rinehart and Co., 1944).

Pozsar, Zoltan., Adrian, Tobias., Ashcraft, Adam., and Boesky, Hayley. 'Shadow banking', (New York: Federal Reserve Bank of New York, Staff Papers, no. 458, 2010).

Przeworski, Adam and Teune, Henry. *The Logic of Comparative Social Inquiry*. (New York: Wiley-Interscience, 1970).

Queiroz, Carlos A. R. 'A política monetária num contexto de indexação: o caso brasileiro', *Revista Brasileira de Economia*, 34/2 (1980): 165–202.

Ramalho, Valdir. 'Elementos para uma avaliação de confisco monetários', *Revista Brasileira de Economia*, 47/4 (1993): 533–564.

Rangel, Inácio. *A Inflação Brasileira*. (São Paulo: Bienal, 1963).

Rippy, J. Fred. *British Investment in Latin América, 1822–45*. (Minneapolis, MN: University of Minnesota Press, 1959).

Rogers, Colin. *Money, Interest and Capital: A Study in the Foundations of Monetary Theory*. (Cambridge: Cambridge University Press, 1989).

Rogoff, Kenneth. 'The Optimal Degree of Commitment to and Intermediate Monetary Target', *Quarterly Journal of Economics*, 100 (1985): 1169–1190.

Ronci, Marcio. 'Contribuição de Simonsen à economia política brasileira', *Revista Brasileira de Economia*, 52 (1998): 137–145.

Sachsida, A., Ribeiro M. and Santos C. H. 'A curva de Phillips e a experiência brasileira'. (Textos para Discussão IPEA, no. 1429, 2009).

Saliba, Elias T. (ed). *Idéias Econômicas de Cincinato Braga*. (Brasilia: Senado Federal, 1983).

Santiso, Javier. 'Wall Street and Emerging Democracies: Financial Markets and the Brazilian Presidential Elections', in Lourdes Sola and Laurence Whitehead (eds.). *Statecrafting Monetary Authority: Democracy and Financial Order in Brazil*. (Oxford: University of Oxford Centre for Brazilian Studies, 2006), pp. 269–324.

Sartori, Giovanni. 'From the Sociology of Politics to a Political Sociology', *Government and Opposition*, 4/2 (1969): 195–214.

Scharpf, Fritz. 'Monetary Union, Fiscal Crisis and the Preemption of Democracy.' (Cologne: Max Plank Institute for the Study of Societies, MPIfG Discussion paper, 11/11, 2011).

Schclarek Curutchet, Alfredo. 'The Counter-Cyclical Behaviour of Public and Private Banks: An Overview of the Literature', in Butzbach, Olivier and Kurt Mettenheim, (eds.). *Alternative Banking and Financial Crisis*. (London: Pickering and Chatto, 2014), pp. 43–50.

Schumpeter, Joseph. *History of Economic Analysis*. (London: Routledge, 1954).

Schwartz, Roberto. *Misplaced Ideas: Essays on Brazilian Culture*. (London: Verso, 1996).

Shaw, Eduard. *Financial Deepening in Economic Development*. (New York: Oxford University Press, 1973).

Shonfield, Andrew. *Modern Capitalism*. (Oxford: Oxford University Press, 1965).

Simonsen, Mario H. *Inflação: Gradualismo x Tratamento de Choque*. (Rio de Janeiro: APEC, 1970).

Simonsen, Mario H. *Trinta anos de indexação*. (Rio de Janeiro: Editora FGV, 1995).

Smith, Adam. *An Inquiry into the Nature and Causes of the Wealth of Nations*. (New York: Modern Library, Cannan Edition, 1937[1776]).

Smith, Adam. *The Wealth of Nations*. (New York: Modern Library, 2000).

Soares, Fabio V., Ribas, Rafael P., and Osorio, Rafael G. 'Evaluating the impact of Brazil's Bolsa Família: cash transfer programs in comparative perspective'. *Latin American Research Review*, 45 (2010): 173–90.

Sola, Lourdes. *Idéias Econômicas, Decisões Políticas*, (São Paulo, EDUSP, 1998).

Sola, Lourdes and Kugelmas, Eduardo. 'Crafting economic stabilisation: Political discretion and technical innovation in the implementation of the real plan', in Lourdes Sola and Laurence Whitehead (eds.). *Statecrafting Monetary Authority: Democracy and Financial Order in Brazil*. (Oxford: Centre for Brazilian Studies, 2006), pp. 85–116.

Sola, Lourdes and Marques, Moisés. 'Central banking, democratic governance, and the quality of democracy.' in Sola, Lourdes and Whitehead, Laurence (eds.). *Statecrafting*

Monetary Authority: Democracy and Financial Order in Brazil. (Oxford: Centre for Brazilian Studies, 2006), pp. 143–204.

Sola, Lourdes and Whitehead, Laurence (eds.). *Statecrafting Monetary Authority: Democracy and Financial Order in Brazil.* (Oxford: University of Oxford Centre for Brazilian Studies, 2006).

Souza, Maria do C. C. *Estado e partidos políticos no Brasil (1930 a 1964).* (São Paulo: Paz e Terra, 1976).

Strange, Susan. 'The Politics of International Currencies', *World Politics*, 23/2 (1971): 215–231.

Strange, Susan. *Sterling and British Policy.* (Oxford: Oxford University Press, 1971).

Suzigan, Wilson. 'Política cambial brasileira, 1889–1946', *Revista Brasileira de Economia*, 25/3 (1971): 93–111.

Syrud, Donald. 'Estrutura e política de juros no Brasil – 1960 / 1970'. *Revista Brasileira de Economia*, 26/1: 117–139.

Tavares, Maria da C. *Da Substituição de Importações ao Capitalismo Financeiro.* (Rio de Janeiro: Zahar, 1972).

Taylor, Matthew. 'Institutional Development through Policy Making: A Case Study of the Brazilian Central Bank', *World Politics*, 61/3 (2009): 487–515.

Tilly, Charles (ed.). *The Formation of Nation States in Western Europes.* (Princeton, NJ: Princeton University Press, 1975).

Topik, Steven. *The Political Economy of the Brazilian State, 1889–1930.* (Austin, TX: University of Texas Press, 1987).

Tsibelis, George. *Veto Players.* (Princeton: Princeton University Press, 2002).

Urani, André and Winograd, Carlos. 'Distributional effects of the stabilization. policies in a dual economy: the case of Brazil 1981–1988', *Revista Brasileira de Economia*, 48/1 (1994): 71–84.

Viera, Dorival T. *Evolução do Sistema Monetário Brasileiro.* (São Paulo: Gráfica da FFCL, 1962).

Villela, Anibal V. and Suzigan, Wilson. *Política do Governo e Crescimento da Economia Basileira, 1889–1945.* (Rio de Janeiro: IPEA/INPES, 1973).

Walsh, Carl. 'Optimal Contracts for Central Bankers', *American Economic Review.* 85/1 (1995): 150–167.

Webb, Michael C. 'Capital Mobility and the Possibilities for International Policy Coordination', *Policy Sciences*, 27 (1994): 395–423.

Werlang, Sérgio and Fraga, Armínio. 'Os bancos estadiais e o descontrole fiscal: alguns aspectos', *Revista Brasileira de Economia*, 49/2 (1995): 165–175.

Whitehead, Laurence. *Democratization: Theory and Experience.* (Oxford: Oxford University Press, 2002).

Williamson, John (ed). *Latin American Adjustment, How Much Has Happened?* (Washington, DC: Institute for International Economics, 1990).

Wirth, John. *The Politics of Brazilian Development.* (Stanford, CA: Stanford University Press, 1970).

Wooley, John. T. 'The Politics of Monetary Policy: A Critical Review', *Journal of Public Policy*, 114 (1994): 57–85.

Wray, Randall. *Money and Credit in Capitalist Economies: The Endogenous Money Approach.* (Aldershot: Eduard Elgar, 1990).

Zini, Jr., Álvaro A. (1986). 'Teoria da determinação da taxa de câmbio', *Revista Brasileira de Economia*, 40/3 (1986): 257–283.

Zysman, John. *Governments, Markets and Growth Financial Systems and the Politics of Industrial Change.* (Ithaca, NY: Cornell University Press, 1983).

Index

For Product Safety Concerns and Information please contact our EU
representative GPSR@taylorandfrancis.com Taylor & Francis Verlag GmbH,
Kaufingerstraße 24, 80331 München, Germany

Printed and bound by CPI Group (UK) Ltd, Croydon, CR0 4YY
01/05/2025
01858355-0003